Foundations of Semantic Databases

C.A.R. Hoare, Series Editor

BACKHOUSE, R. C., *Program Construction and Verification*
BACKHOUSE, R. C., *Syntax of Programming Languages: Theory and practice*
DE BAKKER, J. W., *Mathematical Theory of Program Correctness*
BIRD, R. and WADLER, P., *Introduction to Functional Programming*
BJÖRNER, D. and JONES, C. B., *Formal Specification and Software Development*
BORNAT, R., *Programming from First Principles*
BUSTARD, D., ELDER, J. and WELSH, J., *Concurrent Program Structures*
CLARK, K. and McCABE, F. G., *micro-Prolog: Programming in Logic*
CROOKES, D., *Introduction to Programming in Prolog*
DROMEY, R. G., *How to Solve it by Computer*
DUNCAN, F., *Microprocessor Programming and Software Development*
ELDER, J., *Construction of Data Processing Software*
ELLIOTT, R. J. and HOARE, C. A. R. (eds), *Scientific Applications of Multiprocessors*
GOLDSCHLAGER, L. and LISTER, A., *Computer Science: A modern introduction (2nd edn)*
GORDON, M. J. C., *Programming Language Theory and its Implementation*
HAYES, I. (ed.), *Specification Case Studies*
HEHNER, E. C. R., *The Logic of Programming*
HENDERSON, P., *Functional Programming: Application and implementation*
HOARE, C. A. R., *Communicating Sequential Processes*
HOARE, C. A. R. and JONES, C. B. (eds), *Essays in Computing Science*
HOARE, C. A. R. and SHEPHERDSON, J. C. (eds), *Mechanical Logic and Programming Languages*
HUGHES, J. G., *Database Technology: A software engineering approach*
INMOS LTD, *occam Programming Manual*
INMOS LTD, *occam 2 Reference Manual*
JACKSON, M. A., *System Development*
JOHNSTON, H., *Learning to Program*
JONES, C. B., *Software Development: A rigorous approach (OOP)*
JONES, C. B., *Systematic Software Development Using VDM (2nd edn)*
JONES, C. B. and SHAW, R. C. F. (eds), *Case Studies in Systematic Software Development*
JONES, G., *Programming in occam*
JONES, G. and GOLDSMITH, M., *Programming in occam 2*
JOSEPH, M., PRASAD, V. R. and NATARAJAN, N., *A Multiprocessor Operating System*
LEW, A., *Computer Science: A mathematical introduction*
MACCALLUM, I., *Pascal for the Apple*
MACCALLUM, I., *UCSD Pascal for the IBM PC*
MARTIN, J. J., *Data Types and Data Structures*
MEYER, B., *Introduction to the Theory of Programming Languages*
MEYER, B., *Object-oriented Software Construction*
MILNER, R., *Communication and Concurrency*
PEYTON JONES, S. L., *The Implementation of Functional Programming Languages*
POMBERGER, G., *Software Engineering and Modula-2*
REYNOLDS, J. C., *The Craft of Programming*
RYDEHEARD, D. E. and BURSTALL, R. M., *Computational Category Theory*
SLOMAN, M. and KRAMER, J., *Distributed Systems and Computer Networks*
SPIVEY, J. M., *The Z Notation: A reference manual*
TENNENT, R. D., *Principles of Programming Languages*
WATT, D. A., *Programming Language Concepts and Paradigms*
WATT, D. A., WICHMANN, B. A. and FINDLAY, W., *ADA: Language and methodology*
WELSH, J. and ELDER, J., *Introduction to Modula-2*
WELSH, J. and ELDER, J., *Introduction to Pascal (3rd edn)*
WELSH, J., ELDER, J. and BUSTARD, D., *Sequential Program Structures*
WELSH, J. and HAY, A., *A Model Implementation of Standard Pascal*
WELSH, J. and McKEAG, M., *Structured System Programming*
WIKSTRÖM, Å., *Functional Programming using Standard ML*

Foundations of Semantic Databases

Bert de Brock

State University of Groningen
The Netherlands

Academic Service
Schoonhoven

Prentice Hall
New York London Toronto Sydney Tokyo Singapore

First published in English in 1995 by
Prentice Hall International (UK) Ltd
Campus 400, Maylands Avenue
Hemel Hempstead, Herts HP2 7EZ
A division of
Simon & Schuster International Group

and

Academic Service, Schoonhoven, Holland

A co-publication between Prentice Hall International (UK) Ltd
and Academic Service, Schoonhoven

Original Dutch language edition, *De grondslagen van semantische databases*,
published by Academic Service, Schoonhoven, Holland, in 1990

Printed and bound in Great Britain

Library of Congress Cataloging-in-Publication Data

Available from the publisher

British Library Cataloguing in Publication Data

A catalogue record for this book is available from the British Library

ISBN: 0-13-327099-8

1 2 3 4 5 99 98 97 96 95

This book is dedicated to
Audrey, Cherelien, and Daniëlle

Contents

Preface xi

Basic Mathematical Concepts 1
1 Sets 1
2 Functions 5
3 The Transitive Closure of a Relation 14

1 From Tables to Database Universes 18
1.1 Tables 18
1.2 Database States 20
1.3 Database Universes 21

2 Some Database Concepts 25
2.1 Concepts concerning Tables 25
2.1.1 Operations on Tables 25
2.1.2 Momentary Dependency 35
2.1.3 Unique Identification 38
2.1.4 Connecting Tables 41
2.2 Concepts concerning Sets of Tables 45
2.2.1 Permanent Dependency 46
2.2.2 Keys and Minimal Keys 49
2.2.3 Some Normal Forms 51
2.3 Concepts concerning Database Universes 53
2.3.1 Operations on Database Universes 55
2.3.2 Permanent Dependency and (Minimal) Keys 57
2.3.3 Some Normal Forms for Database Universes 61
2.3.4 Permanent Connections and Database Functions 63
2.4 Summary 68

3 Constructing Database Universes **76**
3.1 Specifications of Admissible Attribute Values 80
3.2 Specifications of Admissible Tuple Values 84
3.3 Specifications of Admissible Table Values 85
3.4 Specifications of Admissible Database Values 87
3.5 Summary 93

4 A Nontrivial Example of a Database Universe **97**
4.1 Informal Description 98
4.2 Formal Definition 106
4.3 Some Database Functions 115

5 Dynamic Constraints **119**
5.1 Transition Relations 119
5.2 A Nontrivial Example of a Transition Relation 127

6 Retrieval **134**
6.1 Queries 134
6.2 Views 151

7 Maintenance **155**
7.1 Transactions 155
7.2 Some Common Classes of Transactions 164

8 Data Dictionaries **173**
8.1 The Data Definition Part of a Data Dictionary 174
8.2 Summary of the Examples 185

9 Directions for Realization in SQL **188**
9.1 Introduction 188
9.2 Constructing Database Universes 188
9.2.1 Attribute Constraints 189
9.2.2 Tuple Constraints 191
9.2.3 Table Constraints 191
9.2.4 Database Constraints 193
9.2.5 Summary 195
9.3 Retrieval 199
9.3.1 Queries 199
9.3.2 Views 209
9.4 Maintenance 211
9.4.1 Insertion of a Tuple 211
9.4.2 Insertion of a Table 211

9.4.3 Deletion 212
9.4.4 Update 213

References **215**

List of Definitions **219**

Index of Lemmas, Theorems, Examples, Figures, and Exercises **223**

Subject Index **225**

Preface

The complexity of information systems increases rapidly in practice. As a consequence, the need for formal specifications of such complex systems becomes more and more prevalent. This need not only concerns the formal specification of the so-called *data model* of an organization, but also of the so-called *process model*. The data model consists of the data (structures) relevant to this organization, along with the conditions on the data (commonly referred to as *constraints*). The process model includes the relevant queries and transactions on the data. These formal models can serve as guidelines for the implementation and use of such complex systems. Direct translations from such mathematical models to an implementation are becoming increasingly feasible by the current commercially available database management systems. This tendency towards an increasingly smaller distance between formal model and implementation once again emphasizes the growing significance of formal specifications of information systems.

This book shows what such (system independent) formal specifications might look like, and how they are useful (and actually even indispensable) in complex situations in practice. It also explains how a substantial part of the *semantics* of the data can be reflected *in* the formal data- and process model of the organization; this property is based on the fundamental insight that the semantics of the data determines the constraints that both data and operations on these data must satisfy. One of the main themes of this book concerns the way in which these constraints can be included as an essential part in the definition of the mathematical model of the data and their operations. It is the very intention of semantic databases to make the formal model capture as much semantics as possible, which explains the title of this book. The approach presented here has been applied extensively in widely divergent practical situations, and has clearly demonstrated its usefulness in modelling information systems.

This book can be placed in the context of the developments initiated by the introduction of the relational model ([Co 70]) and followed by research topics such as functional models (cf. [Sh 81]), semantic models (cf. [PM 88]), nested relations (cf. [RKS 88]), complex objects (cf. [Ab 89]), and object oriented models (cf. [Ca 93] or [AA

93]). Currently, the developments in these research areas can be followed in conference series such as VLDB (Very Large Data Bases), DOOD (Deductive and Object Oriented Databases), SIGMOD's Conference on the Management of Data, and OOPSLA (Object Oriented Programming, Systems, Languages, and Applications), and in journals such as ACM Transactions On Database Systems, Data Base (of ACM's SIGBIT), SIGMOD Record, Communications of the ACM, and IEEE Transactions on Software Engineering. Sometimes, interesting special issues can also be found in the Journal of the ACM, ACM Computing Surveys, the Journal of Object Oriented Programming, Software Engineering Notes, IEEE Transactions on Knowledge and Data Engineering, ACM Transactions on Office Information Systems, and ACM's SIGOIS Bulletin.

The author has lectured on database systems at the Technical University of Eindhoven (the Netherlands) for five years. The present book results from an extensive revision of his lecture notes, as well as from addition of new material.

The book starts with an introduction that contains the definitions and elementary properties of the general basic mathematical concepts used throughout the book.

In Chapter 1, the three basic concepts of a *table*, a *database state*, and a *database universe* will be formally defined. These notions constitute the basis of the rest of the book.

Chapter 2 treats several central topics from the theory of databases:

- operations on tables (projection, join, renaming, etc.),
- dependencies, (minimal) keys and normal forms,
- referential integrity and database functions, and
- operations on database universes.

Much emphasis will be placed on the important distinction between *incidental* properties (i.e., properties of states) and *structural* properties (i.e., properties of state spaces). Unfortunately, many theoretical and practical treatises do not make a clear distinction between these two levels.

Chapter 3 is dedicated to the systematic construction of database universes in practice. In this chapter, a classification of (static) constraints will be given, illustrated by several practical examples. It will also be shown how *generalization* and *specialization* (alias *differentiation*) can be modelled.

In order to give some insight into the specific problems that can arise in complex databases, Chapter 4 contains an extensive example of a database universe. This well-known hospital case is used in several countries for the evaluation of the functional properties of various leading database management systems (see for example [NGI 88] and [IDT 88/89/90]). Many types of constraints that one might encounter in practice have an analogue in this nontrivial case.

Chapter 5 offers a formal treatment of *dynamic* constraints, i.e., requirements pertaining to allowable state *transitions*. This chapter also contains an elaborate example describing various kinds of dynamic constraints, based on the hospital case from Chapter 4.

Chapter 6 treats the subject of *querying* a database. In this chapter, the notions of a *query* and a *view* will be defined formally and are illustrated by way of numerous examples.

Chapter 7 contains a mathematical treatment of the subject of *maintenance* of a database through (trans)actions, which can vary from basic to highly complex. In this book, the specifications of transactions are neither imperative nor operational, but declarative instead. Next to the general notion of a transaction, some specific, SQL-like classes of transactions will also be defined.

Chapter 8 treats the topic of *data dictionaries*. As a formal theory of databases typically abstracts from specific applications, a formal theory of data dictionaries should typically abstract from specific data dictionary systems. Despite the rapidly growing interest in data dictionaries, there is still hardly any formal material on this subject at all. It is the purpose of the last chapter of this book to provide for such a formal description of data dictionaries. In particular, we will closely examine the data definition part of a data dictionary and support our examination by way of some extensive examples.

Chapter 9 shows how we can implement our mathematical constructions in SQL, a widely adopted standard database language. In particular, §9.2 gives translation rules for the construction of database universes (as treated in Chapter 3), §9.3 gives them for retrieval (covering Chapter 6), and §9.4 contains translation rules for our maintenance operations (covering Chapter 7). It is perfectly possible to read these three sections immediately after the chapters they refer to.

This book contains a large selection of exercises covering both theoretical and practical aspects. The reader is strongly urged to perform a major part of these exercises to get a good grasp of the material.

As a last general comment, I want to emphasize that throughout this book considerable attention will be paid to the process of translating informal descriptions to formal specifications, and vice versa. After all, this process provides the link between experts of the application area on the one hand, and system design experts on the other.

I would like to express my gratitude to all those colleagues and students who in the last few years have contributed (be it consciously or unconsciously) to the multitude of experiences and insights that have led to this present book. In particular I would like to mention Frans Remmen; the balance between theory and practice which I hope to have found in my work on databases is greatly inspired by his judgement. Special thanks also go to the reviewers Frank Pieper and Frans Remmen for their very meticulous reading; their suggestions and comments highly improved earlier versions of the original Dutch text. I also want to thank the series editor and the reviewers of the English version for their stimulating comments; e.g., without them Chapter 9 would not have been put on paper. I would also like to thank Suzanne Michiels-Den Ouden for her very competent preparation of the text. In addition, I would like to thank Jan Willem Nienhuys for his assistance in the final preparation and for his design of several troff-macros specially for this book. Last but not least, I want to thank Audrey de Brock-

Blank for her moral support and patience, which were at times vital for completing this book.

Groningen, September 1994

Bert de Brock

Basic Mathematical Concepts

In this preliminary chapter we will establish our conventions concerning basic concepts and notations that we will use. We assume that many readers are more or less familiar with most of these basic concepts. When introducing a basic concept, we will therefore usually restrict ourselves to giving the formal definition and summing up some elementary properties of that concept, usually in the form of a lemma (without offering a proof). It is possible though that some "well-known" concepts are defined in a slightly different (or more general) way than the reader is used to.

In view of the elementary character of this chapter no exercises have been included (although we can regard every lemma as an exercise to prove that very lemma). For those readers who want a more elaborate treatment of the concepts introduced in this chapter, we refer to [DDS 76] for example.

1 Sets

We assume familiarity with the elementary notion of a *set*. We recall that sets are not ordered and have no duplicates; the way in which we describe the elements is also irrelevant. We know for instance that

$\{3, 2, 2, 1, 2+1, 2-1\} = \{3, 2, 1\} = \{1, 2, 3\}.$

We also assume familiarity with the following expressions:

Expression	Meaning
$x \in A$	x is an element of A
$x \notin A$	x is not an element of A
$\vert A \vert$	the number of elements of A
$\varnothing$	the empty set
$\mathbb{Z}$	the set of all integers
$m \bmod n$	the remainder of m after integer division by n
$m \operatorname{div} n$	m divided by n, ignoring the remainder

For any $m \in \mathbb{Z}$ and any $n \in \mathbb{Z}$ for which $n \neq 0$, we have
$(m \operatorname{div} n) \in \mathbb{Z}$,
$0 \leq m \bmod n < n$, and
$m = n * (m \operatorname{div} n) + m \bmod n$.
We will also make frequent use of the following abbreviations:

Notation	Meaning
$\forall x \in A$:	for each element x of A it holds that:
$\exists x \in A$:	for at least one element x of A it holds that:
$\Leftrightarrow$	if and only if
$\overset{D}{\Leftrightarrow}$	by definition if and only if
$\overset{D}{=}$	is defined as

For "$\Leftrightarrow$" we will sometimes write "iff" (for "if and only if"). Furthermore we note that the symbol "$\square$" will be used to denote the end of an example, a proof, or a series of exercises.

As an illustration of the notations introduced above, we can concisely and accurately represent the (true) statement that for any given integer there exists a smaller integer as follows:

$$\forall x \in \mathbb{Z} : \exists y \in \mathbb{Z} : y < x$$

Finally we also assume familiarity with the notion of an *ordered pair*. The ordered pair with *first coordinate* x and *second coordinate* y is denoted by $(x ; y)$. Conversely, if p is an ordered pair, then the first coordinate of p can be written as $\pi_1(p)$ and the second coordinate of p as $\pi_2(p)$.

We note that two ordered pairs are equal if and only if both their first and their second coordinates are equal:

$$(x ; y) = (x' ; y') \quad \text{iff} \quad x = x' \text{ and } y = y'.$$

Hence $(2; 3) \neq (3; 2)$, whereas $\{2, 3\} = \{3, 2\}$.

The set of all natural numbers (including 0) is denoted by $\mathbb{N}$:

DEFINITION 1:
$I\!N \overset{D}{=} \{k \in \mathbb{Z} \mid k \geq 0\}.$

If $n \in I\!N$, then Chs(n) denotes the set of all strings of at most n characters. For each $n \in I\!N$, the empty string (i.e., the string consisting of zero characters) belongs to Chs(n). After Example 2 (at the end of this chapter) we will return to this concept. For each $n \in I\!N$, Chs(n) is a finite set.

We continue our notational conventions with the formal definitions of *set inclusion*, the *union*, the *intersection*, the *difference*, and the *Cartesian product* of two sets, and finally the *power set* of a set:

DEFINITION 2:
If A and B are sets, then:

(a) $A \subseteq B \overset{D}{\Longleftrightarrow} \forall x \in A : x \in B$;
(b) $B \supseteq A \overset{D}{\Longleftrightarrow} A \subseteq B$;
(c) $A \subset B \overset{D}{\Longleftrightarrow} A \subseteq B$ and $A \neq B$;
(d) $A \cup B \overset{D}{=} \{x \mid x \in A \text{ or } x \in B\}$;
(e) $A \cap B \overset{D}{=} \{x \mid x \in A \text{ and } x \in B\}$;
(f) $A - B \overset{D}{=} \{x \mid x \in A \text{ and } x \notin B\}$;
(g) $A \times B \overset{D}{=} \{(x\,;y) \mid x \in A \text{ and } y \in B\}$;
(h) $\mathbf{P}(A) \overset{D}{=} \{X \mid X \subseteq A\}$.

We emphasize that the elements of a set can be sets themselves. The power set $\mathbf{P}(A)$ of A is an example of such a set of sets.

In the following definitions we introduce notations for some useful subsets of $\mathbb{Z}$:

DEFINITION 3:
If $m \in \mathbb{Z}$ and $n \in \mathbb{Z}$, then:

(a) $[m \mathinner{..} n] \overset{D}{=} \{k \in \mathbb{Z} \mid m \leq k \text{ and } k \leq n\}$;
(b) $[m \mathinner{..} n) \overset{D}{=} \{k \in \mathbb{Z} \mid m \leq k \text{ and } k < n\}$;
(c) $[m \mathinner{..}) \overset{D}{=} \{k \in \mathbb{Z} \mid m \leq k\}$.

DEFINITION 4:
If $n \in I\!N - \{0\}$, then:

(a) $\text{Snn}(n) \overset{D}{=} [10^{n-1} \mathinner{..} 10^n - 1]$;
(b) $\text{Int}(n) \overset{D}{=} [-(10^n - 1) \mathinner{..} 10^n - 1]$.

Hence, Snn(n) is the set of all *natural* numbers that (in decimal notation) consist of *precisely n* digits, and Int(n) is the set of all *integers* consisting of *at most n* digits in decimal notation (when we disregard the sign). For example,

Snn(4) = [1000 .. 9999] and Int(4) = [–9999 .. 9999].

A frequently used notation for summation is

$$\sum_{\phi_x} u_x$$

where ϕ_x expresses the domain *over which* the summation takes place, and u_x expresses the set of *terms* being summated. Since such expressions ϕ_x can often be long in practice, we will instead write summations as

$$\sum \phi_x : u_x$$

For example, the expression

$$\sum n \in [0\,..\,199] \text{ and } (n \bmod 3) \neq 0 : n^2$$

represents the sum of the squares of all natural numbers less than 200 that are not divisible by three.

The definition of the (generalized) union of *a set of* sets is a generalization of the definition of the union of *two* sets (cf. Lemma 1 (2)).

DEFINITION 5:
If W is a set of sets, then:
$\bigcup W \stackrel{D}{=} \{x \mid \exists A \in W : x \in A\}$.

The following lemma describes special cases in which the set W has 0, 1, or 2 elements.

LEMMA 1:
If A and B are sets, then:
(0) $\bigcup \varnothing = \varnothing$;
(1) $\bigcup \{A\} = A$;
(2) $\bigcup \{A, B\} = A \cup B$.

If R is a set of ordered pairs, then *the domain of R*, denoted by dom(R), is defined as the set of all first coordinates in R. Analogously, *the range of R*, denoted by rng(R), is defined as the set of all second coordinates in R. The set R^{-1}, *the inverse of R*, denotes the set of the "inverses" of each of the elements of R:

DEFINITION 6:
If R is a set of ordered pairs, then:
(a) $\mathrm{dom}(R) \stackrel{D}{=} \{x \mid (x\,;y) \in R\}$;
(b) $\mathrm{rng}(R) \stackrel{D}{=} \{y \mid (x\,;y) \in R\}$;
(c) $R^{-1} \stackrel{D}{=} \{(y\,;x) \mid (x\,;y) \in R\}$.

A set of ordered pairs is often referred to as a *relation* in mathematics, whereas "relation" is often used in database theory for what we will call a *table* (cf. Definition 1.1).

The following lemma sums up a few elementary properties of the domain, the range, and the inverse of some compound sets of ordered pairs.

LEMMA 2:
If R and P are sets of ordered pairs and $D \subseteq R$, then:

(a) $R \cup P$, $R \cap P$, $R - P$, D and R^{-1} are also sets of ordered pairs;

(b) $\text{dom}(R \cup P) = \text{dom}(R) \cup \text{dom}(P)$ and $\text{rng}(R \cup P) = \text{rng}(R) \cup \text{rng}(P)$;

(c) $\text{dom}(R \cap P) \subseteq \text{dom}(R) \cap \text{dom}(P)$ and $\text{rng}(R \cap P) \subseteq \text{rng}(R) \cap \text{rng}(P)$;

(d) $\text{dom}\,(R - P) \supseteq \text{dom}(R) - \text{dom}(P)$ and $\text{rng}(R - P) \supseteq \text{rng}(R) - \text{rng}(P)$;

(e) $\text{dom}(D) \subseteq \text{dom}(R)$ and $\text{rng}(D) \subseteq \text{rng}(R)$;

(f) $\text{dom}(R^{-1}) = \text{rng}(R)$ and $\text{rng}(R^{-1}) = \text{dom}(R)$;

(g) $(R \cup P)^{-1} = R^{-1} \cup P^{-1}$ and $(R \cap P)^{-1} = R^{-1} \cap P^{-1}$ and
$(R - P)^{-1} = R^{-1} - P^{-1}$ and $(R^{-1})^{-1} = R$.

2 Functions

We define the well-known concept of a *function* as follows:

DEFINITION 7:
F is a **function** $\overset{D}{\Longleftrightarrow}$ F is a set of ordered pairs and
$\forall(x\,;y) \in F : \forall(x'\,;y') \in F :$ if $x = x'$ then $y = y'$.

In other words, F is a function if F is a set of ordered pairs such that for each $x \in \text{dom}(F)$ there exists *exactly one* y such that $(x\,;y) \in F$. For each function f and each $x \in \text{dom}(f)$, $f(x)$ denotes the unique y for which $(x\,;y) \in f$. Read $f(x)$ as: *f applied to x*. Conversely, f inv y, *the pre-image of y under f*, stands for the set of all $x \in \text{dom}(f)$ such that $(x\,;y) \in f$. Hence, $f \text{ inv } y = \{x \in \text{dom}(f) \mid f(x) = y\}$.

An element of dom(f) is called an *argument of f* and an element of rng(f) a *value of f* or an *image under f*. In particular, $f(x)$ is called *the value of f for x* or *the image of x under f*. If $f(x) = x$, then x is called a *fixed point of f*.

For illustration purposes, we define the set f1 as follows:

f1 = {(EMPNO; 10), (DEPNO; 6), (SAL; 1962)}

According to Definition 7, the set f1 is a function and f1(EMPNO) = 10, f1(DEPNO) = 6, and f1(SAL) = 1962. The set {(EMPNO; 10), (DEPNO; 6), (SAL; 1962), (DEPNO; 8)} is not a function. A straightforward (and classical) example of a function is the so-called *successor function* for natural numbers, defined as $\{(x\,;x+1) \mid x \in \mathbb{N}\}$. The set $\{((k\,;n)\,;k^2+n) \mid (k\,;n) \in \mathbb{Z} \times \mathbb{N}\}$ is an example of a function "of two variables".

Since every function is a set of ordered pairs, each concept and each lemma that applies to sets in general, or to sets of ordered pairs in particular, also applies to functions! Thus, for instance, the intersection and the union of two functions are defined, as are the domain and the range of a function. For example, dom(f1) = {EMPNO, DEPNO, SAL} and rng(f1) = {6, 10, 1962}; the afore-mentioned function "of two variables" has domain $\mathbb{Z} \times \mathbb{N}$ and range $\mathbb{N}$.

It goes without saying that Lemma 2 applies to functions as well. As a result, for all functions f and g, the sets $f \cup g$, $f \cap g$, and $f - g$ are sets of ordered pairs. But are they also *functions*? This question is answered in the following lemma.

LEMMA 3:
If f and g are functions and $D \subseteq f$, then:

(a) D is a function;

(b) $f \cap g$ and $f - g$ are functions;

(c) $|\operatorname{rng}(f)| \leq |\operatorname{dom}(f)|$;

(d) $\varnothing$ is a function and $\operatorname{dom}(\varnothing) = \operatorname{rng}(\varnothing) = \varnothing$.

Apparently, the union of two functions does not have to be a function itself. Consider the function f2 defined as follows:

f2 = {(DEPNO; 6), (SAL; 2100), (AGE; 26)}.

Now f1 $\cup$ f2 is not a function, because we have both (SAL; 1962) $\in$ f1 $\cup$ f2 and (SAL; 2100) $\in$ f1 $\cup$ f2.

If f and g are functions such that $f \cup g$ is also a function, then we call f and g *joinable* (or *compatible*):

DEFINITION 8:
If f and g are functions, then:
***f* and *g* are joinable** $\overset{D}{\Longleftrightarrow}$ $f \cup g$ is a function.

We note that every function is joinable with itself. If the functions f and g are joinable and the functions g and h are joinable as well, then f and h do not have to be joinable. (Verify this.) In Lemma 13 on page 12 we will establish some criteria for joinability of two functions.

The following lemma gives some useful criteria for proving inclusion or equality of functions:

LEMMA 4:
If f and g are functions, then:
(a) $f \subseteq g$ iff $\text{dom}(f) \subseteq \text{dom}(g)$ and $\forall x \in \text{dom}(f) : f(x) = g(x)$;
(b) $f = g$ iff $\text{dom}(f) = \text{dom}(g)$ and $\forall x \in \text{dom}(f) : f(x) = g(x)$.

Part (a) is deducible from Definition 7, and part (b) follows from (a).

We introduce the following terminology:

DEFINITION 9:
If A is a set, then:
(a) f is a **function over** $A \overset{D}{\Longleftrightarrow} f$ is a function and $\text{dom}(f) = A$;
(b) f is a **function from** $A \overset{D}{\Longleftrightarrow} f$ is a function and $\text{dom}(f) \subseteq A$;
(c) f is a **function into** $A \overset{D}{\Longleftrightarrow} f$ is a function and $\text{rng}(f) \subseteq A$;
(d) f is a **function onto** $A \overset{D}{\Longleftrightarrow} f$ is a function and $\text{rng}(f) = A$.

In the literature, a function from A is sometimes referred to as a *partial* function over A. A function over A is also called a (*total*) function *from A* in expressions such as "(*total*) function *from A into B*" and "(*total*) function *from A onto B*".

We note that every function f is a function *from* dom(f) *onto* rng(f).

For each set A we define id(A), *the identity function on A*, as the function that assigns to each element of A that same element:

DEFINITION 10:
If A is a set, then:
$\text{id}(A) \overset{D}{=} \{(x\,;x) \mid x \in A\}$.

LEMMA 5:
If A and B are sets, then:
(a) id(A) is a total function from A onto A;
(b) $\text{id}(A \cup B) = \text{id}(A) \cup \text{id}(B)$;
(c) $\text{id}(A \cap B) = \text{id}(A) \cap \text{id}(B)$;
(d) $\text{id}(A - B) = \text{id}(A) - \text{id}(B)$.

The set of all total functions from A into B is denoted by $A \twoheadrightarrow B$, and the set of all "partial" functions from A into B is denoted by $A \overset{\sim}{\twoheadrightarrow} B$:

DEFINITION 11:
If A and B are sets, then:

(a) $A \rightarrowtriangle B \stackrel{D}{=} \{f \mid f \text{ is a function and } \mathrm{dom}(f) = A \text{ and } \mathrm{rng}(f) \subseteq B\}$;

(b) $A \tilde{\rightarrowtriangle} B \stackrel{D}{=} \{f \mid f \text{ is a function and } \mathrm{dom}(f) \subseteq A \text{ and } \mathrm{rng}(f) \subseteq B\}$.

From the definition it follows that $(A \rightarrowtriangle B) \subseteq (A \tilde{\rightarrowtriangle} B)$.

We can apply these notations consecutively; thus $A \rightarrowtriangle (B \rightarrowtriangle C)$ is the set of all functions that assign to each element of A a function from B into C. Conversely, $(A \rightarrowtriangle B) \rightarrowtriangle C$ is the set of all functions that assign to each function from A into B an element of C.

In the literature "$f \in A \rightarrowtriangle B$" is often written as "$f : A \to B$", and $A \rightarrowtriangle B$ is often written as B^A.

If R is a set of ordered pairs, then R is called *injective* iff for each $y \in \mathrm{rng}(R)$ there is *exactly one* x such that $(x\,;y) \in R$:

DEFINITION 12:
If R is a set of ordered pairs, then:
R is **injective** $\stackrel{D}{\Leftrightarrow} \forall (x\,;y) \in R : \forall (x'\,;y') \in R$: if $y = y'$ then $x = x'$.

Note that the above requirement is in fact the reverse of the one in Definition 7.

For functions, injectivity amounts to the following:

LEMMA 6:
If f is a function, then:
f is injective $\Leftrightarrow \forall x \in \mathrm{dom}(f) : \forall x' \in \mathrm{dom}(f)$: if $f(x) = f(x')$ then $x = x'$.

An injective function is also called an *injection* or a *one-to-one function*.

LEMMA 7:
If R is a set of ordered pairs, then:

(a) R is injective iff R^{-1} is a function;

(b) if R is an injective function, then $|\,\mathrm{dom}(R)\,| = |\,\mathrm{rng}(R)\,|$.

In connection with part (b) of the foregoing lemma (and part (c) of Lemma 3), we mention the following useful equivalences:

LEMMA 8:
If A and B are sets, then:

(a) $|\,A\,| \geq |\,B\,|$ iff $\exists f \in A \rightarrowtriangle B : \mathrm{rng}(f) = B$;

(b) $|\,A\,| \leq |\,B\,|$ iff $\exists f \in A \rightarrowtriangle B : f$ is injective;

(c) $|\,A\,| = |\,B\,|$ iff $\exists f \in A \rightarrowtriangle B : f$ is injective and $\mathrm{rng}(f) = B$.

A function as mentioned under (c) is called a *bijection from A to B*:

DEFINITION 13:
If A and B are sets, then:
f is a **bijection from A to B** $\overset{D}{\Longleftrightarrow}$ f is an injective function and $\text{dom}(f) = A$ and $\text{rng}(f) = B$.

We sometimes use the notation "$\lambda x \in A : u_x$" (where u_x represents some expression in x) as an abbreviation for "$\{(x\,;\,u_x) \mid x \in A\}$". Hence $\lambda x \in A : u_x$ represents a function over A. For instance, we can write the successor function for the natural numbers as $\lambda x \in \mathbb{N} : x + 1$, and the aforementioned function "of two variables" as $\lambda (k\,;\,n) \in \mathbb{Z} \times \mathbb{N} : k^2 + n$. Furthermore, for every set A, we can write the identity function on A as follows:

$$\text{id}(A) = \lambda x \in A : x$$

In addition, we will also use the notation "$\lambda x \in A$ and $\phi_x : u_x$" (where ϕ_x represents some condition for x) as an abbreviation for "$\{(x\,;\,u_x) \mid x \in A \text{ and } \phi_x\}$".

We define the *composition of g after f* for every pair of functions f and g (and not only in the case of $\text{rng}(f) \subseteq \text{dom}(g)$, which is common):

DEFINITION 14:
If f and g are functions, then:
$g \circ f \overset{D}{=} \{(x\,;\,g(f(x))) \mid x \in \text{dom}(f) \text{ and } f(x) \in \text{dom}(g)\}$.

In λ-notation: $g \circ f = \lambda x \in \text{dom}(f)$ and $f(x) \in \text{dom}(g) : g(f(x))$.

To take just one practical application of this (somewhat more general) definition of function composition, consider the function h1 and (the aforementioned function) f1:

h1 = {(DNO; DEPNO), (ENO; EMPNO), (CT; CITY)}
f1 = {(DEPNO; 6), (EMPNO; 10), (SAL; 1962)}

From the definition of function composition, it follows that f1 $\circ$ h1 is the set {(DNO; 6), (ENO; 10)}. Moreover, we have h1 $\circ$ f1 = $\varnothing$, since there is no $x \in$ dom(f1) such that f1(x) $\in$ dom(h1).

The following lemma, which sums up several useful properties of function composition, will be used frequently in subsequent chapters.

LEMMA 9:
If f, g, and h are functions, then:

(a) $g \circ f$ is a function;

(b) $\text{dom}(g \circ f) \subseteq \text{dom}(f)$;

(c) $\text{rng}(g \circ f) \subseteq \text{rng}(g)$;

(d) if $\text{rng}(f) \subseteq \text{dom}(g)$, then $\text{dom}(g \circ f) = \text{dom}(f)$;

(e) if $\text{dom}(g) \subseteq \text{rng}(f)$, then $\text{rng}(g \circ f) = \text{rng}(g)$;

(f) $h \circ (g \circ f) = (h \circ g) \circ f$;

(g) if $\text{dom}(f) = \text{dom}(g)$, then $\text{dom}(f \circ h) = \text{dom}(g \circ h)$;

(h) $f \circ h = g \circ h \Leftrightarrow f \circ \text{id}(\text{rng}(h)) = g \circ \text{id}(\text{rng}(h))$;

(i) if $f \circ h = g \circ h$ and $\text{dom}(f) \subseteq \text{rng}(h)$, then $f \subseteq g$;

(j) if $f \circ h = g \circ h$ and $\text{dom}(f) = \text{dom}(g) \subseteq \text{rng}(h)$, then $f = g$.

The following lemma shows that composition with the identity function on B, both "before" and "after", can be considered as a kind of "filter". We also see that the composition of the identity functions on two sets is equal to the identity function on the intersection of those sets.

LEMMA 10:
If f is a function and A and B are sets, then:

(a) $f \circ \text{id}(B) = \{(x\,;y) \in f \mid x \in B\}$;

(b) $\text{id}(B) \circ f = \{(x\,;y) \in f \mid y \in B\}$;

(c) $\text{id}(A) \circ \text{id}(B) = \text{id}(A \cap B)$.

For every function f and every set B the set mentioned under (a) is called *the restriction of f to B*, i.e., the set of all elements of f such that the first coordinates belong to B. The restriction of f to B is denoted by $f \upharpoonright B$; the remaining elements of f constitute the set $f \not\upharpoonright B$:

DEFINITION 15:
If f is a function and B is a set, then:

(a) $f \upharpoonright B \stackrel{D}{=} \{(x\,;y) \in f \mid x \in B\}$;

(b) $f \not\upharpoonright B \stackrel{D}{=} \{(x\,;y) \in f \mid x \notin B\}$.

For example, f1 $\upharpoonright$ {EMPNO, SAL} = {(EMPNO; 10), (SAL; 1962)} and f1 $\not\upharpoonright$ {EMPNO, SAL} = {(DEPNO; 6)}. For the function h1 we have h1 $\upharpoonright$ {EMPNO, SAL} = ∅, and h1 $\not\upharpoonright$ {EMPNO, SAL} = h1 (since EMPNO and SAL do not occur in h1 as first coordinates).

LEMMA 11:
If f is a function and B and B' are sets, then:

(a) $f \upharpoonright B$ is a function over $\text{dom}(f) \cap B$;

(b) $f \not\upharpoonright B$ is a function over $\text{dom}(f) - B$;

(c) $f \upharpoonright B$ and $f \not\upharpoonright B$ are joinable;

(d) $f = (f \upharpoonright B) \cup (f \not\upharpoonright B)$;

(e) $f \upharpoonright B = \lambda x \in \mathrm{dom}(f) \cap B : f(x)$;

(f) $f \not\upharpoonright B = \lambda x \in \mathrm{dom}(f) - B : f(x)$;

(g) $f \not\upharpoonright B = f \upharpoonright (\mathrm{dom}(f) - B)$;

(h) $f \upharpoonright B = f \circ \mathrm{id}(B)$;

(i) $(f \not\upharpoonright B) \not\upharpoonright B' = f \not\upharpoonright (B \cup B')$;

(j) $(f \upharpoonright B) \upharpoonright B' = f \upharpoonright (B \cap B')$;

(k) $(f \upharpoonright B) \not\upharpoonright B' = f \upharpoonright (B - B')$;

(l) $f \upharpoonright \varnothing = \varnothing$ and $\varnothing \upharpoonright B = \varnothing$;

(m) $f \not\upharpoonright \varnothing = f$ and $\varnothing \not\upharpoonright B = \varnothing$.

Lemma 11(h) restates explicitly that restriction is in fact a special case of function composition.

DEFINITION 16:
If f and g are functions and A is a set, then:
$f \equiv g$ **on** $A \overset{D}{\Longleftrightarrow} f \upharpoonright A = g \upharpoonright A$.

In the case above we say that f and g *match on A*.

Sometimes a given function f is "not exactly" the function we want, in the sense that some pairs $(x\,;y)$ are missing or some arguments are not mapped to the "right" images. The "adjustment" on f can be represented by a function, with the "result of the adjustment" being defined as follows:

DEFINITION 17:
If f and g are functions, then:
$f \,\theta\, g \overset{D}{=} (f \not\upharpoonright \mathrm{dom}(g)) \cup g$.

For instance, for the functions f1 and f2 given before, we have

f1 θ f2 = {(EMPNO; 10), (DEPNO; 6), (SAL; 2100), (AGE; 26)} and
f2 θ f1 = {(EMPNO; 10), (DEPNO; 6), (SAL; 1962), (AGE; 26)}

We call $f \,\theta\, g$ the *modification of f according to g*. In [SP 89], this operation is called *functional overriding*.

LEMMA 12:
If f, g, and h are functions, then:

(a) $f \,\theta\, g$ is a function over $\mathrm{dom}(f) \cup \mathrm{dom}(g)$;

(b) if $\text{dom}(f) = \text{dom}(g)$, then $f \,\theta\, g = g$;
(c) $(f \,\theta\, g) \,\theta\, h = f \,\theta\, (g \,\theta\, h)$;
(d) $f \,\theta\, \varnothing = \varnothing \,\theta\, f = f$;
(e) $f \,\theta\, f = f$.

We are now able to give some alternative definitions of joinability.

LEMMA 13:
If f and g are functions, then the following statements are equivalent:
(a) f and g are joinable;
(b) $f \cup g$ is a function;
(c) f and g match on $\text{dom}(f) \cap \text{dom}(g)$;
(d) $\text{dom}(f \cap g) = \text{dom}(f) \cap \text{dom}(g)$;
(e) $f \,\theta\, g = g \,\theta\, f$;
(f) $f \,\theta\, g = f \cup g$.

Note that from part (c) onwards, this lemma can be said to give four alternative definitions of joinability. The lemma also shows that joinable pairs of functions have various interesting properties. In Chapter 2 we will discuss joinable pairs of functions in greater detail. The following lemma gives a few properties of joinable pairs of functions.

LEMMA 14:
If f, g, and h are functions and f and g are joinable, then:
(a) $f \circ h$ and $g \circ h$ are joinable;
(b) $(f \circ h) \cup (g \circ h) = (f \cup g) \circ h$;
(c) $(h \circ f) \cup (h \circ g) = h \circ (f \cup g)$.

Note that the value of a function may be a set or even a function. For example, $\lambda n \in \mathbb{N}$: $[0 \,..\, (n-1)]$ is the "set-valued" function over $\mathbb{N}$ that assigns to each natural number the set of all its predecessors in $\mathbb{N}$, and $\lambda n \in \mathbb{N} : (\lambda k \in \mathbb{Z} : k^n)$ is the "function-valued" function over $\mathbb{N}$ that assigns to each natural number n the n-th power function over $\mathbb{Z}$.

A set-valued (*) function is also called a *set function*:

(*) For readers familiar with axiomatic set theory, we note that we use a naive set theory in which we do not presuppose that everything is a set.

DEFINITION 18:
F is a **set function** $\stackrel{D}{\Leftrightarrow}$ F is a function and
$\forall x \in \text{dom}(F) : F(x)$ is a set.

EXAMPLE 1:
For illustration purposes, we present two examples of set functions. These functions, FE and FD, will be used frequently later on. To make things a bit more vivid, we give behind the vertical bar a possible interpretation of what this example could mean in practice.

FE = {(NO ; $\mathbb{N}$),	identity number of an *employee*
(NAME ; Chs(40)),	name
(SAL ; $\mathbb{N}$),	salary
(SEX ; { 'M', 'F'}),	sex
(DEPNO ; [1 .. 99])}	department number
FD = {(DNO ; $\mathbb{N}$),	number of a *department*
(NAME ; Chs(45)),	department name
(MANNO; $\mathbb{N}$)}	identity number of the manager

□ Example 1.

If F is a set function, then $\Pi(F)$ denotes the set of all functions over dom(F) that determine a "choice" from the set $F(x)$ for each $x \in \text{dom}(F)$, and $\tilde{\Pi}(F)$ denotes the set of all functions that determine a choice from $F(x)$ for "some" of the elements $x \in \text{dom}(F)$:

DEFINITION 19:
If F is a set function, then:
(a) $\Pi(F) \stackrel{D}{=} \{f \mid f$ is a function over dom(F) and $\forall x \in \text{dom}(f) : f(x) \in F(x)\}$;
(b) $\tilde{\Pi}(F) \stackrel{D}{=} \{f \mid f$ is a function from dom(F) and $\forall x \in \text{dom}(f) : f(x) \in F(x)\}$.

We call $\Pi(F)$ *the generalized product of F*. From the definition it follows that $\Pi(F) \subseteq \tilde{\Pi}(F)$.

For the set function FD mentioned above, Π(FD) is the set of all functions of the form

{(DNO; n), (NAME; α), (MANNO; m)},

where $n \in \mathbb{N}$, $\alpha \in$ Chs(45), and $m \in \mathbb{N}$.

For all sets A and B, we can describe the concepts introduced in Definition 11 in an alternative way by using Definition 19 and the function $\lambda a \in A : B$ (i.e., the (constant) set function that assigns to each element of A the set B):

LEMMA 15:
If A and B are sets, then:

(a) $A \twoheadrightarrow B = \Pi(\lambda a \in A : B)$;

(b) $A \tilde{\twoheadrightarrow} B = \tilde{\Pi}(\lambda a \in A : B)$.

If V is a set of functions, then He(V) denotes *the heading of V* (or *the complete domain of V*), which by definition is equal to the union of the domains of all elements of V:

DEFINITION 20:
If V is a set of functions, then:
$\text{He}(V) \stackrel{D}{=} \bigcup \{\text{dom}(f) \mid f \in V\}$.

Thus we have, for example, He({f1, f2}) = {EMPNO, DEPNO, SAL, AGE}, where

f1 = {(EMPNO; 10), (DEPNO; 6), (SAL; 1962)}
f2 = {(DEPNO; 6), (SAL; 2100), (AGE; 26)}

The following lemma treats some special cases.

LEMMA 16:
If A and B are sets and F is a set function, then:

(a) $\text{He}(\Pi(F)) = \text{dom}(F)$ if $\Pi(F) \neq \varnothing$;

(b) $\text{He}(A \twoheadrightarrow B) = A$ if $B \neq \varnothing$;

(c) $\text{He}(A \twoheadrightarrow \varnothing) = \varnothing$;

(d) $\text{He}(\varnothing) = \varnothing$.

3 The Transitive Closure of a Relation

Before we define the transitive closure of a relation, we first introduce the notion of a *sequence*:

DEFINITION 21:
If $n \in \mathbb{N}$, then:
r is a **sequence of length** n $\stackrel{D}{\Leftrightarrow}$ r is a function and $\text{dom}(r) = [0 .. n)$.

EXAMPLE 2:
Some examples of sequences are:

r1 = {(0; 37), (1; 29), (2; 37)}
r2 = {(0; 29), (1; 37), (2; 37)}
r3 = {(0; 29), (1; 37)}

The functions r1 and r2 are sequences of length 3 whereas r3 is a sequence of length 2.
We sometimes denote sequences as follows:

r1 = <37; 29; 37>
r2 = <29; 37; 37>
r3 = <29; 37>

Note that r1 ≠ r2, r2 ≠ r3, and r3 ≠ r1.

□ Example 2.

For each $n \in \mathbb{N}$ we can also consider Chs(n) as a set of sequences:

$$\text{Chs}(n) = \{r \mid \exists k \in [0 \,..\, n]\text{: } r \text{ is a sequence of length } k \text{ and rng}(r) \subseteq C\},$$

where C is the set of characters (of which no further specification is given here). For example, when we replace the number 37 in Example 2 by the character 'D' and the number 29 by the character 'A', then we obtain the representations of the strings 'DAD', 'ADD', and 'AD', respectively.

Should duplicates, if any, and the order in which objects occur be relevant, as in the preceding example (in which after all r1 ≠ r2 and r2 ≠ r3), then sequences can prove to be very useful.

If r and r' are sequences such that $r \subseteq r'$, then we call r an *initial subsequence of* r', and, conversely, r' an *extension of* r. These two names may become clear from Example 2, in which r3 ⊆ r2 (but not r3 ⊆ r1). Also, if r and r' are elements of Chs(n), then $r \subseteq r'$ indeed expresses the fact that the character sequence r is an initial subsequence of the character sequence r'. For instance, 'AD' is an initial subsequence of 'ADD' but not an initial subsequence of 'DAD'.

We conclude the treatment of sequences with the remark that it follows from Definition 21 that the length of a sequence r is always $|r|$ and that $\varnothing$ is the only sequence of length 0.

DEFINITION 22:
If $n \in \mathbb{N} - \{0\}$ and R is a relation, then:

$$R \uparrow n \stackrel{D}{=} \{(r(0)\,;\, r(n)) \mid r \text{ is a sequence of length } n+1 \text{ and } \forall i \in [0 \,..\, n) : (r(i)\,;\, r(i+1)) \in R\}.$$

LEMMA 17:

(a) $R \uparrow 1 = R$ for each relation R;

(b) $\varnothing \uparrow n = \varnothing$ for each $n \in \mathbb{N} - \{0\}$.

EXAMPLE 3:

We define the relation R1 as follows:

R1 = {(1; 2), (2; 3), (3; 4), (1; 4), (3; 1)}

Such a set of ordered pairs can also be depicted as follows:

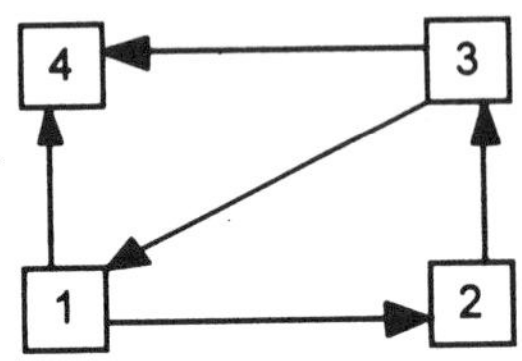

Figure 1: A graphical representation of R1

From Definition 22 we infer that

R1 $\uparrow$ 2 = {(1; 3), (2; 4), (2; 1), (3; 2), (3; 4)},
R1 $\uparrow$ 3 = {(1; 4), (1; 1), (2; 2), (2; 4), (3; 3)}, and
R1 $\uparrow$ 4 = R1

Furthermore it holds for every $m \in I\!N$ and every $k \in \{1,2,3\}$ that R1 $\uparrow (3m + k)$ = R1 $\uparrow k$.

□ Example 3.

In terms of the graphical representation of R, we can describe $R \uparrow n$ informally as the set of (starting point; end point)-pairs of all possible "walks" of exactly n steps in the graphical representation of R.

By *the transitive closure of* a relation R, denoted by Tcl(R), we mean the set of (starting point; end point)-pairs of all possible *non-empty* walks in the graphical representation of R. We call R *cyclic* iff real "tours" are possible in R; otherwise R is called *acyclic*. To be precise:

DEFINITION 23:

If R is a relation, then:

(a) $\text{Tcl}(R) \stackrel{D}{=} \bigcup \{R \uparrow n \mid n \in I\!N - \{0\}\}$;

(b) R is **cyclic** $\stackrel{D}{\Longleftrightarrow} \exists (x\,;y) \in \text{Tcl}(R) : x = y$;

(c) R is **acyclic** $\stackrel{D}{\Longleftrightarrow} \forall (x\,;y) \in \text{Tcl}(R) : x \neq y$.

By elaborating on part (a), and using Definition 22, we see that $(x\,;y) \in \text{Tcl}(R)$ if there is an n belonging to $I\!N - \{0\}$ and a sequence r of length n + 1 such that $x = r(0)$ and $y = r(n)$ and $(r(i)\,;r(i+1)) \in R$ for all i belonging to [0 .. n).

For the relation R1, from Example 3, we have
$\mathrm{Tcl}(\mathrm{R1}) = (\mathrm{R1} \uparrow 1) \cup (\mathrm{R1} \uparrow 2) \cup (\mathrm{R1} \uparrow 3) = \{1, 2, 3\} \times \{1, 2, 3, 4\}$.
Hence, the relation R1 is cyclic.

LEMMA 18:
If R is a relation, then:

(a) $R \subseteq \mathrm{Tcl}(R)$;

(b) $\mathrm{Tcl}(\mathrm{Tcl}(R)) = \mathrm{Tcl}(R)$;

(c) $\mathrm{Tcl}(\varnothing) = \varnothing$;

(d) if R is acyclic, then R is *irreflexive* (i.e., $\forall (x\, ; y) \in R : x \neq y$);

(e) R is acyclic $\Longleftrightarrow$ $\mathrm{Tcl}(R)$ is irreflexive.

CHAPTER 1

From Tables to Database Universes

In this chapter, we introduce the important basic notions of *table*, ***database state***, and *database universe*.

1.1 Tables

By a *table over* a set A we mean a set of functions over A:

DEFINITION 1.1:
If A is a set, then:
T is a **table over** A $\overset{D}{\Leftrightarrow}$ T is a set and
$\forall t \in T$: t is a function over A.

An element of a table is called a *tuple*.

EXAMPLE 1.1:

Figure 1.1(a) represents a table T1 over {DEPNO, SEX, NAME, NO, SAL}, and Figure 1.1(b) represents a table T2 over {DNO, MANNO, NAME}. T1 has three elements and T2 has two elements.

NO	NAME	SAL	SEX	DEPNO
8	JOHNSON	2200	M	1
7	JOHNSON	3109	F	2
9	DECKER	2995	M	1

(a) A table over {NO, NAME, SAL, SEX, DEPNO}

DNO	NAME	MANNO
2	PLANNING	7
1	PRODUCTION	9

(b) A table over {DNO, NAME, MANNO}

Figure 1.1

The two elements of T2 are the functions

t1 = {(DNO; 2), (MANNO; 7), (NAME; 'PLANNING')}, and
t2 = {(DNO; 1), (MANNO; 9), (NAME; 'PRODUCTION')}.

Hence, t1(DNO) = 2, t1(MANNO) = 7, etc. We see that dom(t1) = dom(t2) = {DNO, MANNO, NAME}, which is consistent with Definition 1.1.

Note that T1 $\subseteq \Pi$(FE) and T2 $\subseteq \Pi$(FD), where FE and FD are the set-valued functions defined in Example 1 on page 13.

We can think of NO, NAME, SAL, SEX and DEPNO in Figure 1.1(a) as representing an employee's number, name, salary, sex, and department number, respectively. Much in the same way DNO, NAME, and MANNO in Figure 1.1(b) can be thought of as representing department number, department name, and employee number of the manager of a department, respectively. Clearly these "possible" meanings, elucidatory as they might be, are not necessary for a formal understanding.

□ Example 1.1.

Since every table is a (special) set, every concept defined for sets also applies to tables. Thus, for example, the notions of union and intersection of two tables make sense; see also §2.1.1.

From Definition 1.1 it follows that ∅ is a table over *any* set. (Verify this.) For each set A and for each *non-empty* table T over A, however, A is the only set over which T is a table. This fact is proven as follows:
Let T be a non-empty table over A *and* over A'. Since T is non-empty, there exists a $t_0 \in T$; but then t_0 is a function over A and over A'. Hence, $\text{dom}(t_0) = A$ and $\text{dom}(t_0) = A'$. Conclusion: $A' = A$. Therefore, A is the only set over which T is a table.

Exercises 1.1 and 1.2 give alternative definitions of the concepts of table and table over A.

EXERCISES

1.1. Prove the following equivalence. (Hint: take A = He(V) for the "$\Leftarrow$"-part.)

$$\text{V is a table} \iff \text{V is a set of functions and}$$
$$\forall f \in V : \forall f' \in V : \text{dom}(f) = \text{dom}(f').$$

1.2. If A is a set, then:
T is a table over A $\iff$ $T \subseteq A \rightarrow B$ for some set B.
Prove this. (Hint: take $B = \bigcup \{\text{rng}(t) \mid t \in T\}$ in the "$\Rightarrow$"-part.)

□

1.2 Database States

EXAMPLE 1.2:

Figure 1.1 can be considered as a representation of (the relevant part of) the state of some (small) organization. This state can be represented formally by a function v1 over a set of two elements, say over {EMPL, DEP}, such that

v1 (EMPL) = T1 and v1(DEP) = T2.

If, in addition, g1 is the function over {DEP, EMPL} defined by

g1(DEP) = {DNO, MANNO, NAME} and
g1(EMPL) = {DEPNO, SEX, NAME, NO, SAL},

then v1 is called a *database state* (or briefly DB state) *over* g1.

□ Example 1.2.

We define the concept of a DB state for any set function g:

DEFINITION 1.2:

If g is a set function, then:
v is a **DB state over** g $\overset{D}{\iff}$ v is a function over dom(g) and
$\forall E \in \text{dom}(g) : v(E)$ is a table over $g(E)$.

Since every DB state is a function, every concept defined for functions also applies to DB states. Thus we can speak about the domain and the range of a DB state, for example.

EXERCISES

1.3. What is the domain and what is the range of the DB state v1 from Example 1.2?

1.4. Is it possible for a DB state to be defined over more than one set function? (Remember the empty set.)

□

1.3 Database Universes

The DB state v1 mentioned in Example 1.2 represents the state of some organization *at a certain point in time*. Assuming that we remain interested in the same characteristics, the state of the organization in question can always be represented by a DB state over g1. Conversely, not every DB state over g1 represents an admissible state of that organization.

The set of admissible states (to be determined by the organization in question) is therefore some set of DB states over g1. We call such a set a *database universe* (or briefly DB universe) *over* g1. In general:

DEFINITION 1.3:
If *g* is a set function, then:
U is a **DB universe over** *g* $\overset{D}{\Longleftrightarrow}$ *U* is a set of DB states over *g*.

If *U* is a DB universe over *g*, then we call *g the DB skeleton of U*, an element *E* of dom(*g*) a *table index* (or "table name") *of U*, *g* (*E*) *the heading of E in U*, and an element of *g* (*E*) an *attribute* (or "attribute name") *of E in U*. We call an element of *U* a *DB state consistent with U*.

EXAMPLE 1.3:

For the organization mentioned in Example 1.2, we will define a DB universe EXU over g1, in which the following requirements are incorporated:

(1) Every employee is determined uniquely by the employee number.

(2) Every department is determined uniquely by the department number.

(3) Every department is also determined uniquely by the department name.

(4) Every department number in the employee table also occurs (as a department number) in the department table.

(5) Every manager number in the department table also occurs as an employee number in the employee table.

In order to define our DB universe EXU, we make use of the set-valued functions FE and FD from the preceding chapter, of two sets of tables, namely WE and WD (representing the admissible employee tables and the admissible department tables, respectively), and of an auxiliary function HF (establishing the links between table indices and sets of tables):

$$\begin{aligned}
\text{FE} = \{&(\text{NO} \;;\; \mathbb{N}),\\
&(\text{NAME} \;;\; \text{Chs}(40)),\\
&(\text{SAL} \;;\; \mathbb{N}),\\
&(\text{SEX} \;;\; \{\text{'M'}, \text{'F'}\}),\\
&(\text{DEPNO} \;;\; [1\,..\,99])\};
\end{aligned}$$

$$\begin{aligned}
\text{FD} = \{&(\text{DNO} \;;\; \mathbb{N}),\\
&(\text{NAME} \;;\; \text{Chs}(45)),\\
&(\text{MANNO} \;;\; \mathbb{N})\};
\end{aligned}$$

$$\begin{aligned}
\text{WE} = \{T \mid\; &T \subseteq \Pi(\text{FE}) \text{ and}\\
&\forall t \in T : \forall t' \in T : \text{if } t \neq t' \text{ then } t(\text{NO}) \neq t'(\text{NO})\}; && (1)
\end{aligned}$$

$$\begin{aligned}
\text{WD} = \{T \mid\; &T \subseteq \Pi(\text{FD}) \text{ and}\\
&\forall t \in T : \forall t' \in T : \text{if } t \neq t' \text{ then } t(\text{DNO}) \neq t'(\text{DNO}) \text{ and} && (2)\\
&\qquad\qquad t(\text{NAME}) \neq t'(\text{NAME})\}; && (3)
\end{aligned}$$

$$\begin{aligned}
\text{HF} = \{&(\text{EMPL} \;;\; \text{WE}),\\
&(\text{DEP} \;;\; \text{WD})\};
\end{aligned}$$

$$\begin{aligned}
\text{EXU} = \{v \mid\; &v \in \Pi(\text{HF}) \text{ and}\\
&\{e(\text{DEPNO}) \mid e \in v(\text{EMPL})\} \subseteq \{d(\text{DNO}) \mid d \in v(\text{DEP})\} \text{ and} && (4)\\
&\{d(\text{MANNO}) \mid d \in v(\text{DEP})\} \subseteq \{e(\text{NO}) \mid e \in v(\text{EMPL})\}\} && (5)
\end{aligned}$$

□ Example 1.3.

Since every DB universe is a (special) set, each concept defined for sets applies to DB universes as well. Moreover, formally speaking, a DB universe over a set function g is also a table over dom(g):

THEOREM 1.1:
If g is a set function and U is a DB universe over g,
then U is a table over dom(g).

Proof:
From Definition 1.3 it follows that U is a set, and
from Definition 1.2 it follows that each element of U is a function over dom(g).
Hence U satisfies Definition 1.1.

□

Thus, the table indices of U act as the attributes of the "super table" U, the DB states as the tuples of that table, and the tables in such a DB state as the "attribute values" in the table U. For example, EXU is a table over {EMPL, DEP}.

EXERCISES

1.5. For a DB universe U over a set function g with $E \in \text{He}(U)$, we define:

(a) U is **consistent** $\overset{D}{\Longleftrightarrow} U \neq \varnothing$;

(b) E is **consistent in** U $\overset{D}{\Longleftrightarrow} \exists v \in U : v(E) \neq \varnothing$;

(c) U is **regular** $\overset{D}{\Longleftrightarrow}$ U is consistent and $\forall E' \in \text{He}(U) : E'$ is consistent in U.

Prove the following statements:

(a) If U is consistent, then dom(g) is unique.

(b) If E is consistent in U, then $g(E)$ is unique.

(c) If U is regular, then g is unique.

By "unique" we mean successively that

(a) $\text{dom}(g) = \text{dom}(g')$, (b) $g(E) = g'(E)$, and (c) $g = g'$

for each set function g' over which U is also a DB universe.

1.6. Prove that in each part of Exercise 1.5 "if and only if" holds.

1.7. Does it hold for each DB universe U that
U is regular $\Longleftrightarrow \exists v \in U : \forall E \in \text{He}(U) : v(E) \neq \varnothing$?
(Give for both implications either a proof or a counterexample.)

1.8. Verify that $\{\varnothing\}$ is a DB universe.
Is $\{\varnothing\}$ (formally speaking) a regular DB universe?
If so, what is the (unique) DB skeleton of $\{\varnothing\}$?

1.9. If U is a non-empty DB universe over g, then $\text{dom}(g) = \text{He}(U)$. Prove this.

1.10. (a) Is the function v1 from Example 1.2 an element of EXU?

(b) Give an(other) element of EXU.

(c) Is $\varnothing$ an element of WE? Is it an element of WD?

(d) Are there elements v of EXU such that $v(\text{DEP}) = \varnothing$?
If so, which elements are they?

1.11. A sales organization wants to keep track of data on its *customers*, on the *articles* that it sells, and on the *orders* that these customers place with this organization for these articles.
For each customer, the customer number and the name of that customer are to be recorded. Every customer is determined uniquely by his customer number. A customer number is a six-digit number; to be precise, it is an element of Snn(6).

For each article, its number, name and price are to be recorded. Every article is determined uniquely by its (five-digit) article number.
For each order, the following data is to be recorded: the order number, the number of the customer who placed the order, the article number of the article mentioned in the order, and the quantity ordered. (Thus every order concerns only one article, but possibly in any quantity.) Every order is determined uniquely by its (seven-digit) order number. The customer number of each order must also occur in the customer table. Likewise, the article number of each order must occur in the article table.
Transfer this informal (and somewhat incomplete) description into the formal definition of a DB universe EXU2.

1.12. Define a (small) DB universe EXU3 for some organization (for example, a sporting club or an educational institute).

1.13. We can "convert" each relation R into a table over $\{1,2\}$ as follows:

$$\text{crt}(R) \stackrel{D}{=} \{\{(1\,;x),\,(2\,;y)\} \mid (x\,;y) \in R\}$$

Conversely, every table T over $\{1,2\}$ can be "converted" into a relation:

$$\text{ctr}(T) \stackrel{D}{=} \{(t(1)\,;t(2)) \mid t \in T\}$$

From the conversion result of a table over $\{1,2\}$ (or of a relation) we can reconstruct the original table (relation) unambiguously, by applying "the other" conversion:

(a) $\text{crt}(\text{ctr}(T)) = T$ for each table T over $\{1,2\}$;
(b) $\text{ctr}(\text{crt}(R)) = R$ for each relation R.

Prove (a) and (b).

□

CHAPTER 2

Some Database Concepts

2.1 Concepts concerning Tables

2.1.1 Operations on Tables

We are interested in those operations that assign tables to one or more tables.

Since each table is a set, all operations that apply to sets apply to tables as well. Many of these operations assign to a table a table again. (As a consequence, these operations can be applied repeatedly.) Some of these operations will be treated in this subsection.

In general, every subset of a table over A is also a table over A (Lemma 2.1); in particular, the intersection and the difference of two tables over A are also tables over A (Lemma 2.2). Moreover, the union of two tables over A is a table over A as well (Lemma 2.3).

LEMMA 2.1:
If A is a set and T is a table over A and $D \subseteq T$, then D is also a table over A.

Proof:
T is a table over A and $D \subseteq T$, so D is a set and $t \in D$ implies $t \in T$. But then, by Definition 1.1, t is also a function over A. Thus, we see that, besides T, also D satisfies Definition 1.1.

□

LEMMA 2.2:
If A is a set, and T and T' are tables over A, then $T \cap T'$ and $T - T'$ are tables over A as well.

Proof:
$T \cap T' \subseteq T$ and $T - T' \subseteq T$, so, by Lemma 2.1,
$T \cap T'$ and $T - T'$ are also tables over A.

□

LEMMA 2.3:
If A is a set, and T and T' are tables over A, then $T \cup T'$ is a table over A as well.

Proof:
$T \cup T'$ is a set, and $t \in T \cup T'$ implies $t \in T$ or $t \in T'$; in both cases t is a function over A. In short, $T \cup T'$ satisfies Definition 1.1.

□

Examples of the constructs above (where T1 and T2 are taken from Example 1.1):

(a) $\{t \in \mathrm{T1} \mid t(\mathrm{NO}) \notin \{a(\mathrm{MANNO}) \mid a \in \mathrm{T2}\}\}$;

(b) $\{t \in \mathrm{T1} \mid t(\mathrm{SAL}) > 2500 \text{ and } t(\mathrm{DEPNO}) = 1\}$, or
$\{t \in \mathrm{T1} \mid t(\mathrm{SAL}) > 2500\} \cap \{t \in \mathrm{T1} \mid t(\mathrm{DEPNO}) = 1\}$;

(c) $\{t \in \mathrm{T1} \mid t(\mathrm{NAME}) \neq \text{'JOHNSON'}\}$, or
$\mathrm{T1} - \{t \in \mathrm{T1} \mid t(\mathrm{NAME}) = \text{'JOHNSON'}\}$;

(d) $\{t \in \mathrm{T1} \mid t(\mathrm{SEX}) = \text{'F'} \text{ or } t(\mathrm{DEPNO}) = 1\}$, or
$\{t \in \mathrm{T1} \mid t(\mathrm{SEX}) = \text{'F'}\} \cup \{t \in \mathrm{T1} \mid t(\mathrm{DEPNO}) = 1\}$.

Lemma 2.1 shows that the deletion of a number of "rows" from a table yields another table. Lemma 2.4 will show that the "orthogonal" operation of deleting a number of "columns" from a table yields a table as well.

This operation is defined formally as follows:

DEFINITION 2.1:
If T is a set of functions and B is a set, then:

$T \upharpoonright\!\upharpoonright B \stackrel{D}{=} \{t \upharpoonright B \mid t \in T\}$.

We call $T \upharpoonright\!\upharpoonright B$ *the projection of* T *on* B. While having defined $T \upharpoonright\!\upharpoonright B$ for *each* set of functions and for *each* set B, we are mainly interested in those cases in which T is a table over a set A and, moreover, $B \subseteq A$.

EXAMPLE 2.1:

Figure 2.1 represents the projection of the table T1 of Figure 1.1(a) on the set {SEX, DEPNO}. Note that $\mathrm{T1} \upharpoonright\!\upharpoonright \{\mathrm{DEPNO, SEX}\}$ has fewer elements than T1.

DEPNO	SEX
1	M
2	F

Figure 2.1: The table T1 $\Vert\!\!\upharpoonright$ {DEPNO, SEX}

□ Example 2.1.

LEMMA 2.4:
If A and B are sets and T is a table over A, then:

(a) $T \Vert\!\!\upharpoonright B$ is a table over $A \cap B$;

(b) $|T \Vert\!\!\upharpoonright B| \leq |T|$.

Proof:

(a) $T \Vert\!\!\upharpoonright B = \{t \upharpoonright B \mid t \in T\}$, which is (by Lemma 11(a) on page 10) a set of functions over $B \cap A$; in other words, $T \Vert\!\!\upharpoonright B$ is a table over $A \cap B$.

(b) According to Lemma 8(a) on page 8 it suffices to give a function f with domain T and range $T \Vert\!\!\upharpoonright B$. Let $f = \lambda t \in T : t \upharpoonright B$; obviously, this function suffices.

□

The following operation is called the *natural join:*

DEFINITION 2.2:
If T and T' are sets of functions, then:
$T \bowtie T' \stackrel{D}{=} \{t \cup t' \mid t \in T \text{ and } t' \in T' \text{ and } t \cup t' \text{ is a function}\}$.

Hence, we quantify over all pairs $(t;t') \in T \times T'$ for which t and t' are joinable (see Definition 8 on page 6).

EXAMPLE 2.2:

Figure 2.2 represents

(a) a table V1 over $\{a, b, c\}$ of 4 elements,

(b) a table V2 over $\{b, c, d\}$ of 5 elements, and

(c) V1 $\bowtie$ V2, a table over $\{a, b, c, d\}$, consisting of 7 elements.

To put it in an informal way, each element of V1 is "combined" with *all* elements of V2 that "look the same" on $\{b, c\}$. Note that the elements that have no "equivalent" counterpart in the other set do not occur in the end result.

a	b	c
1	1	2
2	1	2
3	2	1
4	2	2

(a) V1

b	c	d
1	1	2
1	2	2
1	2	3
1	2	4
2	2	5

(b) V2

a	*b*	*c*	*d*
1	1	2	2
1	1	2	3
1	1	2	4
2	1	2	2
2	1	2	3
2	1	2	4
4	2	2	5

(c) V1 $\bowtie$ V2

Figure 2.2

□ Example 2.2.

The following lemma lists some interesting properties of the natural join:

LEMMA 2.5:
If A, A', and A'' are sets and T is a table over A, T' is a table over A', and T'' is a table over A'', then:

(a) $T \bowtie T'$ is a table over $A \cup A'$;

(b) $|T \bowtie T'| \leq |T| * |T'|$;

(c) $T \bowtie T' = T' \bowtie T$, in other words, the natural join is *commutative*;

(d) $T \bowtie (T' \bowtie T'') = (T \bowtie T') \bowtie T''$, i.e., the natural join is *associative*;

(e) if $A = A'$, then $T \bowtie T' = T \cap T'$;

(f) $T \bowtie T = T$ and $T \bowtie \{\varnothing\} = T$ and $T \bowtie \varnothing = \varnothing$.

Proof:

(a) It is clear from the definition of the natural join that $T \bowtie T'$ is a set of functions. If $u \in T \bowtie T'$, then there exist $t \in T$ and $t' \in T'$ such that $u = t \cup t'$; therefore $\text{dom}(u) = \text{dom}(t \cup t') = \text{dom}(t) \cup \text{dom}(t') = A \cup A'$.

(b) We define $f = \{((t;t');\ t \cup t') \mid (t;t') \in T \times T' \text{ and } t \cup t' \text{ is a function}\}$; f is a function and $T \bowtie T' = \text{rng}(f)$ and $\text{dom}(f) \subseteq T \times T'$; therefore, using Lemma 8(a) on page 8:
$|T \bowtie T'| = |\text{rng}(f)| \leq |\text{dom}(f)| \leq |T \times T'| = |T| * |T'|$.

(c) $T \bowtie T'$
$= \{t \cup t' \mid t \in T \text{ and } t' \in T' \text{ and } t \cup t' \text{ is a function}\}$
$= \{t' \cup t \mid t' \in T' \text{ and } t \in T \text{ and } t' \cup t \text{ is a function}\}$
$= T' \bowtie T$.

(d) $T \bowtie (T' \bowtie T'')$
$= \{t \cup x \mid t \in T \text{ and } x \in T' \bowtie T'' \text{ and } t \cup x \text{ is a function}\}$
$= \{t \cup (t' \cup t'') \mid t \in T \text{ and } t' \in T' \text{ and } t'' \in T'' \text{ and}$
$t' \cup t'' \text{ is a function and } t \cup (t' \cup t'') \text{ is a function}\}$; (1)

$(T \bowtie T') \bowtie T''$
$= \{y \cup t'' \mid y \in T \bowtie T' \text{ and } t'' \in T'' \text{ and } y \cup t'' \text{ is a function}\}$
$= \{(t \cup t') \cup t'' \mid t \in T \text{ and } t' \in T' \text{ and } t'' \in T'' \text{ and}$
$t \cup t' \text{ is a function and } (t \cup t') \cup t'' \text{ is a function}\}$; (2)

it is clear from Lemma 3(a) on page 6 that in (1) and (2) the last requirement implies the last requirement but one, which can therefore be omitted.
Subsequently, it is easy to see that
$T \bowtie (T' \bowtie T'') = (T \bowtie T') \bowtie T''$.

The remainder of the proof is left as an exercise to the reader (in Exercise 2.8).

□

In order to illustrate the practical use of joins, we will give yet another example of a join.

EXAMPLE 2.3:

If in Figure 1.1(a) of Example 1.1 DEPNO is replaced by DNO and NAME by EMPLNM, we get (the representation of) a table T3. By Lemma 2.5(a), T3 $\bowtie$ T2 is a table over {NO, EMPLNM, SAL, SEX, DNO, NAME, MANNO}. This table of three elements is depicted in Figure 2.3.

NO	EMPLNM	SAL	SEX	DNO	NAME	MANNO
8	JOHNSON	2200	M	1	PRODUCTION	9
7	JOHNSON	3109	F	2	PLANNING	7
9	DECKER	2995	M	1	PRODUCTION	9

Figure 2.3: The table T3 $\bowtie$ T2

Apparently, T3 $\bowtie$ T2 contains for each employee the data of that employee *plus* the data of his department.

□ Example 2.3.

In Example 2.3 we informally described a way to obtain a table from another table, namely by substitution of "column names" by other column names. We are now faced with the question of how to formally define this (useful) operation on tables. For that purpose we use a "renaming function" (or *attribute transformation*) *h* that assigns to each "new" column name *b* the old column name that was replaced by *b*:

DEFINITION 2.3:
If *T* is a set of functions and *h* is a function, then:

$T \infty h \stackrel{D}{=} \{t \circ h \mid t \in T\}$.

EXAMPLE 2.4:

The attribute transformation used in Example 2.3, is the function h3 over {NO, EMPLNM, SAL, SEX, DNO} defined as follows:

h3(DNO) = DEPNO,
h3(EMPLNM) = NAME, and
h3(*x*) = *x* for each $x \in$ {NO, SAL, SEX}.

We note that h3 is a *bijection* onto {NO, NAME, SAL, SEX, DEPNO}, which is exactly the set over which T1 is a table. The table T3 described in Example 2.3 can now be written as T1 ∞ h3. Let us now take a closer look at the effect for one of the elements of T1; if t3 is the element of T1 for which t3(NO) = 9, then t3 ∘ h3 indeed displays the desired behaviour:

t3 ∘ h3(DNO) = t3(h3(DNO)) = t3(DEPNO) = 1.

The renaming is represented in Figure 2.4.

NO	EMPLNM	SAL	SEX	DNO
NO	NAME	SAL	SEX	DEPNO

(a) The attribute transformation h3

NO	NAME	SAL	SEX	DEPNO
9	DECKER	2995	M	1
8	JOHNSON	2200	M	1
7	JOHNSON	3109	F	2

(b) The table T1

NO	EMPLNM	SAL	SEX	DNO
9	DECKER	2995	M	1
8	JOHNSON	2200	M	1
7	JOHNSON	3109	F	2

(c) The table T1 ∞ h3

Figure 2.4

□ Example 2.4.

We emphasize that the attribute transformation assigns the old attributes to the new attributes, and not the other way around.

Definition 2.3 admits the possibility of replacing one "old" attribute by two or more "new" attributes. It follows from the definition that in that case we have "copies" of the old column under each of those new attributes. These new attributes can in fact be regarded as "synonyms" of each other.

Lemma 2.6 confirms our conjecture that renaming of attributes in a table yields a table with the same number of elements.

LEMMA 2.6:

If h is a function and T is a table over $\text{rng}(h)$, then:

(a) $T \infty h$ is a table over $\text{dom}(h)$;

(b) $| T \infty h | = | T |$;

(c) $T \infty h = \varnothing$ iff $T = \varnothing$.

Proof:

(a) It follows from Lemma 9 on page 9, parts (a) and (d), that $t \circ h$ is a function for each $t \in T$. Moreover, since $\text{rng}(h) = \text{dom}(t)$, we have $\text{dom}(t \circ h) = \text{dom}(h)$. Hence, $T \infty h$ is a table over $\text{dom}(h)$.

(b) It is easy to see that $\lambda t \in T: t \circ h$ is a function from T onto $T \infty h$.
The function is also injective:
Let $t \in T$ and $t' \in T$ be such that $t \circ h = t' \circ h$; for each $y \in \text{dom}(t)$ it holds that $y \in \text{rng}(h)$; in other words, there is an $x \in \text{dom}(h)$ such that $h(x) = y$;
then $t(y) = t(h(x)) = t'(h(x)) = t'(y)$. From Lemma 4(b) on page 7 it now follows that $t = t'$.
In short, the function $\lambda t \in T: t \circ h$ from T onto $T \infty h$ is also injective (see Lemma 6 on page 8).

(c) This result follows immediately from (b), because $\varnothing$ is the only set with 0 elements.

□

EXERCISES

2.1. (a) Can we summarize lemmas 2.2 and 2.3 by saying that the union as well as the intersection and the difference of each pair of tables is also a table?

(b) Describe in words the four sets of employee tuples given in the examples following Lemma 2.3 on page 26.

2.2. If A is a set and W is a set of tables over A, then $\bigcup W$ is also a table over A. Prove this.

2.3. Explain why T1 $|\!\upharpoonright$ {DEPNO,SEX} has fewer elements than T1. (Compare, for example, Figure 2.1 with Figure 2.4(b).)

2.4. If T is a set of functions and B is a set, then:

(a) $T \,|\!\upharpoonright B = \varnothing$ iff $T = \varnothing$;

(b) $T \,|\!\upharpoonright B = \{\varnothing\}$ iff $T \neq \varnothing$ and $B \cap \text{He}(T) = \varnothing$.

Prove this.

2.5. Does part (b) of Lemma 2.4 also hold if T is an arbitrary set of functions? (Give a proof or a counterexample.)

2.6. Prove that the following hold for all sets A, B, and B' and for all tables T and T' over A:

(a) $(T \cup T') \,|\!\upharpoonright B = (T \,|\!\upharpoonright B) \cup (T' \,|\!\upharpoonright B)$;

(b) $(T \cap T') \,|\!\upharpoonright B \subseteq (T \,|\!\upharpoonright B) \cap (T' \,|\!\upharpoonright B)$;

(c) $(T - T') \,|\!\upharpoonright B \supseteq (T \,|\!\upharpoonright B) - (T' \,|\!\upharpoonright B)$;

(d) $(T \,|\!\upharpoonright B') \,|\!\upharpoonright B = T \,|\!\upharpoonright (B' \cap B)$.

Give counterexamples for the two "missing" inclusions.

2.7. The formula in Exercise 2.6(a) can be phrased as follows: "Projection *distributes to the right* over union".

(a) Does projection also "distribute to the left" over union? (First indicate what we mean by that.)

(b) Does projection distribute to the left over intersection or over difference?

2.8. Prove the remainder of Lemma 2.5.

2.9. Substitution of MANNO by NO, and NAME by DNM in Figure 1.1(b) yields (the representation of) a table T4.

(a) Determine T1 $\bowtie$ T4.

(b) Determine T3 $\bowtie$ T4, where T3 is the table introduced in Example 2.3.

(c) Determine T1 $\bowtie$ T5 and T3 $\bowtie$ T5, where T5 = T4 $\cup$ {t5}, and t5 = {(DNO; 3), (DNM; 'PURCHASE'), (NO; 7)}.

(d) Give informal descriptions of tables T1 $\bowtie$ T5 and T3 $\bowtie$ T5.

2.10. Determine the natural join of T1 and T2 from Example 1.1. Also try to give an informal description of what T1 $\bowtie$ T2 represents.

2.11. Prove the following for all sets A and A' and for all tables T over A and T' over A':

(a) $(T \bowtie T') \upharpoonright A \subseteq T$;

(b) if $T \upharpoonright A' \subseteq T' \upharpoonright A$, then $(T \bowtie T') \upharpoonright A = T$;

(c) if $A' \subseteq A$, then $T \bowtie T' = \{t \in T \mid t \upharpoonright A' \in T'\}$;

(d) if $A \cap A' = \varnothing$, then $|\, T \bowtie T' \,| = |\, T \,| * |\, T' \,|$.

2.12. Use the results from the preceding exercise to prove that for each element v of the DB universe EXU from Example 1.3 the following holds. Here, h3 is the attribute transformation previously defined in Example 2.4 as follows:

h3(DNO) = DEPNO, h3 (EMPLNM) = NAME, and
h3(x) = x for each $x \in$ {NO, SAL, SEX}.

For the DB skeleton g1, introduced in Example 1.2, we recall that
g1(DEP) = {DNO, MANNO, NAME}.

(a) (v (DEP) $\bowtie$ (v (EMPL) ∞ h3)) $\upharpoonright$ g1(DEP) $\subseteq$ v(DEP);

(b) (v (DEP) $\bowtie$ (v(EMPL) ∞ h3)) $\upharpoonright$ dom(h3) = v(EMPL) ∞ h3;

(c) v (DEP) $\bowtie$ (v(EMPL) ∞ {(MANNO; NO)}) = v(DEP).

2.13. If A is a set and T is a table over A, and $B \subseteq A$ and $C \subseteq A$, then $T \upharpoonright (B \cup C) \subseteq (T \upharpoonright B) \bowtie (T \upharpoonright C)$.
Prove this.

2.14. Prove that for all sets A and A', and for all tables T over A and T' and T'' over A', the following hold:

(a) $T \bowtie (T' \cap T'') = (T \bowtie T') \cap (T \bowtie T'')$;

(b) $T \bowtie (T' - T'') = (T \bowtie T') - (T \bowtie T'')$;

(c) $T \bowtie (T' \cup T'') = (T \bowtie T') \cup (T \bowtie T'')$.

2.15. Exercise 2.14 can be rephrased as follows: "The natural join ***distributes to the left*** over intersection, difference, and union".

(a) Does the natural join "distribute to the right" over difference as well? (First formulate what is meant by this.)

(b) Does the natural join also distribute to the right over intersection and over union?

2.16. Give a formal definition of the attribute transformation used in Exercise 2.9, i.e., a function h2 such that T4 = T2 ∞ h2 (where T2 is the table from Figure 1.1(b)).

2.17. If T is a set of functions, and h and h' are functions, then:

(a) $T \infty (h \circ h') = (T \infty h) \infty h'$;

(b) $T \infty (h \cup h') \subseteq (T \infty h) \bowtie (T \infty h')$ if h and h' are joinable.

Prove this.

2.18. Prove the following for all functions h and for all tables T and T' over rng(h):

(a) $(T \cup T') \infty h = (T \infty h) \cup (T' \infty h)$;

(b) $(T \cap T') \infty h = (T \infty h) \cap (T' \infty h)$;

(c) $(T - T') \infty h = (T \infty h) - (T' \infty h)$;

(d) if $T \subseteq T'$ then $T \infty h \subseteq T' \infty h$;

(e) if h is injective, then:
$T \subseteq T' \Longleftrightarrow T \infty h \subseteq T' \infty h$.

2.19. Prove the following:
If T is a set of functions, and B is a set and h is a function, then:

(a) $T \|\!\upharpoonright B = T \infty \mathrm{id}(B)$;
(b) $(T \infty h) \|\!\upharpoonright B = T \infty (h \upharpoonright B)$;
(c) $(T \|\!\upharpoonright B) \infty h = T \infty (\mathrm{id}(B) \circ h)$.

2.20. Prove the following:
If A and A' are sets, and T is a table over A and T' is a table over A' and h is a function, then:

(a) $(T \bowtie T') \infty h \subseteq (T \infty h) \bowtie (T' \infty h)$;

(b) $(T \bowtie T') \infty h = (T \infty h) \bowtie (T' \infty h)$ if $A \cap A' \subseteq \mathrm{rng}(h)$.

2.21. Derive the following property from the preceding exercise:
If A and A' are sets, and T is a table over A and T' is a table over A' and B is a set, then:

(a) $(T \bowtie T') \|\!\upharpoonright B \subseteq (T \|\!\upharpoonright B) \bowtie (T' \|\!\upharpoonright B)$;

(b) $(T \bowtie T') \|\!\upharpoonright B = (T \|\!\upharpoonright B) \bowtie (T' \|\!\upharpoonright B)$ if $A \cap A' \subseteq B$.

2.22. If T is a set of functions and B is a set, then we define:

$$T \not\!\|\!\upharpoonright B \overset{D}{=} \{t \not\upharpoonright B \mid t \in T\}.$$

Use Lemma 11 on page 10 and the properties of projection to serve as a guideline for deriving some properties of this new concept.

□

2.1.2 Momentary Dependency

If T is a table over A while B and C are subsets of A, then C is said to be ***momentarily dependent on B in T*** iff each pair of elements of T that match on B also match on C. For the sake of brevity this property is denoted by: $B \rightarrow C$ in T. (This notation should not be confused with the notation "$B \twoheadrightarrow C$" from Definition 11 on page 8; see also Exercise 2.25(b).) The concept of momentary dependency is formally defined as follows:

DEFINITION 2.4:
If A, B, and C are sets and T is a table over A, then:

$$B \rightarrow C \textbf{ in } T \overset{D}{\Longleftrightarrow} \forall t \in T : \forall t' \in T : \text{if } t \upharpoonright B = t' \upharpoonright B \text{ then } t \upharpoonright C = t' \upharpoonright C.$$

Although we defined momentary dependency in a table over A for all sets B and C, only those cases are interesting in which $B \subseteq A$ and $C \subseteq A$. (Formally speaking, we do not even need the other cases; see Exercise 2.25(a).)

EXAMPLE 2.5:

Examination of the table T1 over {NO, NAME, SAL, SEX, DEPNO}, introduced in Example 1.1 (see Figure 2.5), reveals that:

(a) {NO} → {NO, NAME, SAL, SEX, DEPNO} in T1;

(b) {SAL} → {NO, NAME, SAL, SEX, DEPNO} in T1;

(c) {SEX} → {DEPNO} in T1;

(d) {DEPNO} → {SEX} in T1;

(e) {NAME, SEX} → {SAL} in T1;

(f) {NAME, DEPNO} → {NO, SAL, SEX} in T1;

(g) not {NAME} → {NO, SAL, SEX, DEPNO} in T1;

(h) not {DEPNO} → {NO, SAL, SEX, NAME} in T1.

NO	NAME	SAL	SEX	DEPNO
7	JOHNSON	3109	F	2
8	JOHNSON	2200	M	1
9	DECKER	2995	M	1

Figure 2.5: The table T1

□ Example 2.5.

We continue by giving four lemmas; Lemma 2.7 contains three important elementary properties of momentary dependency, Lemma 2.8 gives some of their immediate consequences, Lemma 2.9 treats cases involving the empty set and, finally, Lemma 2.10 gives an alternative characterization of momentary dependency.

LEMMA 2.7:
If A is a set, and T is a table over A and $B \subseteq A$ and $C \subseteq A$ and $D \subseteq A$, then:

(a) if $C \subseteq B$, then $B \to C$ in T;

(b) if $B \to C$ in T and $C \to D$ in T, then $B \to D$ in T;

(c) $B \to C$ in T iff $\forall c \in C : B \to \{c\}$ in T.

Proof:

(a) Let $t \in T$ and $t' \in T$ such that $t \upharpoonright B = t' \upharpoonright B$;
but then, for $C \subseteq B$, we also have $t \upharpoonright C = t' \upharpoonright C$;
hence, $B \to C$ in T.

(b) $B \to C$ in T, so $\forall t \in T : \forall t' \in T$: if $t \upharpoonright B = t' \upharpoonright B$ then $t \upharpoonright C = t' \upharpoonright C$; (1)
$C \to D$ in T, so $\forall t \in T : \forall t' \in T$: if $t \upharpoonright C = t' \upharpoonright C$ then $t \upharpoonright D = t' \upharpoonright D$; (2)
from (1) and (2) we derive
$\forall t \in T : \forall t' \in T$: if $t \upharpoonright B = t' \upharpoonright B$ then $t \upharpoonright D = t' \upharpoonright D$;
hence, $B \to D$ in T.

(c) $t \upharpoonright C = t' \upharpoonright C$ iff $\forall c \in C : t(c) = t'(c)$;
in other words, $t \upharpoonright C = t' \upharpoonright C$ iff $\forall c \in C : t \upharpoonright \{c\} = t' \upharpoonright \{c\}$; therefore:
$B \to C$ in T
$\Leftrightarrow \forall t \in T : \forall t' \in T$: if $t \upharpoonright B = t' \upharpoonright B$ then $\forall c \in C : t \upharpoonright \{c\} = t' \upharpoonright \{c\}$
$\Leftrightarrow \forall c \in C : \forall t \in T : \forall t' \in T$: if $t \upharpoonright B = t' \upharpoonright B$ then $t \upharpoonright \{c\} = t' \upharpoonright \{c\}$
$\Leftrightarrow \forall c \in C : B \to \{c\}$ in T.

□

LEMMA 2.8:
If A is a set, and T is a table over A and $B \subseteq A$ and $C \subseteq A$ and $D \subseteq A$ and $E \subseteq A$, then:

(a) $B \to B$ in T;

(b) if $B \to C$ in T and $B \subseteq D$, then $D \to C$ in T;

(c) if $B \to C$ in T and $D \subseteq C$, then $B \to D$ in T;

(d) if $B \to C$ in T and $D \to E$ in T, then $B \cup D \to C \cup E$ in T.

Lemma 2.8 can be proven directly from Lemma 2.7, i.e., without reverting to the actual *definition* of momentary dependency. (We could even say that the properties in Lemma 2.7, the so-called *Armstrong axioms*, precisely characterize all possible dependency structures in tables; see [Ar 74] for the details.)

Proof:

(a) Choose C to be equal to B in Lemma 2.7(a).

(b) $B \subseteq D$, so $D \to B$ in T, according to Lemma 2.7(a);
since also $B \to C$ in T, it follows from Lemma 2.7(b) that $D \to C$ in T.

(c) Analogous to the proof of (b).

(d) $B \to C$ in T and $B \subseteq B \cup D$, so $B \cup D \to C$ in T, according to part (b);
likewise, $B \cup D \to E$ in T;
now it follows from Lemma 2.7(c) that
$(\forall c \in C : B \cup D \to \{c\}$ in $T)$ and $(\forall c \in E : B \cup D \to \{c\}$ in $T)$;
in short, $\forall c \in C \cup E : B \cup D \to \{c\}$ in T;
finally, we use Lemma 2.7(c) once more and conclude that
$B \cup D \to C \cup E$ in T.

□

LEMMA 2.9:
If A is a set, and T is a table over A and $B \subseteq A$ and $C \subseteq A$, then:

(a) $B \to C$ in $\varnothing$;

(b) $B \to \varnothing$ in T;

(c) $\varnothing \to C$ in T iff $| T \upharpoonright\!\upharpoonright C | \leq 1$.

Proof:

(a) Follows directly from Definition 2.4.

(b) Choose C to be equal to $\varnothing$ in Lemma 2.7(a).

(c) $\varnothing \to C$ in T
$\Leftrightarrow \forall t \in T : \forall t' \in T$: if $t \upharpoonright \varnothing = t' \upharpoonright \varnothing$ then $t \upharpoonright C = t' \upharpoonright C$ (by Definition 2.4)
$\Leftrightarrow \forall t \in T : \forall t' \in T$: if $\varnothing = \varnothing$ then $t \upharpoonright C = t' \upharpoonright C$ (by Lemma 11(l))
$\Leftrightarrow \forall t \in T : \forall t' \in T : t \upharpoonright C = t' \upharpoonright C$
$\Leftrightarrow \forall x \in T \upharpoonright\!\upharpoonright C : \forall x' \in T \upharpoonright\!\upharpoonright C : x = x'$
$\Leftrightarrow | T \upharpoonright\!\upharpoonright C | \leq 1$.

□

LEMMA 2.10:
If A is a set, and T is a table over A and $B \subseteq A$ and $C \subseteq A$, then:
$B \to C$ in T iff $\{(t \upharpoonright B\, ; t \upharpoonright C) \mid t \in T\}$ is a function.

Proof:
$\{(t \upharpoonright B\, ; t \upharpoonright C) \mid t \in T\}$ is a function
$\Leftrightarrow \forall t \in T : \forall t' \in T$: if $t \upharpoonright B = t' \upharpoonright B$ then $t \upharpoonright C = t' \upharpoonright C$ (by Definition 7, page 5)
$\Leftrightarrow B \to C$ in T (by Definition 2.4)

□

In the preceding lemmas we usually "varied" the attribute sets while "keeping T constant". In the following lemma we will "vary" the table while "keeping the attribute sets constant", in order to see to what extent momentary dependency is preserved under the operations in §2.1.1. That question is also investigated in the exercises 2.27 and 2.28.

LEMMA 2.11:

If A is a set, and T is a table over A and $B \subseteq A$ and $C \subseteq A$ and $B \rightarrow C$ in T, then:

(a) if $T' \subseteq T$, then $B \rightarrow C$ in T';

(b) if B' is a set such that $B \subseteq B'$, then $B \rightarrow C$ in $T \upharpoonright B'$;

(c) if A' is a set and T' is a table over A', then $B \rightarrow C$ in $T \bowtie T'$;

(d) if h is a function and $B' \subseteq \mathrm{dom}(h)$ such that $B \subseteq \mathrm{rng}(h \upharpoonright B')$, then $B' \rightarrow \{a \in \mathrm{dom}(h) \mid h(a) \in C\}$ in $T \infty h$.

EXERCISES

2.23. Find all momentary dependencies in table T1 of Figure 2.5 which are of the form $B \rightarrow \{c\}$, where $c \in$ {NO, NAME, SAL, SEX, DEPNO} $- B$, and where B is minimal in the following sense: $\forall B' \subseteq B$: if $B' \rightarrow \{c\}$ in T1 then $B' = B$.

2.24. Explain why the collection of momentary dependencies of the form above suffice, in principle, to describe *all* momentary dependencies in a table over some finite attribute set.

2.25. If A, B, and C are sets and T is a table over A, then:

(a) $B \rightarrow C$ in $T \Leftrightarrow (B \cap A) \rightarrow (C \cap A)$ in T;

(b) $B \rightarrow C$ in $B \twoheadrightarrow C$.

Prove this.

2.26. Prove Lemma 2.11.

2.27. Show by means of an example that in general momentary dependency is not preserved under the union of two tables over the same set A.

2.28. Prove the following:
If A and A' are sets, and T is a table over A and T' is a table over A' and $B \subseteq A$ and $C \subseteq A \cap A'$ and $D \subseteq A'$, then:
if $B \rightarrow C$ in T and $C \rightarrow D$ in T', then $B \rightarrow D$ in $T \bowtie T'$.

□

2.1.3 Unique Identification

If T is a table over a set A, and $B \subseteq A$, then B is called *uniquely identifying* (or in short *u.i.*) *in T* iff two different elements of T always have different restrictions to B. Unique identification is in fact an important special case of momentary dependency (see Lemma 2.12). We call B *minimally u.i in T* iff B is u.i. in T and every proper subset of B is not u.i. in T. These concepts are formally defined as follows:

DEFINITION 2.5:
If A and B are sets and T is a table over A, then:
B is u.i. in T $\overset{D}{\Longleftrightarrow} \forall t \in T : \forall t' \in T$: if $t \restriction B = t' \restriction B$ then $t = t'$.

DEFINITION 2.6:
If A and B are sets and T is a table over A, then:
B is minimally u.i. in T $\overset{D}{\Longleftrightarrow} B$ is u.i. in T and
$\forall B' \subset B : B'$ is not u.i. in T.

EXAMPLE 2.6:
For table T1 from Example 2.5 the following hold:

(a) {NAME, NO} is u.i. in T1;

(b) {NAME, SAL} is u.i. in T1;

(c) {NAME} is not u.i. in T1;

(d) {SEX, DEPNO} is not u.i. in T1;

(e) each of the sets {NO}, {SAL}, {NAME, SEX}, and {NAME, DEPNO} is minimally u.i. in T1;

(f) no set other than those mentioned under (e) is minimally u.i. in T1.

□ Example 2.6.

The following lemmas offer elementary properties of unique identification. Most of these properties follow directly from the lemmas in §2.1.2.

LEMMA 2.12:
If A is a set, and T is a table over A and $B \subseteq A$ and $C \subseteq A$ and $D \subseteq A$, then:

(a) B is u.i. in T iff $B \rightarrow A$ in T;

(b) B is u.i. in T iff $\forall a \in A - B : B \rightarrow \{a\}$ in T;

(c) A is u.i. in T;

(d) if B is u.i. in T and $B \subseteq C$, then C is u.i. T;

(e) if B is u.i. in T and $C \rightarrow B$ in T, then C is u.i. in T;

(f) if $B \rightarrow C$ in T and $D \rightarrow (A - C)$ in T, then $B \cup D$ is u.i. in T;

(g) $\varnothing$ is u.i. in T iff $|\, T \,| \leq 1$.

LEMMA 2.13:
If A is a set, and T is a table over A and $B \subseteq A$ and B is u.i. in T, then:

(a) if $T' \subseteq T$, then B is u.i. in T';

(b) if $B \subseteq B'$, then B is u.i. in $T \Vert\!\restriction B'$;

(c) if h is a function and $B \subseteq \mathrm{rng}(h)$, then $\mathrm{dom}(h)$ is u.i. in $T \infty h$.

LEMMA 2.14:

If A and A' are sets, and T is a table over A and T' is a table over A' and $B \subseteq A$ and $B' \subseteq A'$ and B is u.i. in T and B' is u.i. in T', then:

(a) $B \cup B'$ is u.i. in $T \bowtie T'$;

(b) if $B' \subseteq A$, then B is u.i. in $T \bowtie T'$.

We offer only the proof of Lemma 2.14(a). The other proofs are left to the reader in the exercises.

Proof of Lemma 2.14(a):

B is u.i. in T and B' is u.i. in T', (given)
hence $B \to A$ in T and $B' \to A'$ in T', (by Lemma 2.12(a))
hence $B \to A$ in $T \bowtie T'$ and $B' \to A'$ in $T' \bowtie T$, (by Lemma 2.11(c))
hence $B \cup B' \to A \cup A'$ in $T \bowtie T'$, (by Lemma 2.8(d) and 2.5(c))
hence $B \cup B'$ is u.i. in $T \bowtie T'$ (by Lemma 2.12(a) and 2.5(a))

□

EXERCISES

2.29. Rewrite the definitions of WE and WD, given in Example 1.3, in terms of unique identification.

2.30. Determine the sets that are minimally u.i. in the following tables.

(a) T2 from Example 1.1;

(b) T5 from Exercise 2.9(c).

2.31. Prove Lemma 2.12.

2.32. Prove Lemma 2.13.

2.33. Prove Lemma 2.14(b).

2.34. Momentary dependency can also be defined in terms of unique identification, since for all tables T and all sets B and C we have:

$$B \to C \text{ in } T \Leftrightarrow B \text{ is u.i. in } T \upharpoonright (B \cup C).$$

Prove this.

2.35. Prove the following equivalences (cf. Exercise 1.13).
If R is a relation, then:

(a) R is a function $\Leftrightarrow$ {1} is u.i. in crt(R);

(b) R is injective $\Leftrightarrow$ {2} is u.i. in crt(R).

□

2.1.4 Connecting Tables

We proceed by introducing a new concept by means of an example offered below.

EXAMPLE 2.7:

In Example 1.1 we observe that each "(DNO; MANNO)-combination" in table T2 also occurs as a "(DEPNO; NO)-combination" in table T1 (see also Figure 2.6).

T2:

MANNO	DNO	NAME
9	1	PRODUCTION
7	2	PLANNING

MANNO	DNO

h4: ↓ ↓

T1:

NO	DEPNO	NAME	SAL	SEX
8	1	JOHNSON	2200	M
9	1	DECKER	2995	M
7	2	JOHNSON	3109	F

Figure 2.6: The attribute transformation h4 connects T2 with T1

In other words, we could say that the projection of T2 on {DNO, MANNO} "almost" results in a subset of the projection of T1 on {DEPNO, NO}, except for a renaming of the attributes. The intended renaming can be represented by the following attribute transformation:

h4 = {(DNO; DEPNO), (MANNO; NO)}

The attribute transformation h4 thus assigns to each of the relevant attributes of T2 the "corresponding" attribute of T1. According to our definition of function composition, the projection of T2 on {DNO, MANNO} is indeed a subset of the "renamed" table $\{t \circ \text{h4} \mid t \in \text{T1}\}$. (The latter is indeed a table over {DNO, MANNO}.) Using Definition 2.3, we can formally describe our initial observation as follows:

$$\text{T2} \;\|\!\upharpoonright \text{dom(h4)} \subseteq \text{T1} \infty \text{h4}$$

In this case we say that the attribute transformation h4 *connects* the table T2 *with* the table T1.

□ Example 2.7.

This concept of connecting is defined formally as follows:

DEFINITION 2.7:
If T and T' are sets of functions and h is a function, then:
h connects T with T' $\stackrel{''}{\iff} T \;\|\!\upharpoonright \mathrm{dom}(h) \subseteq T' \infty h.$

Two alternative formulations are:

(1) h connects T with $T' \iff \{t \upharpoonright \mathrm{dom}(h) \mid t \in T\} \subseteq \{t' \circ h \mid t' \in T'\}$;

(2) h connects T with $T' \iff \forall t \in T : \exists t' \in T' : t \upharpoonright \mathrm{dom}(h) = t' \circ h.$

We are usually interested in those cases where T is a table over a set A, T' is a table over a set A', and h is an injective function such that $\mathrm{dom}(h) \subseteq A$ and $\mathrm{rng}(h) \subseteq A'$. Now let $B = \mathrm{dom}(h)$ and $B' = \mathrm{rng}(h)$; we can then give the following informal description of the concept of connecting tables:

h connects T with T' if and only if all B-values in T also occur as B'-values in T', where h indicates which attributes in B correspond to which attributes in B'.

In practice, $\mathrm{rng}(h)$ is often uniquely identifying in T'. In addition, the attributes in B are often equal to the corresponding attributes in B'; in that case h is the identity function on B.

In some situations, connecting not only amounts to set inclusion (as in Definition 2.7), but even to set equality. We then say that *h connects T bilaterally with T'*. Thus, in Example 2.7, the function {(DEPNO; DNO)} connects the table T1 bilaterally with the table T2.

DEFINITION 2.8:
If T and T' are sets of functions and h is a function, then:
h connects T bilaterally with T' $\stackrel{''}{\iff} T \;\|\!\upharpoonright \mathrm{dom}(h) = T' \infty h.$

For an injective function h, bilateral connection can easily be expressed in terms of "ordinary" connection:

LEMMA 2.15:
If T and T' are sets of functions and h is an injective function, then:
h connects T bilaterally with T' $\Leftrightarrow$ h connects T with T' and h^{-1} connects T' with T.

The proof of this lemma is left as an exercise to the reader.

If T and T' are sets of functions and h is a function, then we call

$$\{(t\,;t') \in T \times T' \mid t \upharpoonright \text{dom}(h) = t' \circ h\}$$

the association on $T \times T'$ *(or between* T *and* T'*) induced by* h.

Such an association thus results, informally speaking, in the set of all pairs of tuples that "match" with respect to the "criterion" h.

Using this notion of an induced association, we can give some simple alternative descriptions of the concepts of connection and bilateral connection, as seen in Lemma 2.16. Besides, unique identification of rng(h) in T' or of dom(h) in T turns out to result in some interesting properties of the induced association.

LEMMA 2.16:
If T and T' are sets of functions, and h is a function and R is the association on $T \times T'$ induced by h, i.e.,

$$R = \{(t\,;t') \in T \times T' \mid t \upharpoonright \text{dom}(h) = t' \circ h\},$$

then:

(1) $R \subseteq T \times T'$;

(2) h connects T with T' $\Leftrightarrow$ dom(R) = T;

(3) h connects T bilaterally with T' $\Leftrightarrow$ dom(R) = T and rng(R) = T';

(4) if rng(h) is u.i. in T', then R is a function;

(5) if dom(h) is u.i. in T, then R is injective.

Proof:

(1) It follows directly from the description of R that $R \subseteq T \times T'$.
(Hence, in particular, dom(R) $\subseteq T$ and rng(R) $\subseteq T'$.)

(2) h connects T with T'
$\Leftrightarrow$ $\{t \upharpoonright \text{dom}(h) \mid t \in T\} \subseteq \{t' \circ h \mid t' \in T'\}$
$\Leftrightarrow$ $\forall t \in T : \exists t' \in T' : t \upharpoonright \text{dom}(h) = t' \circ h$
$\Leftrightarrow$ $T \subseteq \text{dom}(R)$;
(2) now follows from (1) and the preceding equivalences.

(3) h connects T bilaterally with T'
$\Leftrightarrow$ $\{t \upharpoonright \text{dom}(h) \mid t \in T\} = \{t' \circ h \mid t' \in T'\}$
$\Leftrightarrow$ $(\forall t \in T : \exists t' \in T' : t \upharpoonright \text{dom}(h) = t' \circ h)$ and
$(\forall t' \in T' : \exists t \in T : t \upharpoonright \text{dom}(h) = t' \circ h)$
$\Leftrightarrow$ $T \subseteq \text{dom}(R)$ and $T' \subseteq \text{rng}(R)$;
(3) now follows from (1) and the preceding equivalences.

(4) Let $(t\,;t') \in R$ and $(t\,;t'') \in R$; we now have to prove that $t' = t''$.
From $(t\,;t') \in R$ and $(t\,;t'') \in R$ it follows that $t' \in T'$ and $t'' \in T'$ and that $t \restriction \mathrm{dom}(h) = t' \circ h$ and $t \restriction \mathrm{dom}(h) = t'' \circ h$;
hence $t' \circ h = t'' \circ h$; as a consequence, $t' \restriction \mathrm{rng}(h) = t'' \restriction \mathrm{rng}(h)$;
knowing that $\mathrm{rng}(h)$ is u.i. in T', we now have that $t' = t''$.

(5) Let $(t\,;t') \in R$ and $(s\,;t') \in R$; we now have to prove that $t = s$.
From $(t\,;t') \in R$ and $(s\,;t') \in R$ it follows that $t \in T$ and $s \in T$ and that $t \restriction \mathrm{dom}(h) = t' \circ h$ and $s \restriction \mathrm{dom}(h) = t' \circ h$;
hence $t \restriction \mathrm{dom}(h) = s \restriction \mathrm{dom}(h)$;
and since $\mathrm{dom}(h)$ is u.i. in T, it follows that $t = s$.

□

EXERCISES

2.36. Check the correctness of each of the following statements regarding tables T1 and T2 in Example 2.7.

- (a) {(DNO; DEPNO)} connects T2 with T1;
- (b) {(DEPNO; DNO)} connects T1 with T2;
- (c) {(MANNO; NO)} connects T2 with T1;
- (d) {(NO; MANNO)} connects T1 with T2;
- (e) $\mathrm{h4}^{-1}$ connects T1 with T2.

2.37. Answer the following questions regarding the attribute transformation h4 in Example 2.7.

- (a) Is dom(h4) (minimally) u.i. in T2?
- (b) Is rng(h4) (minimally) u.i. in T1?
- (c) Is the association on T2 × T1 induced by h4 an <u>injective</u> <u>function</u> <u>from</u> T2 <u>onto</u> T1? (Check each of the four underlined properties.)

2.38. Is it true for each pair of tables T and T' that $\varnothing$ connects T with T'?

2.39. If T and T' are sets of functions, and h is a function and h connects T with T' and $h' \subseteq h$, then h' also connects T with T'. Prove this.

2.40. Prove Lemma 2.15.

2.41. Does the "if and only if" property hold for parts (4) and (5) of Lemma 2.16? (Give either a proof or a counterexample.)

2.42. Rewrite the definition of EXU in Example 1.3 using the concept of (bilateral) connection.

□

2.2 Concepts concerning Sets of Tables

The concepts introduced in §2.1.2 and §2.1.3, defined for *tables*, will be generalized in §2.2.1 and §2.2.2 to their counterparts at the level of *sets* of tables. In order to clearly discern the different levels, which is often neglected in the literature and in practice, we will use different terms for the corresponding concepts at different levels.

In Example 1.3, we have already seen examples of sets of tables, namely the sets WE and WD. Another example of a set of tables is offered below.

EXAMPLE 2.8:

We define the set WP of tables (referring to persons) by means of three auxiliary functions, namely F1, F2 and F3. The functions F1 and F2 will be used in the definition of the set function F3. To the right of these definitions we offer some informal explanation.

Definitions	*Explanation*
F1 = {(HNO ; [1 .. 5000]),	house number
(STR ; Chs(50))};	street
F2 = {(DAY ; [1 .. 31]),	day
(MNT ; [1 .. 12]),	month
(YR ; $\mathbb{N}$)};	year
F3 = {(NO ; $\mathbb{N} - \{0\}$),	identity number
(NM ; Chs(40)),	name
(ADDR ; Π(F1)),	address
(PC ; Chs(7)),	zipcode
(TOWN ; Chs(30)),	city
(BDT ; Π(F2)),	date of birth
(BPL ; Chs(30)),	place of birth
(NMC ; $\mathbf{P}$ (Chs(30)))};	names of children

WP = {$T \subseteq \Pi$(F3) | {NO} is u.i. in T and
{PC} $\rightarrow$ {TOWN} in T and
{ADDR,TOWN} $\rightarrow$ {PC} in T and
$\forall t \in T$: if t(NO) $\neq 1$ then $\exists t' \in T$: t'(NO) = t(NO) $- 1$}

Figure 2.7 represents an element TP of WP.

NO	NM	ADDR		PC	TOWN	BDT			BPL	NMC
		STR	HNO			DAY	MNT	YR		
1	E.F. CODD	PARK LANE	85	HP3 4AY	YORK	10	6	1962	CORK	∅
2	C.J. DATE	WALL STR.	34	99970	NY	26	2	1988	NY	{JOHN, PETE, PAT}
3	R. FAGIN	CHURCH STR.	269	15011	NY	16	1	1925	LA	{ANN, JOHN}
4	M.E. SENKO	52ND STREET	1	56653	LA	5	10	1953	ROME	{MARY}

Figure 2.7: The table TP, an element of WP

□ Example 2.8.

We have also shown in Example 2.8 that attributes can have "sub-attributes" themselves, namely if the attribute values are functions. Examples are the attributes ADDR and BDT, having {HNO, STR} and {DAY, MNT, YR} as sets of sub-attributes, respectively. We also emphasize that attributes can be "set-valued", like the attribute NMC.

In principle, such a "hierarchy" of nested and set-valued attributes can of course reach any depth in (our) theory. That does not imply, however, that current database management systems can deal with such constructions.

2.2.1 Permanent Dependency

We call the counterpart of momentary dependency at the level of sets of tables *permanent dependency*. In particular, we call *C permanently dependent on B in W* if *C* is momentarily dependent on *B* in every element of *W*. We also call permanent dependency *structural dependency* (and momentary dependency *incidental dependency*). In order to distinguish from the notation "$B \rightarrow C$ in T" for momentary dependency in a table T, we will use the notation "$B \hat{\rightarrow} C$ in W" for the generalized concept of permanent dependency in a set of tables W.

DEFINITION 2.9:
If A, B, and C are sets and W is a set of tables over A, then:
$B \hat{\rightarrow} C$ **in** W $\overset{D}{\Longleftrightarrow} \forall T \in W : B \rightarrow C$ in T.

Again, as in the case of individual tables (see Definition 2.4), we are mainly interested in those cases in which $B \subseteq A$ and $C \subseteq A$.

In much of the database literature, the term *functional dependency* is often used; however, it is often not clear whether momentary or permanent dependency is meant.

EXAMPLE 2.9:

With the set of tables WE from Example 1.3 in mind, we take a closer look at the momentary dependencies in Example 2.5. We will find from the definition of WE that the *momentary* dependency in T1 mentioned in Example 2.5(a) is also a *permanent* dependency in WE:

(a) $\{NO\} \hat{\rightarrow} \{NO, NAME, SAL, SEX, DEPNO\}$ in WE.

The dependencies mentioned in (g) and (h) of Example 2.5 appeared not to be valid in T1, let alone in WE (since T1 ∈ WE). For the other dependencies as well, however, we can give counterexamples. Let for example T12 be the table obtained from table T1 by changing the department number in the tuple with employee number 8 from a 1 to a 2; cf. Figure 2.8. It is then easily verified that T12 ∈ WE. The dependencies in (c), (d) and (f) of Example 2.5, however, do not hold in T12, and therefore neither do they hold in WE. Cases (b) and (e) will be treated in Exercise 2.44.

NO	NAME	SAL	SEX	DEPNO
7	JOHNSON	3109	F	2
8	JOHNSON	2200	M	2
9	DECKER	2995	M	1

Figure 2.8: The table T12

□ Example 2.9.

EXERCISES

2.43. This exercise concerns Example 2.8.

(a) Describe the requirement pertaining to the last line of the definition of WP in words.

(b) Does WP have infinitely many elements?

(c) Does WP have infinitely large elements?

(d) Does WP have finite elements of each possible size?

Let F30 be the set function obtained by replacing $\mathbb{N} - \{0\}$ by $\mathbb{N}$ in the Definition of F3 in Example 2.8. Furthermore, let WP0 be the set of tables obtained by replacing the generalized product Π(F3) by Π(F30) in the definition of WP.

(e) Check whether Π(F3) is included in Π(F30), and vice versa.

(f) Check whether WP is included in WP0, and vice versa.

Let FI be the set function obtained by substituting $\mathbb{N}$ in the definition of F30 by $\mathbb{Z}$, and let WI be the set of tables obtained by substituting the generalized product Π(F30) in the definition of WP0 by Π(FI).

(g) Check whether Π(F30) is included in Π(FI), and vice versa.

(h) Check whether WP0 is included in WI, and vice versa.

2.44. Show that the momentary dependencies listed in (b) and (e) of Example 2.5 are not permanent dependencies in WE.

2.45. Each of the properties of momentary dependency mentioned in the lemmas 2.7 through 2.10 have natural counterparts at the level of permanent dependency. Formulate (and prove) these properties.

2.46. (a) Verify in Example 2.8 that {NO} $\hat{\rightarrow}$ {NO, ADDR, TOWN} in WP, {ADDR, TOWN} $\hat{\rightarrow}$ {PC} in WP, and {ADDR, PC} $\hat{\rightarrow}$ {TOWN} in WP.

(b) Is {NO} permanently dependent on {NM, ADDR, TOWN} in WP?

2.47. Figure 2.9 represents two tables; let T6 be the table depicted in (a) and T7 be the table depicted in (b). We define W1 = {T1, T6, T7} and W2 = W1 ∪ {∅}, where T1 is the table from Example 2.5. Determine all permanent dependencies in W1 and in W2 of the form $B \hat{\rightarrow} \{c\}$, where $c \in$ {NO, NAME, SAL, SEX, DEPNO} $- B$ and B is minimal in the following sense:
$\forall B' \subseteq B$: if $B' \hat{\rightarrow} \{c\}$ in W1 (or in W2, respectively) then $B' = B$.

NO	NAME	SAL	SEX	DEPNO
8	JOHNSON	2451	M	1
2	HACKING	3109	M	2
3	HACKING	2451	M	3
9	DECKER	3235	M	4

(a) The table T6

NO	NAME	SAL	SEX	DEPNO
8	JOHNSON	2452	M	1
1	JOHNS	2452	F	1

(b) The table T7

Figure 2.9

2.48. Let WP1 be the set of all elements T of the set of tables WP, defined in Example 2.8, obeying the requirement that each pair of tuples in T having the same zip-code and the same house number also has the same address.

(a) Define WP1 formally.

(b) Has the requirement previously mentioned the form of a permanent dependency in WP1?

(c) Is WP1 a proper subset of WP?
Explain your answer.

□

2.2.2 Keys and Minimal Keys

We call B a *key* of a set of tables W if B is uniquely identifying in each element of W. If in addition no proper subset of B is a key of W, then we call B a *minimal key* of W. To be precise:

DEFINITION 2.10:
If A is a set and W is a set of tables over A, then:
B is a **key of** $W \overset{D}{\Longleftrightarrow} B$ is a set and
$\forall T \in W$: B is u.i. in T.

DEFINITION 2.11:
If A is a set and W is a set of tables over A, then:
B is a **minimal key of** $W \overset{D}{\Longleftrightarrow} B$ is a key of W and
$\forall B' \subset B : B'$ is not a key of W.

We note that the term *key* in the literature is used in the sense of Definition 2.11 as well, while the term *superkey* only occurs in the sense of Definition 2.10.

EXAMPLE 2.10:

The sets {NO, NAME} and {NO} are examples of keys of the set WE of tables from Example 1.3; consequently, {NO, NAME} is not a *minimal* key of WE. Since $\varnothing$ is not a key of WE, the key {NO} of WE, however, is minimal.

The set of tables WD from Example 1.3 has exactly two minimal keys, namely {DNO} and {NAME}.

□ Example 2.10.

For *sets* of tables, Lemma 2.17 is the counterpart of Lemma 2.12.

LEMMA 2.17:
If A is a set and W is a set of tables over A, and $B \subseteq A$ and $C \subseteq A$ and $D \subseteq A$, then:

(a) B is a key of W iff $B \hat{\rightarrow} A$ in W;

(b) B is a key of W iff $\forall a \in A - B : B \hat{\rightarrow} \{a\}$ in W;

(c) A is a key of W;

(d) if B is a key of W and $B \subseteq C$, then C is also a key of W;

(e) if B is a key of W and $C \hat{\rightarrow} B$ in W, then C is also a key of W;

(f) if $B \hat{\rightarrow} C$ in W and $D \hat{\rightarrow} (A - C)$ in W, then $B \cup D$ is a key of W;

(g) $\varnothing$ is a key of W iff $\forall T \in W : |T| \leq 1$.

We conclude §2.2.2 by introducing some additional concepts and notations concerning minimal keys of sets of tables. Let W be a set of tables over a set A. Let us start by noting that, except for a few exceptional cases concerning W, the set A is expressible in terms of W: $A = \text{He}(\bigcup W)$; cf. Exercise 2.56. Therefore we will call He($\bigcup W$) *the heading of* W, denoted by Head(W). Furthermore, we denote the set of all minimal keys of W by Mk(W):

DEFINITION 2.12:
If A is a set and W is a set of tables over A, then:

(a) $\text{Head}(W) \stackrel{D}{=} \text{He}(\bigcup W)$;

(b) $\text{Mk}(W) \stackrel{D}{=} \{B \subseteq \text{Head}(W) \mid B \text{ is a minimal key of } W\}$.

An element of Head(W) is called an *attribute of* W. An element of a minimal key of W is called a *primary* attribute of W; the other attributes of W are called *secondary* attributes. The set of all primary attributes of W is denoted by Prim(W), and the set of all secondary attributes of W is denoted by Sec(W):

DEFINITION 2.13:
If A is a set and W is a set of tables over A, then:

(a) $\text{Prim}(W) \stackrel{D}{=} \bigcup \text{Mk}(W)$;

(b) $\text{Sec}(W) \stackrel{D}{=} \text{Head}(W) - \text{Prim}(W)$.

EXAMPLE 2.11:

In Exercise 2.49 it is asked to prove that

$$\text{Mk(WD)} = \{\{\text{DNO}\}, \{\text{NAME}\}\} \text{ and } \text{Mk(WE)} = \{\{\text{NO}\}\}.$$

Using Definition 2.13 (and Lemma 1 on page 4), the sets of primary attributes of WE and WD can be derived as follows:

$$\begin{aligned}
\text{Prim(WE)} &= \bigcup \text{Mk(WE)} = \bigcup \{\{\text{NO}\}\} = \{\text{NO}\} \text{ and} \\
\text{Prim(WD)} &= \bigcup \text{Mk(WD)} = \bigcup \{\{\text{DNO}\}, \{\text{NAME}\}\} \\
&= \{\text{DNO}\} \cup \{\text{NAME}\} = \{\text{DNO, NAME}\}.
\end{aligned}$$

□ Example 2.11.

EXERCISES

2.49. Prove that the sets of attributes {DNO} and {NAME} of WD and {NO} of WE in Example 1.3 are the only minimal keys of those sets of tables.

2.50. Prove Lemma 2.17.

2.51. Formulate and prove the counterpart of Lemma 2.13 for sets of tables.

2.52. (a) Determine the set of all minimal keys of WP from Example 2.8.
(b) Determine the set of all minimal keys of W1 from Exercise 2.47.

2.53. Let A be a set and W be a set of tables over A, and $B' \subseteq A$ and $B \subseteq B'$ and B be a minimal key of W and $W' \subseteq W$ and h be an injection onto B. Does the following hold?
(a) B is a minimal key of W'
(b) B is a minimal key of $\{T \upharpoonright B' \mid T \in W\}$
(c) dom(h) is a minimal key of $\{T \infty h \mid T \in W\}$
Give in each case either a proof or a counterexample.

2.54. Prove that every finite key of a set of tables W includes a minimal key of W.

2.55. Show by way of an example that not all (infinite) keys include a minimal key.

2.56. (a) For which sets of tables W over a set A is A uniquely determined by W?
(b) Prove that in that case $A = \text{He}(\bigcup W)$.
(c) Compute $\text{He}(\bigcup W)$ in the other cases.

□

2.2.3 Some Normal Forms

In the literature, several so-called "normal forms" for sets of tables are distinguished. In this section we will merely treat two main normal forms, namely the *Boyce-Codd normal form* (in short: BCNF) and the *third normal form* (in short: 3NF).

First, we define when a set of tables is in Boyce-Codd normal form:

DEFINITION 2.14:
If A is a set and W is a set of tables over A, then:
W **is in BCNF** $\overset{D}{\Longleftrightarrow} \forall B \subseteq \text{Head}(W) : \forall a \in \text{Head}(W)$: if $B \hat{\rightarrow} \{a\}$ in W and $a \notin B$ then B is a key of W.

In much of the literature, in order for a set of tables to be in BCNF or 3NF, this set must meet the additional requirement that it is in 1NF (*first normal form*), i.e., every attribute value is "atomic". The notion "atomic" is usually described as "nondecomposable by the underlying database management system"; see for example [Ya 86]. (As a critical side-remark we note that a DBMS is usually quite capable of, say, decomposing strings into substrings . . . Does this mean that the DBMS is too powerful or that strings are not admissible as attribute values?)

We shall drop the (rather vague) 1NF-requirement for all our normal forms, not only for BCNF and 3NF, but also later when we define 2NF and 4NF (in the exercises at the end of Chapter 2). The reason is not only that this requirement is in fact not appropriately formalizable, but especially that in our opinion this (DBMS-dependent) requirement does not belong at this level. What's more, "non-1NF databases" are often desirable in various applications. For developments in this area, we refer to [RKS 88], [Ab 89], and the journals mentioned in the Preface.

The original definitions of 3NF and BCNF can be found in [Co 72] and [Co 74], respectively.

We now give our definition of 3NF:

DEFINITION 2.15:

If A is a set and W is a set of tables over A, then:

W is in 3NF $\overset{D}{\Longleftrightarrow} \forall B \subseteq \text{Head}(W) : \forall a \in \text{Sec}(W)$: if $B \mathrel{\hat{\rightarrow}} \{a\}$ in W and $a \notin B$ then B is a key of W.

We can phrase the two normal forms informally as follows: W is in BCNF iff each attribute set B that "determines" an attribute outside B is a key, and W is in 3NF iff each attribute set B that "determines" a *secondary* attribute outside B is a key. BCNF is therefore a stronger property than 3NF:

LEMMA 2.18:

If A is a set and W is a set of tables over A, then:
If W is in BCNF, then W is also in 3NF.

EXAMPLE 2.12:

We give an example of a set of tables in 3NF that is not in BCNF.

FPCB =	{(HNO	; Chs(6)),	house number
	(STR	; Chs(50)),	street
	(PC	; Chs(7)),	zipcode
	(TOWN	; Chs(40))};	city

WPCB = $\{T \mid T \subseteq \Pi(\text{FPCB})$ and
{STR, HNO, TOWN} is u.i. in T and
{PC, HNO} is u.i. in T and
$\{\text{PC}\} \rightarrow \{\text{TOWN}\}$ in $T\}$

We note that Mk(WPCB) = {{STR, HNO, TOWN}, {PC, HNO}}, hence all attributes of WPCB are primary attributes. It now follows trivially that WPCB is in 3NF. WPCB is not in BCNF, however, since {PC} $\hat{\rightarrow}$ {TOWN} in WPCB, whereas {PC} is not a key of WPCB.

□ Example 2.12.

EXERCISES

2.57. Check whether the following sets of tables are in BCNF.

- (a) WP from Example 2.8;
- (b) WP1 from Exercise 2.48;
- (c) W1 from Exercise 2.47;
- (d) W2 from Exercise 2.47;
- (e) $\{\varnothing\}$;
- (f) $\varnothing$.

2.58. Let W be a set of tables over a set A, and $C \subseteq A$ and $W' \subseteq W$ and W be in BCNF. Are W' and $\{T \Vert\!\upharpoonright C \mid T \in W\}$ in BCNF as well?
Let W' be in BCNF. Is W then in BCNF as well?

2.59. Prove that Mk(WPCB) in Example 2.12 is indeed equal to {{HNO, STR, TOWN}, {ZC, HNO}}.

2.60. Prove Lemma 2.18.

2.61. Check for all sets of tables in Exercise 2.57 whether they are in 3NF.

2.62. Let W be a set of tables over a set A, and $C \subseteq A$ and $W' \subseteq W$ and W be in 3NF. Are W' and $\{T \Vert\!\upharpoonright C \mid T \in W\}$ also in 3NF?
Let W' be in 3NF. Is W then in 3NF as well?

□

2.3 Concepts concerning Database Universes

In §2.3.1 we will begin by treating properties of some operations on database universes.

We want to use the concepts of *permanent dependency* and a *(minimal) key*, introduced in §2.2, at the level of database universes as well. The exact terms and corresponding notations will be introduced in §2.3.2.

In §2.3.3 we will generalize the normal forms, defined in §2.2.3 for sets of tables, to normal forms for DB universes. In fact, we are more interested in normal forms for a DB universe as a whole, rather than normal forms for a "loose" set of tables.

In §2.3.4 we will commence with a generalization of the concept of connecting, introduced in §2.1.4. In this section we will also define the important concept of a *database function*.

Up till now, we have given merely one example of a database universe, namely the DB universe EXU in Example 1.3. Therefore, we will first give another example of a DB universe before turning our attention to particular concepts concerning DB universes.

EXAMPLE 2.13:

The "modules" F1, F2, F3 and WP in Example 2.8 are listed below, and we will extend this example to a DB universe U1 (concerning persons and municipalities). This is done by adding a set function F4 (a so-called "object characterization"), a set of tables WT, a set function F5 (a so-called "database characterization"), and finally the DB universe U1.

Definition	
F1 = {(HNO ; [1 .. 5000]),	house number
(STR ; Chs(50))};	street
F2 = {(DAY ; [1 .. 31]),	day
(MNT ; [1 .. 12]),	month
(YR ; $\mathbb{N}$)};	year
F3 = {(NO ; $\mathbb{N} - \{0\}$),	identity number
(NM ; Chs(40)),	name
(ADDR ; Π(F1)),	address
(PC ; Chs(7)),	zipcode
(TOWN ; Chs(30)),	city
(BDT ; Π(F2)),	birth date
(BPL ; Chs(30)),	birth place
(NMC ; **P** (Chs(30)))};	names of children

WP = $\{T \subseteq \Pi(\text{F3})$ | {NO} is u.i. in T and
{PC} $\rightarrow$ {TOWN} in T and
{ADDR,TOWN} $\rightarrow$ {PC} in T and
$\forall t \in T$: if $t(\text{NO}) \neq 1$ then $\exists t' \in T$: $t'(\text{NO}) = t(\text{NO}) - 1\}$

Definition	
F4 = {(TOWN ; Chs(30)),	city
(POP ; $\mathbb{N}$),	population
(AREA ; $\mathbb{N}$),	area (in acres)
(NO ; $\mathbb{N}$)};	identity number of the mayor

WT = $\{T \subseteq \Pi(\text{F4})$ | {TOWN} is u.i. in $T\}$;

$$F5 = \{(PERS\ ;WP),\ (TOWN;WT)\};$$

$$U1 = \{v \in \Pi(F5) \mid id(\{TOWN\}) \text{ connects } v(PERS) \text{ with } v(TOWN) \text{ and} \quad (a)$$
$$id(\{NO, TOWN\}) \text{ connects } v(TOWN) \text{ with } v(PERS)\} \quad (b)$$

□ Example 2.13.

2.3.1 Operations on Database Universes

In this section we are interested in operations that assign to one or more DB universes a DB universe again.

Since a DB universe is a set, notions such as subset, union, intersection and difference also apply to DB universes. For the most part, such operations yield DB universes once again, namely over the original DB skeleton; the reader is referred to cases (1), (2), and (3) of Theorem 2.1 for details.

Furthermore, we call to mind Theorem 1.1, stating that each DB universe over a set function g is also a table over dom(g). This means, therefore, that all concepts, notations and operations that we have previously defined for tables apply to DB universes as well!

Hence, in particular, the table operations introduced in §2.1.1 are also applicable to DB universes, each producing tables, according to the results in that section. But does the application of such an operation to DB universes yield a *DB universe* once again, and, if so, over which DB skeleton? From part (4) of Theorem 2.1 on, we will investigate this matter, resulting in several interesting results. First of all, however, we will briefly describe what those operations from §2.1.1 amount to, when applied to DB universes:

- Projection (on a set of table indices) corresponds to the "restriction" of the DB universe (and of the DB states) to a "module" or "subscheme" of table indices (that are related in some sense).
- The join of two DB universes having joinable DB skeletons corresponds to the "integration" of all possible pairs of DB states having the same (table) value for table indices with the same name. Each "integration" results in a DB state containing all table indices of the two original DB states.
- Finally, renaming in the case of DB universes amounts to the renaming of *table indices*.

The enumeration within Theorem 2.1 (up to and including (6)) corresponds to the enumeration given in lemmas in §2.1.1 concerning the same operations.

THEOREM 2.1:
If g and g' are set functions
and U and V are DB universes over g
and U' is a DB universe over g'
and $D \subseteq U$ and $X \subseteq \text{dom}(g)$ and h is a function, then:

(1)	D	is a DB universe over g;
(2)	$U \cap V$	is a DB universe over g and
	$U - V$	is a DB universe over g;
(3)	$U \cup V$	is a DB universe over g;
(4)	$U \Upharpoonright X$	is a DB universe over $g \upharpoonright X$;
(5)	$U \bowtie U'$	is a DB universe over $g \cup g'$ provided that g and g' are joinable;
(6)	$U \infty h$	is a DB universe over $g \circ h$;
(7)	$U \pitchfork X$	is a DB universe over $g \pitchfork X$.

Proof:

(1) Each element of U is a DB state over g, so each element of D is one too.

(2) This follows immediately from (1).

(3) Each element of U is a DB state over g and
each element of V is a DB state over g,
so each element of $U \cup V$ is one as well.

(4) In this part, Lemma 11 on page 10 is extensively (though implicitly) used:
Each element of $U \Upharpoonright X$ is of the form $v \upharpoonright X$, where $v \in U$.
It holds that $\text{dom}(v \upharpoonright X) = X = \text{dom}(g \upharpoonright X)$,
hence $v \upharpoonright X$ is a function over $\text{dom}(g \upharpoonright X)$.
It also holds for each $E \in \text{dom}(g \upharpoonright X)$ that $(v \upharpoonright X)(E) = v(E)$,
hence $(v \upharpoonright X)(E)$ is a table over $g(E)$, i.e., over $(g \upharpoonright X)(E)$.
Then $v \upharpoonright X$ is a DB state over $g \upharpoonright X$, according to Definition 1.2.
Then $U \Upharpoonright X$ is a DB universe over $g \upharpoonright X$, according to Definition 1.3.

(5) In this part, we employ Lemma 2(b), page 5:
Each element of $U \bowtie U'$ is of the form $v \cup v'$,
where $v \in U$ and $v' \in U'$ and $v \cup v'$ is a function.
It holds that
$\text{dom}(v \cup v') = \text{dom}(v) \cup \text{dom}(v') = \text{dom}(g) \cup \text{dom}(g') = \text{dom}(g \cup g')$,
hence $v \cup v'$ is a function over $\text{dom}(g \cup g')$.
It also holds for each $E \in \text{dom}(g \cup g')$ that

- $E \in \text{dom}(v)$, hence $(v \cup v')(E) = v(E)$, being a table over $g(E)$, or
- $E \in \text{dom}(v')$, hence $(v \cup v')(E) = v'(E)$, being a table over $g'(E)$.

Since g and g' are joinable, in either case $(v \cup v')(E)$ is a table over $(g \cup g')(E)$.
Then $v \cup v'$ is a DB state over $g \cup g'$, according to Definition 1.2.
Then $U \bowtie U'$ is a DB universe over $g \cup g'$, according to Definition 1.3.

(6) Each element of $U \infty h$ is of the form $v \circ h$, where $v \in U$.
Since $\text{dom}(v) = \text{dom}(g)$, we have by Lemma 9(g) on page 10 that hence $v \circ h$ is a function over $\text{dom}(g \circ h)$.
We also have for each $E \in \text{dom}(g \circ h)$ that $(v \circ h)(E) = v(h(E))$, which is a table over $g(h(E))$, i.e., over $(g \circ h)(E)$.
Then by Definition 1.2, $v \circ h$ is a DB state over $g \circ h$.
Then by Definition 1.3, $U \infty h$ is a DB universe over $g \circ h$.

(7) The proof of this part is analogous to the proof of (4).
(For the definition of $U \Uparrow X$ we refer the reader to Exercise 2.22.)

□

In the exercises of §2.1.1 we have given various properties of the operations treated in Theorem 2.1, applied to tables. Remember that these properties remain valid when applied to DB universes!

EXERCISES

2.63. Give a detailed description of the DB skeleton of the DB universe U1 defined in Example 2.13.

2.64. Give an informal description of the formal requirements (a) and (b) in the definition of U1.

2.65. Give an element of U1, for instance by using the table TP in Figure 2.7.

2.66. Does the population of a city correspond to the number of persons living in that city in each DB state consistent with U1?
If so, prove this; if not, give a formal definition of the DB universe U2 consisting of all elements of U1 that do indeed obey this property.

2.67. Verify to what extent the lemmas 2.4, 2.5, and 2.6 can be sharpened or refined for DB universes. Explain your results.

□

2.3.2 Permanent Dependency and (Minimal) Keys

We will define the concepts of permanent dependency, of a key, and of a minimal key with respect to a table index E of a DB universe U, by applying the corresponding concepts from §2.2 to the set of tables $\{v(E) \mid v \in U\}$. We will call this set of tables *the universe of E in U* and denote this set by $\text{Un}(E,U)$.

DEFINITION 2.16:
If g is a set function and U is a DB universe over g and $E \in \text{He}(U)$, then:
$\text{Un}(E,U) \overset{D}{=} \{v(E) \mid v \in U\}$.

DEFINITION 2.17:
If g is a set function and U is a DB universe over g, and $E \in$ He(U) and B and C are sets, then:
$B \hat{\rightarrow} C$ **in** E **of** $U \overset{D}{\Longleftrightarrow} B \hat{\rightarrow} C$ in Un(E, U).

DEFINITION 2.18:
If g is a set function and U is a DB universe over g and $E \in$ He(U), then:
(a) B is a **key of** E **in** U $\overset{D}{\Longleftrightarrow} B$ is a key of Un(E, U);
(b) B is a **minimal key of** E **in** U $\overset{D}{\Longleftrightarrow} B$ is a minimal key of Un(E, U).

Much in the same way, we will lift the notations introduced in the definitions 2.12 and 2.13, concerning a set of tables W, to the level of a table index E of a DB universe U. The new notations are easily distinguishable from the old notations with the same name, for they have two parameters instead of one.

DEFINITION 2.19:
If g is a set function, and U is a DB universe over g and $E \in$ He(U), then:
(a) Head(E, U) $\overset{D}{=}$ Head(Un(E, U));
(b) Mk(E, U) $\overset{D}{=}$ Mk(Un(E, U));
(c) Prim(E, U) $\overset{D}{=}$ Prim(Un(E, U));
(d) Sec(E, U) $\overset{D}{=}$ Sec(Un(E, U)).

We will illustrate the concepts above using the DB universe U1, defined in Example 2.13.

EXAMPLE 2.14:
We will first determine the universes of the table indices PERS and TOWN in U1, i.e., the sets Un(PERS, U1) and Un(TOWN, U1). From the definitions of U1 and F5 it immediately follows that

Un(PERS, U1) $\subseteq$ WP and Un(TOWN, U1) $\subseteq$ WT.

It is not so easy to see, however, whether these inclusions are also equalities. First we will show that every $T \in$ WP can indeed be a PERS-table in an appropriately chosen $v_T \in$ U1. For that purpose, we will define the function v_T over {PERS, TOWN} as follows:

v_T (PERS) = T and

$$v_T\,(\text{TOWN}) = \{\{(\text{TOWN}\ ;\ t(\text{TOWN})),\ (\text{POP}\ ;\ 20000),\ (\text{AREA}\ ;\ 6000),\ (\text{NO}\ ;\ t(\text{NO}))\} \mid t \in T \text{ and } \forall t' \in T\text{: if } t(\text{TOWN}) = t'(\text{TOWN}) \text{ then } t(\text{NO}) \leq t'(\text{NO})\} \qquad \text{(c)}$$

The function v_T proves to be an element of U1 (cf. Exercise 2.68(b)). But then WP $\subseteq$ Un(PERS, U1), hence Un(PERS, U1) is equal to WP. (Such a DB state v_T may not seem very realistic, but that is of course irrelevant for that matter.)

We now show that the universe of TOWN in U1 is a *proper* subset of WT. We will even prove slightly more, namely

Un(TOWN, U1) $\subseteq$ $\{T \in$ WT | {NO} is u.i. in $T\}$. (1)

For sake of convenience, $\{T \in$ WT | {NO} is u.i. in $T\}$ will henceforth be called WT2. Since WT2 is a proper subset of WT (see also Exercise 2.69(a)), Un(TOWN, U1) is a proper subset of WT too. (Moreover, Un(TOWN, U1) turns out to be a proper subset of WT2 as well: see Exercise 2.69(b). It is even fairly hard to characterize Un(TOWN, U1) explicitly as a subset of WT: see Exercise 2.73.)

In order to show that the inclusion above indeed holds, we must first prove that

$\forall v \in$ U1: {NO} is u.i. in v(TOWN).

Thus, let $v \in$ U1, $t \in v$(TOWN), $t' \in v$(TOWN) and t(NO) = t'(NO); (2)
we must then prove that $t = t'$, according to the definition of unique
identification. Because of requirement (b) in the definition of U1,
there exist tuples p and p' in v(PERS) such that
t(NO) = p(NO) and t'(NO) = p'(NO) and (3)
t(TOWN) = p(TOWN) and t'(TOWN) = p'(TOWN). (4)
From (2) and (3) it follows that p(NO) = p'(NO). (5)
Since v(PERS) $\in$ WP, {NO} is u.i. in v(PERS),
according to the definition of WP. (6)
It follows from (5) and (6) that $p = p'$.
Using (4) it follows that t(TOWN) = t'(TOWN). (7)
Since v(TOWN) $\in$ WT, {TOWN} is u.i. in v(TOWN).
Using (7), we conclude that $t = t'$.

We have thus established correctness of property (1). In fact {NO} thus turns out to be a key of TOWN in U1, even though {NO} is not a key of the set of tables WT used in the definition of U1! Such side-effects of other specified conditions often occur in practice (sometimes unconsciously).

After this preliminary work, calculation of the sets of actual importance, namely Mk(PERS, U1) and Mk(TOWN, U1), are left to the reader; cf. Exercise 2.71.

To illustrate Definition 2.17, we conclude this somewhat comprehensive example with the straightforward observation that for instance {ADDR, TOWN} $\hat{\rightarrow}$ {PC} in PERS of U1, since {ADDR, TOWN} $\hat{\rightarrow}$ {PC} in WP and Un(PERS, U1) = WP.

□ Example 2.14.

Given a certain DB skeleton, permanent dependencies and keys are preserved under "reduction" of the DB universe:

LEMMA 2.19:
If g is a set function, and U and U' are DB universes over g, and $E \in \text{dom}(g)$ and B and C are sets, then:
(a) If $U' \subseteq U$ and $B \hat{\rightarrow} C$ in E of U, then $B \hat{\rightarrow} C$ in E of U'.
(b) If $U' \subseteq U$ and B is a key of E in U, then B is also a key of E in U'.

The proof of this straightforward lemma is left to the reader (see Exercise 2.74). In subsequent exercises we will investigate the possibilities of extending this lemma.

EXERCISES

2.68. In this exercise we examine the function v_T over {PERS, TOWN}, defined in Example 2.14.

(a) Give an informal description of the formal requirement (c) in the definition of v_T.

(b) Prove that for each $T \in$ WP the function v_T is indeed an element of U1.

2.69. From the definition of WT2 in Example 2.14 it follows immediately that WT2 $\subseteq$ WT.
In Example 2.14 it was also proven that Un(TOWN, U1) $\subseteq$ WT2.

(a) Now prove that WT2 $\subset$ WT.

(b) Also prove that Un(TOWN, U1) $\subset$ WT2.

2.70. Verify which of the following permanent dependencies hold in Example 2.13, and explain each of your answers briefly.

(a) {NO} $\hat{\rightarrow}$ {TOWN} in PERS of U1;

(b) {NO} $\hat{\rightarrow}$ {TOWN} in TOWN of U1;

(c) {TOWN} $\hat{\rightarrow}$ {NO} in PERS of U1;

(d) {TOWN} $\hat{\rightarrow}$ {NO} in TOWN of U1.

2.71. In this exercise we examine the minimal keys of the sets defined in the examples 2.13 and 2.14.

(a) Determine Mk(WT) and Mk(WT2).

(b) Determine Mk(PERS, U1) and Mk(TOWN, U1).

2.72. Determine Mk(EMPL, EXU) and Mk(DEP, EXU), where EXU is the DB universe introduced in Example 1.3.

2.73. In Exercise 2.69 we observed that
Un(TOWN, U1) $\subset$ WT, and moreover,
Un(TOWN, U1) $\subset \{T \in \text{WT} \mid \{\text{NO}\}$ is u.i. in $T\}$.

(a) Attempt to characterize Un(TOWN, U1) explicitly as a subset of WT, or at least approximate Un(TOWN, U1) "top-down", i.e., try to give the strongest possible condition $\phi(T)$ (not mentioning Un(TOWN, U1) itself) such that

Un(TOWN, U1) $\subseteq \{T \in \text{WT} \mid \phi(T)\}$ or even
Un(TOWN, U1) $= \{T \in \text{WT} \mid \phi(T)\}$.

(b) Prove the inclusion or equality that you gave pertaining to (a).

2.74. Prove Lemma 2.19.

2.75. For any given DB skeleton, besides the permanent dependencies and the keys, are the minimal keys preserved under reduction of the DB universe as well? Give a proof or a counterexample.

2.76. Check whether permanent dependencies and keys are also preserved under the other operations on DB universes mentioned in Theorem 2.1.

2.77. Verify to what extent minimal keys are preserved under the other operations on DB universes mentioned in Theorem 2.1.

□

2.3.3 Some Normal Forms for Database Universes

A DB universe U is in Boyce-Codd normal form (or third normal form) if Un(E, U) is in BCNF (or 3NF, respectively) for each table index E of U. We will use the same notations as for the corresponding normal forms for sets of tables. It will be clear from the context which of the two levels is considered.

DEFINITION 2.20:
If g is a set function and U is a DB universe over g, then:

(a) **U is in BCNF** $\overset{D}{\Longleftrightarrow} \forall E \in \text{He}(U) : \text{Un}(E, U)$ is in BCNF;

(b) **U is in 3NF** $\overset{D}{\Longleftrightarrow} \forall E \in \text{He}(U) : \text{Un}(E, U)$ is in 3NF.

Lemma 2.20 is an immediate consequence of Lemma 2.18 (since Lemma 2.18 is applicable to the set of tables $\text{Un}(E, U)$).

LEMMA 2.20:
If g is a set function and U is a DB universe over g, then:
If U is in BCNF, then U is also in 3NF.

EXERCISES

2.78. Is U1 of Example 2.13 in BCNF or in 3NF?

2.79. We define (starting from Example 2.13):

WP2 = $\{T \subseteq \Pi(\text{F3}) \mid \{\text{NO}\}$ is u.i. in $T\}$;

F6 = {(PERS ; WP2),
(TOWN; WT)};

U3 = $\{v \in \Pi(\text{F6}) \mid$ id({TOWN}) connects v(PERS) with v(TOWN) and
id({NO, TOWN}) connects v(TOWN) with v(PERS) and
{(BPL; TOWN)} connects v(PERS) with v(TOWN)}.

At this point we also refer the reader to §2.4 where a summary will be given of all definitions concerning our persons/cities-examples.

(a) Describe in words the "new" requirement given in the definition of U3.

(b) Is U3 in BCNF or in 3NF?

(c) Are U1 and U3 disjoint? Is one included in the other?

(d) Prove that $\Pi(\text{F5}) \subseteq \Pi(\text{F6})$.

2.80. Verify to what extent BCNF is preserved under the operations on DB universes mentioned in Theorem 2.1.

2.81. Go through the same programme for 3NF.
□

2.3.4 Permanent Connections and Database Functions

We want to define the two connection concepts defined in §2.1.4 at the level of DB universes as well. This is done as follows:

DEFINITION 2.21:
If g is a set function and U is a DB universe over g and $M \in \text{He}(U)$ and $D \in \text{He}(U)$ and h is a function, then:

(a) ***h* connects *M* permanently with *D* in *U***
$\overset{D}{\Longleftrightarrow} \forall v \in U : h$ connects $v(M)$ with $v(D)$;

(b) ***h* connects *M* permanently bilaterally with *D* in *U***
$\overset{D}{\Longleftrightarrow} \forall v \in U : h$ connects $v(M)$ bilaterally with $v(D)$.

EXAMPLE 2.15:
From the examples 1.3 and 2.13 we observe the following permanent connections in EXU and U1 respectively:

{(DEPNO; DNO)}	connects	EMPL	permanently with	DEP	in EXU;
{(MANNO; NO)}	connects	DEP	permanently with	EMPL	in EXU;
id({NO, TOWN})	connects	TOWN	permanently with	PERS	in U1;
id({TOWN})	connects	PERS	permanently with	TOWN	in U1.

From the two last permanent connections we can even derive a permanent *bilateral* connection: id({TOWN}) connects TOWN permanently bilaterally with PERS in U1.

□ Example 2.15.

The following concept is again introduced by way of an example.

EXAMPLE 2.16:
From the definition of U1 in Example 2.13 it can be derived that for each v in U1 there exists a function H1(v) from v(PERS) into v(TOWN) that assigns to each "person-tuple" in the DB state v the (uniquely determined) tuple of its town. Note that what we have here is in fact a (function-valued) function H1 over U1. H1 is an example of what we will call a *database function over* U1 *with respect to* (w.r.t.) the ordered pair of table indices (PERS; TOWN).

□ Example 2.16.

The general definition of the concept of a database function reads as follows:

DEFINITION 2.22:
If g is a set function and U is a DB universe over g and $(M;D) \in \mathrm{He}(U) \times \mathrm{He}(U)$, then:
H is a **DB function over** U **w.r.t.** $(M;D)$ $\stackrel{D}{\Longleftrightarrow}$ H is a function over U and
$\forall v \in U : H(v) \in v(M) \twoheadrightarrow v(D)$.

M is called *the source index of H* and D is called *the target index of H.*

An important class of DB functions in practice is given by the following lemma, based on Lemma 2.16. The lemma states the following property: if a function h connects the table index M permanently with a table index D in a DB universe U, and in addition rng(h) is a key of D in U, then the function that assigns to each $v \in U$ the association on $v(M) \times v(D)$ induced by h, is a DB function over U with respect to the pair $(M;D)$.

LEMMA 2.21:
If g is a set function and U is a DB universe over g and $M \in \mathrm{He}(U)$ and $D \in \mathrm{He}(U)$ and h is a function and
(1) rng(h) is a key of D in U and
(2) h connects M permanently with D in U,
then $\lambda v \in U : \{(t;t') \in v(M) \times v(D) \mid t \upharpoonright \mathrm{dom}(h) = t' \circ h\}$ is a DB function over U with respect to $(M;D)$.

Proof:
We shall verify whether this function
$\lambda v \in U : \{(t;t') \in v(M) \times v(D) \mid t \upharpoonright \mathrm{dom}(h) = t' \circ h\}$ obeys Definition 2.22.
In this proof we will call this function H.
From the definition of H it follows immediately that H is a function over U.
Now let $v \in U$. Obviously, $H(v) \subseteq v(M) \times v(D)$. (a)
From (1) we have that rng(h) is u.i. in $v(D)$.
By Lemma 2.16 (4), $H(v)$ is a function. (b)
Furthermore, we have from (2) that h connects the table $v(M)$ with the table $v(D)$.
By Lemma 2.16 (2), we now have that $\mathrm{dom}(H(v)) = v(M)$. (c)
From (a), (b), and (c) it follows that $H(v) \in v(M) \twoheadrightarrow v(D)$ for each $v \in U$.
As a result, H obeys Definition 2.22.

□

Lemma 2.22 indicates how to obtain, by means of *generalized composition,* a "new" DB function from two given DB functions. Generalized composition is defined for each pair of function-valued functions as follows:

DEFINITION 2.23:
If G and H are function-valued functions, then:
$G \odot H \stackrel{D}{=} \lambda x \in \mathrm{dom}(G) \cap \mathrm{dom}(H) : G(x) \circ H(x)$.

In other words, $G \odot H$, *the generalized composition of G after H*, is the function over $\mathrm{dom}(G) \cap \mathrm{dom}(H)$ defined by $(G \odot H)(x) = G(x) \circ H(x)$ for each $x \in \mathrm{dom}(G) \cap \mathrm{dom}(H)$. As yet, we will use generalized composition only if $\mathrm{dom}(G) = \mathrm{dom}(H) = U$, where U is some DB universe. A typical situation is the following lemma that states that the generalized composition of two DB functions with a corresponding source and target index is also a DB function:

LEMMA 2.22:
If U is a DB universe over a set function g and $\{M,D,D'\} \subseteq \mathrm{He}(U)$ and
(1) H is a DB function over U w.r.t. $(M;D)$ and
(2) G is a DB function over U w.r.t. $(D;D')$,
then $G \odot H$ is a DB function over U w.r.t. $(M;D')$.

EXERCISES

2.82. Does {(BPL; TOWN)} connect the table index PERS permanently bilaterally with TOWN in U3 of Exercise 2.79? Give a proof or a counterexample.

2.83. (a) Give a formal definition of the function H1, described informally in Example 2.16.
(b) Is H1 of the form described in Lemma 2.21?

2.84. We define the functions H2 and H3 as follows:

$\mathrm{H2} = \lambda v \in \mathrm{U1} : \{(t;t') \in v(\mathrm{TOWN}) \times v(\mathrm{PERS}) \mid t(\mathrm{NO}) = t'(\mathrm{NO})\}$ and
$\mathrm{H3} = \lambda v \in \mathrm{U1} : \{(t;t') \in v(\mathrm{PERS}) \times v(\mathrm{TOWN}) \mid t(\mathrm{BPL}) = t'(\mathrm{TOWN})\}$,

where U1 is the DB universe defined in Example 2.13.
Give an informal description of H2 and H3. Are H2 and H3 DB functions?
If not, why?

2.85. Prove the following:
If g is a set function and U is a DB universe over g, and $(M;D) \in \mathrm{He}(U) \times \mathrm{He}(U)$ and $a \in g(M)$ and $a' \in g(D)$ and $\{a'\}$ is a key of D in U and $\{t(a) \mid t \in v(M)\} \subseteq \{t'(a') \mid t' \in v(D)\}$ for each $v \in U$,
then $\lambda v \in U : \{(t;t') \in v(M) \times v(D) \mid t(a) = t'(a')\}$ is a DB function over U with respect to $(M;D)$.

2.86. If g is a set function and U is a DB universe over g, and $M \in \mathrm{He}(U)$ and $D \in \mathrm{He}(U)$ and $g(M) \cap g(D)$ is a key of D in U and $\mathrm{id}(g(M) \cap g(D))$ connects $v(M)$ with $v(D)$ for each $v \in U$, and H is defined by

$H = \lambda v \in U : \{(t;t') \in v(M) \times v(D) \mid t \text{ and } t' \text{ match on } g(M) \cap g(D)\}$,

then:

(a) H is a DB function over U w.r.t. $(M\,;D)$ and
(b) $v(M) \bowtie v(D) = \{t \cup H(v)\,(t) \mid t \in v(M)\}$ for each $v \in U$.
Prove this.

2.87. Prove Lemma 2.22.

2.88. Is generalized composition associative?

2.89. Are H2 and H3 from Exercise 2.84 function-valued functions?
If so, give an informal description of:

H2 ⊙ H1, H1 ⊙ H2, H2 ⊙ H3, H3 ⊙ H2, and H3 ⊙ (H2 ⊙ H1),

where H1 is the function described in Example 2.16.
Which of these are DB functions over U1, and with respect to which pairs of indices?

2.90. We define (starting from Example 2.13):

WPF = $\{T \in \text{WP} \mid T \text{ is finite}\}$;
WTF = $\{T \in \text{WT} \mid T \text{ is finite}\}$;
F7 = {(PERS ; WPF),
(TOWN; WTF)}.

These definitions can also be found in the summary at the end of §2.4, along with the definitions in Example 2.13.

(a) Prove that $\Pi(\text{F7}) \subseteq \Pi(\text{F5})$.

(b) Prove that WTF = WT.

(c) Is WTF a finite set?

(d) Prove that $\text{WPF} \subset \text{WP}$.

2.91. Referring to the exercises 2.79, 2.84, and 2.90 (or the summary at the end of §2.4), we furthermore define:

$\text{U4} = \text{U3} \cap \Pi(\text{F7})$,
$\text{H4} = \text{H2} \restriction \text{U4}$, and
$\text{H5} = \text{H3} \restriction \text{U4}$.

(a) Prove that U4 $\subseteq$ U1.
(b) Give an informal description of H4 and H5.
(c) Are H4 and H5 also DB functions?

2.92. Starting from Exercise 2.91, we define (by induction):

$G_0 = \text{H4} \odot \text{H5}$ and $G_{n+1} = G_n \odot G_0$ for each $n \in \mathbb{N}$.

(a) Give an informal description of G_0.
(b) Give for any $n \in \mathbb{N}$ an informal description of G_n.
(c) Prove that for each $n \in \mathbb{N}$ the function G_n is a DB function over U4.
(d) Prove that for each $v \in$ U4 not all $G_n(v)$ are different (i.e., $\forall v \in \text{U4} : \exists n \in \mathbb{N} : \exists m \in \mathbb{N} : n \neq m$ and $G_n(v) = G_m(v)$).
(e) Check whether all G_n are different.

□

2.4 Summary

In Figure 2.10 the concepts introduced in Chapters 1 and 2 have been placed together, grouped around the four main concepts of a *table*, a *set of tables*, a *DB state*, and a *DB universe*. The concepts have been divided into two groups in two "orthogonal" ways:

(1) On the one hand, there is a borderline between
- (a) those notions that in fact already belong to the field of *file theory* (i.e., the theory of separate files), and
- (b) those notions that only play a role in *database theory* (i.e., the theory of several "integrated" files).

(2) On the other hand, there is a borderline between
- (a) those notions concerning a *state*, and
- (b) those notions concerning a *state space*.

Hence, starting from a *table* over a set A we can extend in two "dimensions":

I: on the one hand, we can discern several sorts of tables "at the same time" (i.e., to a *DB state* over a set function g), which we did at the transition from §1.1 to §1.2, and

II: on the other hand, we can discern several tables of the same "sort" (i.e., to a *set of tables* over A), as we did in going from §2.1 to §2.2.

When we extend in *both* "dimensions", we obtain a *DB universe* over g. In Chapter 1 this was attained by first carrying out extension I (from §1.1 to §1.2), and after that extension II (from §1.2 to §1.3). In Chapter 2, however, first extension II was carried out (from §2.1 to §2.2), and afterwards extension I (from §2.2 to §2.3).

	File	**Database**
State (momentary) (incidental) (extensional)	§1.1: T is *table* over A §2.1.1: $T \restriction B$, $T \bowtie T'$, $T \infty h$ §2.1.2: $B \rightarrow C$ in T §2.1.3: B is (minimally) u.i. in T §2.1.4: h connects T (bilaterally) with T'	§1.2: v is a *DB state* over g
State space (permanent) (structural) (intensional)	§2.2: W is a *set of tables* over A §2.2.1: $B \hat{\rightarrow} C$ in W §2.2.2: B is a (minimal) key of W Head(W), Mk(W) Prim(W), Sec(W) §2.2.3: W is in BCNF W is in 3NF	§1.3: U is a *DB universe* over g §2.3.2: Un(E, U) $B \hat{\rightarrow} C$ in E of U B is a (minimal) key of E in U Head(E, U), Mk(E, U) Prim(E, U), Sec(E, U) §2.3.3: U is in BCNF U is in 3NF §2.3.4: h connects M permanently (bilaterally) with D in U H is a DB function over U w.r.t. (M ; D) $G \odot H$

Figure 2.10: Overview of the introduced concepts

As a frame of reference we offer in the last example of this chapter the simple but also well-known and widely used example in the database literature concerning suppliers, parts and shipments (cf. [Da 90]).

EXAMPLE 2.17:

The suppliers/parts/shipments-example is based on the following DB skeleton, which we call g2:

g2 = {(S ; {S#, SNAME, STATUS, CITY}),	suppliers
(P ; {P#, PNAME, COLOR, WEIGHT, CITY}),	parts
(SP; {S#, P#, QTY})}	shipments

Here S# stands for *supplier number*, P# for *part number*, and QTY for *quantity*.

We will successively define three object characterizations, one database characterization, and, finally, the DB universe.

FS = {(S# ; Chs(5)),
(SNAME ; Chs(20)),
(STATUS; Int(4)),
(CITY ; Chs(15))};

FP = {(P# ; Chs(6)),
(PNAME ; Chs(20)),
(COLOR ; Chs(6)),
(WEIGHT ; Int(4)),
(CITY ; Chs(15))};

FSP = {(S# ; Chs(5)),
(P# ; Chs(6)),
(QTY; Int(9))};

SPSC = {(S ; $\{T \subseteq \Pi(\text{FS}) \mid \{\text{S\#}\}$ is u.i. in $T\}$),
(P ; $\{T \subseteq \Pi(\text{FP}) \mid \{\text{P\#}\}$ is u.i. in $T\}$),
(SP; $\{T \subseteq \Pi(\text{FSP}) \mid \{\text{S\#, P\#}\}$ is u.i. in $T\}$)};

SPSU = $\{v \mid v \in \Pi(\text{SPSC})$ and
{(S# ; S#)} connects v(SP) with v(S) and
{(P# ; P#)} connects v(SP) with v(P)}.

We now define the following functions over SPSU:

$$\text{Shipsup} = \lambda v \in \text{SPSU} : \{(t\,;t') \in v(\text{SP}) \times v(\text{S}) \mid t(\text{S\#}) = t'(\text{S\#})\}$$
$$\text{Shippart} = \lambda v \in \text{SPSU} : \{(t\,;t') \in v(\text{SP}) \times v(\text{P}) \mid t(\text{P\#}) = t'(\text{P\#})\}$$

According to Lemma 2.21, Shipsup is a DB function over SPSU with respect to the pair of table indices (SP; S), and Shippart is a DB function over SPSU with respect to the pair (SP; P). For $v \in$ SPSU, Shipsup(v) $\in v(\text{SP}) \twoheadrightarrow v(\text{S})$ is the function assigning to each shipment tuple in state v the "corresponding" supplier tuple, and Shippart(v) $\in v(\text{SP}) \twoheadrightarrow v(\text{P})$ is the function assigning to each shipment tuple in state v the "corresponding" part tuple.

We can represent the two set-memberships Shipsup(v) $\in v(\text{SP}) \twoheadrightarrow v(\text{S})$ and Shippart(v) $\in v(\text{SP}) \twoheadrightarrow v(\text{P})$ schematically as follows:

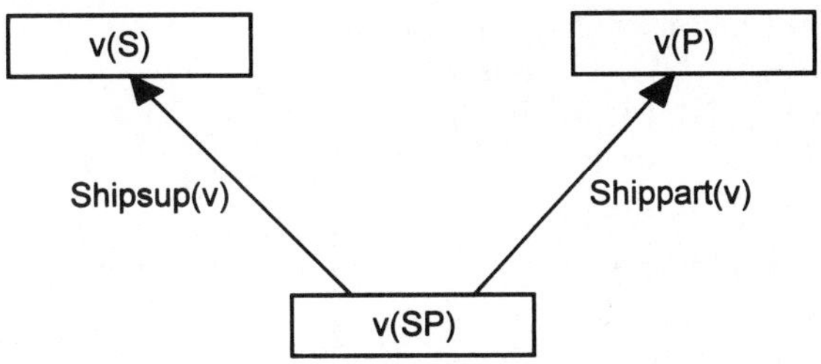

Figure 2.11: Some functional connections

Especially when dealing with a large number of DB functions, which is often the case in practice, such an informal scheme might come in handy. It is perhaps needless to say that, conversely, such an informal sketch is in general insufficient to reconstruct the precise definitions of the depicted functions.

□ Example 2.17.

For sake of convenience, we also give an overview of all our persons/cities-examples, scattered over the examples 2.8, 2.13, and 2.14, and over the exercises 2.79, 2.84, 2.90, and 2.91.

$$\begin{aligned}
\mathrm{F1} = \{&(\mathrm{STR}\ ;\mathrm{Chs}(50)),\\
&(\mathrm{HNO};[1\ ..\ 5000])\};
\end{aligned}$$

$$\begin{aligned}
\mathrm{F2} = \{&(\mathrm{DAY};[1\ ..\ 31]),\\
&(\mathrm{MNT};[1\ ..\ 12]),\\
&(\mathrm{YR}\ \ ;\mathbb{N})\};
\end{aligned}$$

$$\begin{aligned}
\mathrm{F3} = \{&(\mathrm{NO}\ \ ;\mathbb{N}-\{0\}),\\
&(\mathrm{NM}\ \ ;\mathrm{Chs}(40)),\\
&(\mathrm{ADDR}\ ;\Pi(\mathrm{F1})),\\
&(\mathrm{PC}\ \ ;\mathrm{Chs}(7)),\\
&(\mathrm{TOWN};\mathrm{Chs}(30)),\\
&(\mathrm{BDT}\ ;\Pi(\mathrm{F2})),\\
&(\mathrm{BPL}\ ;\mathrm{Chs}(30)),\\
&(\mathrm{NMC}\ ;\mathbf{P}(\mathrm{Chs}(30)))\};
\end{aligned}$$

$$\begin{aligned}
\mathrm{F4} = \{&(\mathrm{TOWN};\mathrm{Chs}(30)),\\
&(\mathrm{POP}\ \ ;\mathbb{N}),\\
&(\mathrm{AREA}\ ;\mathbb{N}),\\
&(\mathrm{NO}\ \ ;\mathbb{N})\};
\end{aligned}$$

$$\begin{aligned}
\mathrm{WP} &= \{T \subseteq \Pi(\mathrm{F3}) \mid \{\mathrm{NO}\} \text{ is u.i. in } T \text{ and}\\
&\qquad \{\mathrm{PC}\} \to \{\mathrm{TOWN}\} \text{ in } T \text{ and}\\
&\qquad \{\mathrm{ADDR}, \mathrm{TOWN}\} \to \{\mathrm{PC}\} \text{ in } T \text{ and}\\
&\qquad \forall t \in T\text{: if } t(\mathrm{NO}) \neq 1 \text{ then } \exists t' \in T : t'(\mathrm{NO}) = t(\mathrm{NO}) - 1\};\\
\mathrm{WT} &= \{T \subseteq \Pi(\mathrm{F4}) \mid \{\mathrm{TOWN}\} \text{ is u.i. in } T\};\\
\mathrm{WP2} &= \{T \subseteq \Pi(\mathrm{F3}) \mid \{\mathrm{NO}\} \text{ is u.i. in } T\};\\
\mathrm{WT2} &= \{T \in \mathrm{WT} \mid \{\mathrm{NO}\} \text{ is u.i. in } T\};\\
\mathrm{WPF} &= \{T \in \mathrm{WP} \mid T \text{ is finite}\};\\
\mathrm{WTF} &= \{T \in \mathrm{WT} \mid T \text{ is finite}\};
\end{aligned}$$

$$\begin{aligned}
\mathrm{F5} &= \{(\mathrm{PERS};\ \mathrm{WP}),\ (\mathrm{TOWN};\ \mathrm{WT})\};\\
\mathrm{F6} &= \{(\mathrm{PERS};\ \mathrm{WP2}),\ (\mathrm{TOWN};\ \mathrm{WT})\};\\
\mathrm{F7} &= \{(\mathrm{PERS};\ \mathrm{WPF}),\ (\mathrm{TOWN};\ \mathrm{WTF})\};
\end{aligned}$$

$$\begin{aligned}
\mathrm{U1} = \{v \in \Pi(\mathrm{F5}) \mid\ & \mathrm{id}(\{\mathrm{TOWN}\}) && \text{connects } v(\mathrm{PERS}) \text{ with } v(\mathrm{TOWN}) \text{ and}\\
& \mathrm{id}(\{\mathrm{NO}, \mathrm{TOWN}\}) && \text{connects } v(\mathrm{TOWN}) \text{ with } v(\mathrm{PERS})\};\\
\mathrm{U3} = \{v \in \Pi(\mathrm{F6}) \mid\ & \mathrm{id}(\{\mathrm{TOWN}\}) && \text{connects } v(\mathrm{PERS}) \text{ with } v(\mathrm{TOWN}) \text{ and}\\
& \mathrm{id}(\{\mathrm{NO}, \mathrm{TOWN}\}) && \text{connects } v(\mathrm{TOWN}) \text{ with } v(\mathrm{PERS}) \text{ and}\\
& \{(\mathrm{BPL};\ \mathrm{TOWN})\} && \text{connects } v(\mathrm{PERS}) \text{ with } v(\mathrm{TOWN})\};\\
\mathrm{U4} = \mathrm{U3} \cap \Pi(\mathrm{F7});\ &
\end{aligned}$$

$$\begin{aligned}
\mathrm{H2} &= \lambda v \in \mathrm{U1}\text{: } \{(t\,;t') \in v(\mathrm{TOWN}) \times v(\mathrm{PERS}) \mid t(\mathrm{NO}) = t'(\mathrm{NO})\};\\
\mathrm{H3} &= \lambda v \in \mathrm{U1}\text{: } \{(t\,;t') \in v(\mathrm{PERS}) \times v(\mathrm{TOWN}) \mid t(\mathrm{BPL}) = t'(\mathrm{TOWN})\};\\
\mathrm{H4} &= \mathrm{H2} \upharpoonright \mathrm{U4};\\
\mathrm{H5} &= \mathrm{H3} \upharpoonright \mathrm{U4}.
\end{aligned}$$

We conclude Chapter 2 with some revisionary exercises.

EXERCISES

2.93. We define the so-called *(left) outer join* of a table T over a set A with a table T' over a set A' as follows:

$$T \mathbin{⟕} T' \overset{D}{=} (T \bowtie T') \cup (T - ((T \bowtie T') \upharpoonright\!\upharpoonright A)).$$

(a) Is the set $T \ltimes T'$ for all tables T and T' a table as well, formally speaking? Give a proof or a counterexample.

(b) If $T \Vert\!\upharpoonright A' \subseteq T' \Vert\!\upharpoonright A$ then $T \ltimes T' = T \bowtie T'$. Prove this.

(c) Is the left outer join commutative?
(In other words, does $T \ltimes T' = T' \ltimes T$ always hold?)

Figure 2.2 in Example 2.2 offers a graphical representation of the tables V1 and V2.

(d) Give the number of elements of the sets V1 $\ltimes$ V2 and V2 $\ltimes$ V1.

(e) Construct graphical representations of V1 $\ltimes$ V2 and V2 $\ltimes$ V1.

2.94. We define the following sets:

(D1) If A and B are sets, $c \notin (A - B)$, and T is a table over A, then:
$\text{Pack}_{B,c}(T) \overset{D}{=} \{t \not\upharpoonright B \cup \{(c\,; t \upharpoonright B)\} \mid t \in T\}$

(D2) If A and B are sets, $a \in A$, $B \cap (A - \{a\}) = \varnothing$, T is a table over A, and $\forall t \in T : t(a)$ is a function over B, then:
$\text{Unpack}_a(T) \overset{D}{=} \{t \not\upharpoonright \{a\} \cup t(a) \mid t \in T\}$.

Answer the following questions.

(a) Are $\text{Pack}_{B,c}(T)$ and $\text{Unpack}_a(T)$ also tables?
If so, over which sets?

Prove the following two equalities and specify in both cases the precise conditions (on a, B, T, etc.).

(b) $\text{Unpack}_a(\text{Pack}_{B,a}(T)) = T$.

(c) $\text{Pack}_{B,a}(\text{Unpack}_a(T)) = T$.

2.95. Does equality hold in Exercise 2.17(b)? Give a proof or a counterexample.

2.96. Let A, B, and C be sets, and let T be a table over A. We define:
$B \twoheadrightarrow C$ in $T \overset{D}{\Leftrightarrow} \forall t \in T : \forall t' \in T$: if $t \upharpoonright B = t' \upharpoonright B$ then $t\,\theta(t' \upharpoonright C) \in T$.
(C is called *multivalued dependent* on B within T.)

(a) If $B \subseteq A$, $C \subseteq A$, and $B \rightarrow C$ in T, then $B \twoheadrightarrow C$ in T.
Prove this.

(b) Give an example of a multivalued dependency that is not a momentary dependency.

(c) Prove the following equivalence:
$B \twoheadrightarrow C$ in $T \Leftrightarrow T = T \Vert\!\upharpoonright (B \cup C) \bowtie T \Vert\!\upharpoonright (B \cup (A - C))$.

2.97. If A, A', and A'' are sets, T is a table over A, T' is a table over A', T'' is a table over A'', and h and h' are injective functions such that $\text{dom}(h) \subseteq A$, and $\text{rng}(h) \subseteq \text{rng}(h')$, $\text{dom}(h') \subseteq A'$, and $\text{rng}(h') \subseteq A''$, h connects T with T', and h'

connects T' with T'', then $h' \circ h$ connects the table T with T''.
Prove this or give a counterexample.

2.98. If A and A' are sets, T is a table over A, T' is a table over A', and h is an injective function such that $\mathrm{dom}(h) \subseteq A$, and $\mathrm{rng}(h) \subseteq A'$, then:

h connects T with T' $\Leftrightarrow$ $T = T \bowtie (T' \infty h)$.

Prove this.

2.99. If T and T' are sets of functions, C is a set, and h is an injective function, then:

(a) $\mathrm{id}(C)$ connects T bilaterally with T' $\Leftrightarrow$ $\mathrm{id}(C)$ connects T' bilaterally with T;

(b) h connects T bilaterally with T' $\Leftrightarrow$ h^{-1} connects T' bilaterally with T.

Prove this.

2.100. In (SQL-)practice, the following equivalence is often employed in the case of some given attribute transformation h and two given tables T and T':

h connects T with T'
$\Leftrightarrow 0 = |\{t \in T \mid 0 = |\{t' \in T' \mid t \restriction \mathrm{dom}(h) = t' \circ h\}|\}|$.

Prove this (rather ugly and also farfetched) equivalence.

2.101. Derive the set of all minimal keys of the set W3 consisting of the following three tables:

T21:

$a1$	$a2$	$a3$	$a4$	$a5$
1	4	9	p	s
1	4	9	q	t

T22:

$a1$	$a2$	$a3$	$a4$	$a5$
1	4	7	p	s
1	6	7	p	s
1	4	9	p	s
2	5	9	q	t
3	5	9	p	t
3	4	7	p	s

T23:

$a1$	$a2$	$a3$	$a4$	$a5$
2	6	7	p	t
2	5	7	p	s
1	4	7	q	t
1	4	9	q	t
2	5	9	p	s

Briefly explain your answer.

2.102. Let A and B be sets, and let W be a set of tables over A. Does the following equivalence hold?

B is a minimal key of W $\Leftrightarrow$ $\forall T \in W : B$ is minimally u.i. in T.

Check the correctness of both implications separately.

2.103. We define another well-known normal form as follows:
If A is a set, and W is a set of tables over A, then:

$$W \textbf{ is in 2NF} \overset{D}{\Longleftrightarrow} \forall a \in \text{Sec}(W) : \forall S \in \text{Mk}(W) : \forall B \subseteq S\text{: if } B \hat{\rightarrow} \{a\} \text{ in } W, \text{ then } B = S.$$

Hence, phrased informally, W is in 2NF (*second normal form*) iff each secondary attribute is "completely dependent" on each minimal key of W.

(a) If W is in 3NF, then W is in 2NF. Prove this.

(b) Is WP in Example 2.8 in 2NF?

2.104. This exercise is a continuation of Exercise 2.96. We introduce the concept of multivalued dependency at the level of sets of tables. In addition, we introduce the *fourth normal form* in this exercise.
If A, B, and C are sets, and W is a set of tables over A, then we define:

(D1) $B \hat{\twoheadrightarrow} C \textbf{ in } W \overset{D}{\Longleftrightarrow} \forall T \in W : B \twoheadrightarrow C \text{ in } T.$

(D2) $W \textbf{ is in 4NF} \overset{D}{\Longleftrightarrow} \forall X \subseteq \text{Head}(W) : \forall Y \subseteq \text{Head}(W)$:
if $X \hat{\twoheadrightarrow} Y$ in W, and $Y \not\subseteq X$, and $X \cup Y \subset \text{Head}(W)$
then X is a key of W.

(a) If W is in 4NF, then W is also in BCNF. Prove this.

(b) Is $\varnothing$ in 4NF?

(c) Is WD in Example 1.3 in 4NF?

□

CHAPTER 3

Constructing Database Universes

In Chapter 1 we defined, theoretically speaking, *what* a DB universe amounts to. In this chapter we will show *how* a DB universe can be constructed in practice.

Definitions of DB universes tend to be quite elaborate in practice. It is not unusual that for activities of a department in an organization several hundred attributes are needed, apart from the description of all the *requirements* that the data should meet. Therefore, DB universes are best constructed in a careful and systematic manner. Moreover, it is sensible to do this in a *modular* way, since (parts of) many existing DB universes are liable to change.

We will distinguish four "phases" in the construction of a DB universe over a *given* DB skeleton *g*, and devote a section to each individual phase. (The definition of the DB skeleton constitutes a phase in itself; see pages 77-80.) These four phases consist of the definitions of

(1) the set of admissible **attribute** values *per* attribute *per* table index,

(2) the set of admissible **tuple** values *per* table index,

(3) the set of admissible **table** values *per* table index, and finally

(4) the set of admissible **database** values.

EXAMPLE 3.1:

In Example 1.3, the sets concerned are (beginning with the DB skeleton g1, previously given in Example 1.2):

(1) the set FE(*a*) for each attribute *a* belonging to the table index EMPL and the set FD(*a*) for each attribute *a* belonging to the table index DEP,

(2) Π(FE) for EMPL and Π(FD) for DEP,

(3) WE for EMPL and WD for DEP, and finally

(4) EXU.

□ Example 3.1.

The sets of values are in fact determined by the requirements that data should meet in all possible states, according to the organization concerned. These requirements on the admissible *states* are referred to as *static constraints* in the literature. Besides static constraints, we will treat *dynamic constraints* in Chapter 5, i.e., requirements pertaining to state *transitions*.

Such requirements, also known as "business rules", reflect to a large extent the "semantics" of the data for the organization concerned! It is one of the objectives of this book to show the reader how to specify this semantics in a formal manner.

As already described in for example [Re82] and [Br 80], we can distinguish four types of static constraints, analogous to the above mentioned phasing of the construction of a DB universe:

(1) **Attribute constraints**;
these are conditions on the values of the individual attributes.

(2) **Tuple constraints** (or "inter-attribute" constraints);
these are conditions on combinations of attribute values within the same tuple.

(3) **Table constraints** (or "inter-tuple" constraints);
these are conditions on combinations of tuples within the same table.

(4) **Database constraints** (or "inter-table" constraints);
these are conditions on combinations of tables within the same DB state.

Note that these four types of static constraints are classified according to increasing "scope".

In each of the phases to be discussed, the material will be enhanced by references to the examples given in the preceding chapters as well as to the main example to be treated in Chapter 4. In addition to this, the discussed material will be illustrated with a small, though varied modelling example, which will be constructed step by step.

The Database Skeleton

In fact, there is also a phase "zero", namely the phase in which the relevant table indices and the relevant attributes per table index - in brief, the right DB skeleton - are determined. In practice, this phase of the design process is quite often underestimated, both in degree of complexity and in duration. The main reason is often that the future users of the database, on further consideration, do not know precisely the actual structure of their organization and its data, nor do they know what is and what is not relevant.

Until now we have given only one explicit example of a DB skeleton, namely the DB skeleton g1 in Example 1.2:

```
g1 = {(DEP    ; {DNO, MANNO, NAME}),
      (EMPL   ; {DEPNO, NO, NAME, SEX, SAL})}
```

The DB skeleton g1 contains both so-called *homonymous* attributes and so-called *synonymous* attributes:

- The attributes NAME of DEP and NAME of EMPL are "homonymous" (i.e., with the same name yet having different "meanings").
- The attributes DNO of DEP and DEPNO of EMPL are "synonymous" (i.e., not with the same name yet having the same "meaning").

The following set function, g2, is the joint DB skeleton of the DB universes U1, U3, and U4, described in the overview at the end of §2.4:

g2 = {(PERS ; {NO, NM, ADDR, PC, TOWN, BDT, BPL, NMC}),
(TOWN ; {TOWN, POP, AREA, NO})}.

The DB skeleton of the DB universe UHPT in §4.2 will consist of 19 table indices with a total of 128 attributes. Examples of table indices in §4.2 will be PAT, SM, MED, and MDP.

EXAMPLE 3.2:

In a certain production company, at least the following data is considered relevant: data on the products made by that company and data on the base products purchased to that end. Furthermore, so-called *Bills Of Material* (briefly, BOMs) are used, i.e., bills listing the direct components of compound products, also indicating how many times each part occurs as a direct part in such a product. Bills Of Material play a central role in production companies and also give cause to all sorts of interesting mathematical problems, many of them being of a recursive nature.

In the production company under consideration, the following attributes are relevant for each *product*: the *product number*, the *description*, the *product type*, the *manufacturing price* a piece, the *sales price* a piece, the *profit* a piece, and the existing *stock*. (All prices are expressed in terms of pennies.) Moreover, it should be known of every product whether or not it is a *compound* product.

Of every *base product*, the *weight* and the *unit of weight* (gram or kilogram) should be known.

Finally, as said before, it should be known which *products* contain which direct *parts*, and in which *number*. For that purpose so-called *BOM rules* are used.

This results in the following DB skeleton:

GBP = {(PROD ; {PNO, DES, TYPE, CPR, SPR, PRFT, STK, COM}),
(BAS ; {PNO, WT, WTU}),
(BOM ; {PNO, PANO, NUM})}.

As an illustration, Figure 3.2 depicts a representative DB state v2 over GBP. First of all, however, we give in Figure 3.1 a graphical representation of the (assembly) data occurring in v2(BOM), together with the descriptions from v2(PROD). In this way the hierarchical product composition is made clear. Conversely, Figure 3.2 shows how to represent such hierarchical structures (like trees and other graphs) by means of tables.

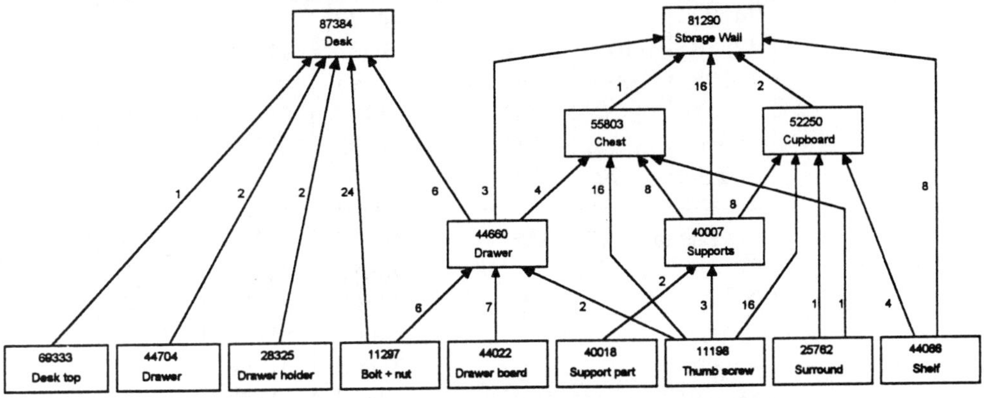

Figure 3.1: A graphical representation of v2(BOM), together with the descriptions from v2(PROD)

PNO	DES	TYPE	CPR	SPR	PRFT	STK	COM
11297	Bolt + nut	BN	10	25	15	1024	N
44660	Drawer	D	2500	5995	3495	400	Y
28325	Drawer holder	DH	5900	11995	6095	101	N
44704	Drawer	D	2500	5995	3495	400	N
87384	Desk	DE	49500	99800	50300	20	Y
11198	Thumb screw	AUX	0	100	100	1001	N
11099	Pen tray	DIV	50	169	119	144	N
69333	Desk top	DT	10000	22500	12500	29	N
81290	Storage wall	SW	127500	255000	127500	4	Y
55803	Chest	C	29000	59800	30800	19	Y
52250	Cupboard	C	25500	59800	34300	37	Y
40007	Supports	AUX	500	1295	795	256	Y
44066	Shelf	DIV	1495	3495	2000	329	N
25762	Surround	SU	12890	25780	12890	0	N
40018	Support part	AUX	200	550	350	597	N
44022	Drawer board	DP	300	750	450	70	N
62931	Desk chair	CH	4900	9900	5000	0	N

(a) The table v2(PROD)

PNO	WT	WTU
62931	9	KG
69333	12	KG
44704	2500	GR
28325	3300	GR
11297	9	GR
44022	178	GR
40018	100	GR
11198	1000	GR
25762	20	KG
44066	1	KG
11099	10	GR

(b) The table v2(BAS)

PANO	PNO	NUM
28325	87384	2
11297	87384	24
44660	87384	6
11297	44660	6
11198	44660	2
44022	44660	7
69333	87384	1
11198	40007	3
11198	55803	16
11198	52250	16
40007	55803	8
40007	52250	8
40007	81290	16
40018	40007	2
44600	55803	4
44660	81290	3
55803	81290	1
52250	81290	2
44066	52250	4
44066	81290	8
25762	52250	1
25762	55803	1
44704	87384	2

(c) The table v2(BOM)

Figure 3.2: The DB state v2 over GBP

□ Example 3.2.

EXERCISE

3.1. Contrive some relevant table indices with relevant attributes for some organization (e.g., a department store, a hospital, or a software house).

□

3.1 Specifications of Admissible Attribute Values

For each table index E in dom(g), the sets of admissible attribute values can be established by means of a set function F over $g(E)$. In other words, F is the function that establishes for each attribute a of E the set of admissible values for a within E. In [Re 82], such a set function is called an *object characterization*.

In the database literature the term *relational schema* sometimes stands for a set of attributes where each attribute is "linked" (implicitly) to a set of values. In that case, a relational schema corresponds in fact to an object characterization. The interested reader is referred to [Mai 83], page 2, for instance. (Often, however, the term relational schema stands for the set $g(E)$, see for example [Ul 82] and [Ya 86], or the pair $(E\,;g(E))$, as in [Ul 82] and [CP 87]).

So far we have seen the following examples of object characterizations:

- FE and FD, introduced in Example 1 on page 13 and used in Example 1.3;
- F3 in Example 2.8, defined by means of the functions F1 and F2, which, despite the syntactical similarities, do not serve as object characterizations in that example;
- FPCB in Example 2.12;
- F4 in Example 2.13.

In §4.2 the reader will find a suitable object characterization for each of the 19 table indices. Examples are the functions FPAT, FSM, and FMDP. Examples of attribute constraints in Chapter 4 are the restricting conditions R03, R04, R05, R06, R46, and R53. R02 is also an attribute constraint. Besides these "numbered" attribute constraints there will also be many non-numbered attribute constraints; examples are the requirements that an internal phone number must be a 4-digit number and that the fee of a specialist must be at least 80 guilders per hour.

Another example of an attribute constraint is the requirement that a bank account number always has to satisfy the so-called *11-test*, that is: 1 times the 9th digit plus 2 times the 8th digit plus ... plus 8 times the 2nd digit plus 1 times the 1st digit is a number divisible by 11. The set of admissible bank account numbers is therefore

$$\{n \in \text{Snn}(9) \mid (\Sigma i \in [1\,..\,9] : i * ((n \text{ div } 10^{i-1}) \bmod 10)) \bmod 11 = 0\}.$$

In most cases, however, a set of admissible attribute values is of the simple "type-plus-length" format, e.g., Chs(30), Snn(9), or Int(4). Other rather common forms of sets of admissible attribute values are intervals (or "subranges"), e.g., [1 .. 31] for the days in a month or [–273..) for temperatures in degrees Celsius.

Sometimes a set of attribute values is given by *enumeration* (that is, by listing all the individual elements), such as the set { 'MAN', 'WOMAN'}, the set { 'Excellent', 'Good', 'Sufficient', 'Poor', 'Bad'} or the set {1, 3, 5, 7, 8, 10, 12} (for the months having 31 days).

Should the enumerative set of values of some attribute *a* be likely to change every now and then, it might be better to choose a somewhat larger set of values for *a*, and introduce a separate "one-column-table". This new table must contain at every instant exactly all values admissible for attribute *a* at that moment. Furthermore the (database) constraint must be added that each *a*-value in the original table also occurs in the above mentioned one-column-table; this database constraint can be said to constitute a "variable attribute constraint". In view of the apparent "semantics" of the three examples of enumerative sets above, the "valuation set" is probably the only candidate for such a flexible solution. In that case, Chs(20) could be taken as the larger set of values, and the new table would (for the moment) consist of five tuples (as shown in Figure 3.3).

SCALE
Excellent
Good
Sufficient
Poor
Bad

Figure 3.3

We will now proceed with the construction of our BOM-example.

EXAMPLE 3.3:

As a continuation of Example 3.2, we now introduce an auxiliary set, namely the set DPN of possible product numbers, and three object characterizations:

DPN = $\{k \in \text{Snn}(5) \mid k \bmod 11 = 0\}$;

FPROD =	{(PNO	; DPN),	product number	(C01)
	(DES	; Chs(30)),	description	
	(TYPE	; Chs(6)),	type of product	
	(CPR	; $\mathbb{N}$),	cost price a piece	
	(SPR	; $\mathbb{N}$),	sales price a piece	
	(PRFT	; $\mathbb{N} - \{0\}$),	profit a piece	(C02)
	(STK	; $\mathbb{N}$),	stock level	
	(COM	; { 'Y', 'N'})};	compound product?	
FBAS =	{(PNO	; DPN),	product number	
	(WT	; $[1 .. 10^6]$),	weight	
	(WTU	; { 'GR', 'KG'})};	weight unit (gram or kilogram)	
FBOM =	{(PNO	; $\{k \in \text{DPN} \mid k \geq 40000\}$),	product number	(C03)
	(PANO	; $\mathbb{N}$),	part number	
	(NUM	; [1 ..))}	number of pieces of that immediate part	

Note that the isolated set $\{k \in \text{Snn}(5) \mid k \bmod 11 = 0\}$ is used at three different places.

It is easily verified that the DB state v2 from Example 3.2 meets the requirements stipulated above, or, to be precise, that

$$v2(PROD) \subseteq \Pi(FPROD) \text{ and } v2(BAS) \subseteq \Pi(FBAS) \text{ and } v2(BOM) \subseteq \Pi(FBOM).$$

□ Example 3.3.

Not only numbers and strings qualify as attribute values. In principle, according to our theory, an attribute value can be any "complex object", e.g.,

- a draft (in a CAD/CAM-environment for example),
- a passport photo (of an employee for example),
- a road map (for a car navigation system for example),
- a compact disc (in a juke box for example),
- a signature (of a manager for example),
- a film excerpt (about an educational subject for example),
- a telephone conversation (with a client for example), or
- an X-ray (of a patient for example).

By the end of the eighties, certain database management systems - some of them even commercially available - already supported such "multi-media" and "object-oriented" possibilities: see for instance [IDT 90]. An important question to be raised in each case is whether the DBMS also offers suitable operations on these special attribute values. For a few examples of the earlier object-oriented databases and their operations, the reader is referred to the survey papers [HK 87] and [PM 88], and the references mentioned in them. More recent developments are described in [Ab 89] and [Bl 90]; see also [Ca 93]. We refer the reader to our Preface for a list of the journals and conference series which cover these developments.

The reason that our theory admits such unorthodox attribute values is that, unlike most of the other database theories, it contains no presuppositions about the nature of the attribute values. Thus, in particular, there is no room for the (questionable) first normal form in our theory.

EXERCISES

3.2. Describe in words conditions C01, C02, and C03 in Example 3.3.

3.3. For each of your table indices from Exercise 3.1 (together with their attributes), construe a plausible object characterization.

□

3.2 Specifications of Admissible Tuple Values

The set of admissible tuples (or table elements) for a table index E with object characterization F is always a subset of $\Pi(F)$. In most cases it is $\Pi(F)$ itself, as in all our examples so far, but in some cases not all of these combinations of attribute values are allowed, in which case the set of admissible tuples is a *proper* subset of $\Pi(F)$. The absence of tuple constraints indicates that the attributes in question appear to represent "mutually independent properties".

In the elaborate example in Chapter 4 the set of admissible tuples of nine of the nineteen table indices will be a proper subset of the generalized product of the object characterization concerned. These proper subsets are TPAT, TSP, TEMP, TGP, TMUN, TDPT, TRM, TADM, and TTTP. These nine sets will be determined by a total of fifteen tuple constraints, namely the conditions R14, R17, R21, R22, R27, R40, R41, R44, R51, R55, R56, R58, R59, and R77.

Other typical examples of requirements at the level of tuples, i.e., requirements *between* attribute values, are: "net amount less than gross amount", "minimum weight (or number, or price, or duration) not exceeding maximum weight (or number, price, duration, respectively)", "(employee number of) department manager different from (that of) the deputy", and "for each affiliated union the (membership numbers of) the chairman, the treasurer, and the secretary are mutually distinct".

In §4.1, requirement R31 (for non-medical personnel) reads as follows: "The monthly allowance should not exceed the monthly salary". Though at first sight seemingly a tuple constraint, R31 will turn out to be a database constraint in §4.2. The reason is that by the use of *generalization* - see §3.4 - the data concerning non-medical personnel is spread over different tables; in this case, the allowance is registered in the NMP-table, yet the monthly salary is registered in the (more general) employee table. This means that R31 should be expressed in terms of the *join* of those two tables. (Within the result of that join, which by Lemma 2.5(a) is also a table, R31 is indeed a "tuple constraint".) Therefore, one of the conclusions of this example is that the classification of a constraint is not an "absolute" property of the constraint itself, but that it may, for example, depend on the chosen DB skeleton.

EXAMPLE 3.4:

We extend Example 3.3 with the following sets of admissible tuples:

$$\begin{aligned}
\text{TPROD} &= \{t \in \Pi(\text{FPROD}) \mid t(\text{SPR}) \geq 2 * t(\text{CPR}) \text{ and} && \text{(C04)}\\
&\qquad t(\text{PRFT}) = t(\text{SPR}) - t(\text{CPR}) \text{ and} && \text{(C05)}\\
&\qquad (t(\text{STK}) \leq 2 \text{ or } t(\text{STK}) * t(\text{CPR}) \leq 10^6)\}; && \text{(C06)}\\
\text{TBAS} &= \{t \in \Pi(\text{FBAS}) \mid \text{if } t(\text{WTU}) = \text{'GR'} \\
&\qquad \text{then } t\,(\text{WT}) < 10000\}; && \text{(C07)}\\
\text{TBOM} &= \{t \in \Pi(\text{FBOM}) \mid t(\text{PANO}) \neq t(\text{PNO})\}. && \text{(C08)}
\end{aligned}$$

Note that {SPR, CPR} → {PRFT} in TPROD; cf. Exercise 3.8.

Since FPROD(PRFT) = $\mathbb{N} - \{0\}$ and FPROD(CPR) = $\mathbb{N}$, it follows from condition C05 that for elements of TPROD the sales price is never equal to 0. This is an example of a "hidden" attribute constraint implied by a tuple constraint.

□ Example 3.4.

EXERCISES

3.4. Describe each of the five conditions in Example 3.4.

3.5. List some elements of TPROD, of TBAS, and of TBOM.

3.6. List some elements of Π(FPROD) – TPROD, of Π(FBAS) – TBAS, and of Π(FBOM) – TBOM.

3.7. Does the DB state v2 in Example 3.2 meet all the requirements given in Example 3.4? (In other words, does it hold that v2(PROD) ⊆ TPROD, v2(BAS) ⊆ TBAS, and v2(BOM) ⊆ TBOM ?)

3.8. Prove the following dependencies:

(a) {CPR, SPR} → {PRFT} in TPROD;

(b) {CPR, PRFT} → {SPR} in TPROD;

(c) {SPR, PRFT} → {CPR} in TPROD.

3.9. Extend your solution in Exercise 3.3 by offering corresponding sets of admissible tuples.

□

3.3 Specifications of Admissible Table Values

If *Y* is the set of admissible tuples for a table index *E*, then the set of admissible tables for *E* is a (usually proper) subset *W* of **P**(*Y*). Hence, each allowed table for *E* is a subset of *Y*, while, conversely, not necessarily each subset of *Y* is an allowed table for *E*.

So far we have seen, for instance, the following examples of such sets of tables *W*:

- WE and WD in Example 1.3;
- WPCB in Example 2.12;
- WP and WT in Example 2.13;
- WT2 (en passant) in Example 2.14;
- WP2 in Exercise 2.79;
- WPF and WTF in Exercise 2.90.

In the exercises 2.47 and 2.101, we gave some "artificial" (definitions of) sets of tables. The reason for this artificiality is that the sets of tables W1 and W2 in Exercise 2.47 and W3 in Exercise 2.101 have been defined by enumerating all individual *elements* instead of the standard procedure of listing their *characterizing properties.*

In §4.2 we will define 19 sets of tables. They will all be used in the definition of FHPT, just before the definition of UHPT. Examples of these sets of tables are WPAT, WSM, WMED, and WMDP. The nineteen sets of tables will be determined by a total of 33 table constraints.

The most important requirements at the level of tables concern *momentary dependency* and *unique identification* in particular (as suggested by our examples). Other possible requirements at the level of tables may concern for instance the average or total salary (per department or otherwise), or serial numbers which may have to be assigned chronologically and consecutively (maybe to the different medicine dispensings of the same patient, to take an example from Chapter 4).

Finally, we mention as a possible requirement at the level of tables that the set of values of one attribute must be contained in the set of values of another (usually uniquely identifying) attribute of the same table. Speaking more generally, this is a table constraint of the form: h connects T with T. Requirement R18 in §4.2 will be an example. Requirement R26 will even go a little further than that. Each of these requirements is an example of an *internal ssr,* where "ssr" stands for *subset requirement.* (In the next section we will go more deeply into this topic.)

EXAMPLE 3.5:

We now extend Example 3.4 with the following sets of admissible tables:

$$\begin{array}{lll} \text{WPROD} = \{T \subseteq \text{TPROD} \mid & \{\text{PNO}\} \text{ is u.i. in } T \text{ and} & \text{(C09)} \\ & (\Sigma t \in T : t(\text{STK}) * t(\text{SPR})) \leq 10^8\}; & \text{(C10)} \\ \text{WBAS} \;\; = \{T \subseteq \text{TBAS} \mid & \{\text{PNO}\} \text{ is u.i. in } T\}; & \text{(C11)} \\ \text{WBOM} \;\; = \{T \subseteq \text{TBOM} \mid & \{\text{PNO, PANO}\} \text{ is u.i. in } T \text{ and} & \text{(C12)} \\ & \{(t(\text{PANO}); t(\text{PNO})) \mid t \in T\} \text{ is acyclic}\}. & \text{(C13)} \end{array}$$

In BOM terminology, the relation $\{(t(\text{PANO}); t(\text{PNO})) \mid t \in T\}$ is called an *assembly relation*, and its inverse, namely the relation $\{(t(\text{PNO}); t(\text{PANO})) \mid t \in T\}$, an *explosion relation.*

The requirement C13 is an example of a so-called *recursive constraint,* because basically it uses *the transitive closure* of a relation (see Definition 23 on page 16).

Note that the tuple constraint C08 has become "redundant" since it follows from the table constraint C13 (by Lemma 18(d) on page 17).

□ Example 3.5.

EXERCISES

3.10. Describe in words the five conditions in Example 3.5.

3.11. Does the DB state v2 from Example 3.2 meet all the requirements listed in Example 3.5?
(First give a somewhat more formal description of this question, in a way similar to Exercise 3.7.)

3.12. Give an element of **P**(TBOM) – WBOM in which {PNO, PANO} is uniquely identifying.

3.13. From C10 we derive the tuple constraint that $t(\text{STK}) * t(\text{CPR}) \leq 10^8$.

(a) Does C06 follow from this tuple constraint?

(b) Does this tuple constraint follow from C06?

3.14. Check whether WPROD, WBAS, and WBOM are in 3NF. Explain your answers.

3.15. Extend your solution of Exercise 3.9 with corresponding sets of admissible tables.

□

3.4 Specifications of Admissible Database Values

The eventual DB universe over g is a (usually proper) subset of $\Pi(H)$ where H is the function over dom(g) that assigns to each E in dom(g) the set of admissible tables chosen for E. In [Re 82], such a "table-set-valued" function is referred to as a *database characterization*.

So far we have seen for instance the following examples of DB universes (with corresponding DB characterizations):

- EXU with DB characterization HF in Example 1.3;
- U1 with DB characterization F5 in Example 2.13;
- U3 with DB characterization F6 in Exercise 2.79.

Furthermore, Exercise 2.91 contains a definition of a DB universe of a somewhat different form:

$$U4 = U3 \cap \Pi(F7),$$

where F7 is the DB characterization defined in Exercise 2.90.

At the end of §4.2 we will find the definition of the DB universe UHPT, based on the DB characterization FHPT that assigns to each of the 19 table indices one of the sets of tables defined earlier. The definition of UHPT contains 35 database constraints.

EXAMPLE 3.6:

In this last example, we introduce the DB characterization HBP and the DB universe UBP (over the DB skeleton GBP mentioned before). We will also introduce the attribute transformation h5; this function will be used in condition C17 (and Exercise 3.18). For sake of completeness, we will repeat all preceding definitions concerning our BOM-example. (Note that there will not be any further explicit use made of the DB skeleton GBP; nevertheless, determination of the underlying DB skeleton in advance is a very important though difficult task in its own right.)

GBP = {(PROD ; {PNO, DES, TYPE, CPR, SPR, PRFT, STK, COM}),
(BAS ; {PNO, WT, WTU}),
(BOM ; {PNO, PANO, NUM})};

h5 =	{(PANO	; PNO),	part number
	(PADES	; DES),	part description
	(PATYPE	; TYPE),	type of part
	(PACPR	; CPR),	cost price part
	(PASPR	; SPR),	sales price part
	(PAPP	; PRFT),	potential profit on part
	(PAST	; STK),	stock level of that part
	(PACOM	; COM)};	compound part?

DPN = $\{k \in \text{Snn}(5) \mid k \bmod 11 = 0\}$;

FPROD =	{(PNO	; DPN),	product number	(C01)
	(DES	; Chs(30)),	description	
	(TYPE	; Chs(6)),	type of product	
	(CPR	; $\mathbb{N}$),	cost price a piece	
	(SPR	; $\mathbb{N}$),	sales price a piece	
	(PRFT	; $\mathbb{N}-\{0\}$),	profit a piece	(C02)
	(STK	; $\mathbb{N}$),	stock level	
	(COM	; {'Y', 'N'})};	compound product?	
FBAS =	{(PNO	; DPN),	product number	
	(WT	; $[1 .. 10^6]$),	weight	
	(WTU	; {'GR', 'KG'})};	weight unit	
FBOM =	{(PNO	; $\{k \in \text{DPN} \mid k \geq 40000\}$),	product number	(C03)
	(PANO	; $\mathbb{N}$),	part number	
	(NUM	; [1 ..))};	number of pieces	

TPROD $= \{t \in \Pi(\text{FPROD}) \mid t(\text{SPR}) \geq 2 * t(\text{CPR})$ and (C04)
$t(\text{PRFT}) = t(\text{SPR}) - t(\text{CPR})$ and (C05)
$(t(\text{STK}) \leq 2$ or $t(\text{STK}) * t(\text{CPR}) \leq 10^6)\};$ (C06)
TBAS $= \{t \in \Pi(\text{FBAS}) \mid$ if $t(\text{WTU}) =$ 'GR' then $t(\text{WT}) < 10000\};$ (C07)
TBOM $= \{t \in \Pi(\text{FBOM}) \mid t(\text{PANO}) \neq t(\text{PNO})\};$ (C08)

WPROD $= \{T \subseteq$ TPROD $\mid$ {PNO} is u.i. in T and (C09)
$(\Sigma t \in T : t(\text{STK}) * t(\text{CPR})) \leq 10^8\};$ (C10)
WBAS $= \{T \subseteq$ TBAS $\mid$ {PNO} is u.i. in $T\};$ (C11)
WBOM $= \{T \subseteq$ TBOM $\mid$ {PNO, PANO} is u.i. in T and (C12)
$\{(t(\text{PANO}); t(\text{PNO})) \mid t \in T\}$ is acyclic}; (C13)

HBP = {(PROD ; WPROD),	products
(BAS ; WBAS),	base products
(BOM ; WBOM)};	Bill Of Material specifications

UBP $= \{v \mid v \in \Pi(\text{HBP})$ and
{(PANO; PNO)} connects v(BOM) with v(PROD) and (C14)
id({PNO}) connects v(BOM) bilaterally
with $\{t \in v(\text{PROD}) \mid t(\text{COM}) =$ 'Y'} and (C15)
id({PNO}) connects v(BAS) bilaterally
with $\{t \in v(\text{PROD}) \mid t(\text{COM}) =$ 'N'} and (C16)
$\forall p \in v(\text{PROD})$:
$(\Sigma t \in v(\text{BOM}) \bowtie (v(\text{PROD}) \infty \text{h5})$
and $t(\text{PNO}) = p(\text{PNO})$:
$t(\text{PACPR}) * t(\text{NUM})) \leq p(\text{CPR})\}.$ (C17)

The latter requirement states that the cost price of a product is at least the sum of the cost prices of the direct components (should they exist).

It follows from condition C14, together with C01, that all PANO-values in the BOM-table are elements of DPN. What we have here is an example of a "hidden" attribute constraint, implied by a database constraint. On the one hand we could well have incorporated this (rather obvious) attribute constraint immediately in the object characterization concerned, whereas on the other hand this requirement turns out to be redundant, in principle.

□ Example 3.6.

By far the most important class of database constraints is the general class of *connection requirements*, also referred to as *subset requirements* (or briefly SSRs). There exist all kinds of connection requirements. Therefore, we now examine some special subclasses.

(A1) The majority of connection requirements in practice have the following (basic) form:

h connects $v(M)$ with $v(D)$

This "standard form" is also known as a *referential integrity constraint.* If moreover, rng(h) is a key of the D-table, as is usually the case, then dom(h) is also called a *foreign key.* In Example 3.6, C14 constitutes an example of such a basic connection requirement where the situation described above arises. The attribute set {PANO} of BOM is indeed a foreign key, according to this terminology.

In the definition of UHPT in §4.2, the first 20 database constraints mentioned there will be of the form above. Strictly speaking, only in the case of (the formulation of) condition R52 do we not have a foreign key. (An equivalent reformulation of R52 within UHPT such that {AMNR} turns out to be a foreign key will still be possible, however.)

(A2) The following form of connection requirement is stronger but occurs less frequently:

h connects $v(M)$ bilaterally with $v(D)$

The classical example is that of orders and order rules. The order number of each order rule should also occur in the order table, while on the other hand each order should contain at least one order rule (so the order number of each order should also occur in the order rule table).

If h is injective, then, by Lemma 2.15, a requirement of the form (A2) can also be written as two separate requirements of the form (A1).

If rng(h) is a key of the D-table and dom(h) is a key of the M-table, then, by Lemma 2.16, in every state v the association induced by h is in fact a bijection from $v(M)$ onto $v(D)$. Hence, in the modelling phase 0, we might just as well have combined the table indices M and D into one table index inheriting both the attributes of M and those of D (minus dom(h), since that set of attributes is already represented by rng(h)).

(B1) Sometimes each M-tuple should correspond with a D-tuple satisfying some special additional condition:

h connects $v(M)$ with $\{t \in v(D) \mid \phi(t)\}$

In other words, the requirement $\phi(t)$ is a prerequisite for a D-tuple t in order to have corresponding M-tuples. This form is therefore a stronger version of the form under (A1). Examples of database constraints of this form are R65, R74, and R84 in §4.2 and the equivalent reformulation of R52 mentioned under (A1).

(B2) The following form is a stronger version of (B1):

$$h \text{ connects } v(M) \text{ bilaterally with } \{t \in v(D) \mid \phi(t)\}$$

In this case the additional condition characterizes *exactly* for which *D*-tuples there also exist corresponding *M*-tuples. Examples of database constraints of this form are C15 and C16 in Example 3.6 and R16, R19, R28, R30, and R67 in §4.2.

As suggested by the examples above, the requirement $\phi(t)$ often appears in the form "$t(a) = w_0$", where the value w_0 does not depend on the tuple t or the DB state v. In that case the database constraint reads as follows:

$$h \text{ connects } v(M) \text{ bilaterally with } \{t \in v(D) \mid t(a) = w_0\}$$

The attribute a is then called an *inspection attribute of D* and w_0 the *inspection value for M*. Note that it can indeed be precisely verified "within the *D*-table itself" for which *D*-tuples there exist corresponding *M*-tuples, namely by inspecting the a-value of the *D*-tuples.

It follows from C15 and C16 in Example 3.6 that COM is an inspection attribute of PROD. The inspection value for BOM is 'Y'; for BAS it is 'N'. Furthermore, it will turn out from R16, R28, and R30 in §4.2 that KDSM is an inspection attribute of SM. The inspection values for the table indices SP, MP, and NMP happen to be 'SP', 'MP', and 'NMP', respectively. According to R67 in §4.2, DISC will be an inspection attribute of ADM where 'YES' is the inspection value for the table index DIS.

This collection of classes of connection requirements is still far from complete, as will become apparent from the connection requirements R24, R08, and R37 in §4.2.

If in one of the preceding subset requirements, *M* and *D* happen to be the same table indices (and if in case of a B1- or B2-form also the additional condition ϕ does not concern other table indices), then the SSR involved is called an *internal SSR*. But then the constraint is in fact a *table* constraint. (Thus, in this case the form (A1) for example reduces to the form: *h* connects *T* with *T*.) Already in §3.3 we mentioned as examples the internal SSRs R18 and R26 from §4.2, where the table constraint R18 is of the form treated under (A1) and R26 of the general form treated under (B1).

If in one of the preceding subset requirements the table indices differ (or the additional condition ϕ does indeed concern other table indices), then we call the SSR involved an *external SSR*. In that case we have a genuine database constraint.

Subset requirements rarely occur "in isolation" (as already suggested earlier): such a database constraint usually occurs in conjunction with the table constraint that rng(h) is uniquely identifying in $v(D)$. By Lemma 2.16(4), we have in that case that the association on $v(M) \times v(D)$ induced by h is a function. The subset requirement that each order number in the order table also occurs in the order rule table, mentioned under (A2), constitutes one of the few counterexamples here.

If, given a subset requirement of one of the forms above, rng(h) is a key of the D-table, and also dom(h) is a key of the M-table, then according to Lemma 2.16 in each state the association induced by h is an injective function from $v(M)$ into $v(D)$. In other words, with each D-tuple there corresponds at most one M-tuple. Therefore we can say that we can look at it as if, in each DB state, some D-tuples have several additional attributes, namely the elements of $g(M) - \text{dom}(h)$, where $g(M)$ is the attribute set of the table index M according to the DB skeleton g.

The situation described above applies for instance to the subset requirement C16 in Example 3.6, where {PNO} is a key of both the BAS-table and the PROD-table. Hence, to some PROD-tuples, the additional attributes WT and WTU (weight and weight unit) from the BAS-table apply. Note that this (not all that surprising) *formal conclusion*, according to the last observation in the preceding paragraph, is at least consistent with the original *informal description* given in Example 3.2. Other examples of subset requirements for which the situation above occurs include R33, R16, R19, R28, R30, R67, and R49 in §4.2 and the last requirement in the definition of U1 in Example 2.13. Applying the last observation in the preceding paragraph to the subset requirement from Example 2.13, we come to the "conclusion" that town attributes can be conceived of as mayor attributes, which is indeed surprising! Application to the subset requirement R49 in §4.2 will lead to the conclusion that department attributes can also be conceived of as attributes of assistant managers in that example. Only when treating dynamic constraints in §5.2 (C00 in particular), will we realize that the *department* number is "more essential" to a DPT-tuple than the *assistant manager* number. (See also the remarks on primary keys and alternate keys in §5.1.)

If in any state v of a DB universe U, the association induced by h is an injective function from $v(M)$ into $v(D)$, then M is called a *specialization* or *differentiation* of D. In some cases M is also called a *subtype* of D. According to this terminology, BAS is a specialization of PROD in Example 3.6 (by C16), CE a specialization of EMP in §4.2 (by R33), and DIS a specialization of ADM in §4.2 (by R67).

A table index D is called a *generalization* of a set of table indices X in a DB universe U, whenever each element M of X is a specialization of D and, moreover, in each state of U exactly one tuple of exactly one table index from X is associated to each D-tuple. Generalization does not apply to the three cases of specialization mentioned above. Yet, in §4.2 the table index SM is a generalization of {SP, EMP}, and EMP itself is a generalization of {MP, NMP}.

We note furthermore that bilateral subset requirements give rise to a so-called *chicken/egg-problem*: a new dom(h)-value intended for the M-table also asks for a new rng(h)-value for the D-table, and . . . the other way round. Hence, this means that at the transition to another DB state, both an M-tuple and a D-tuple must be added "in one go"! More generally speaking, a chicken/egg-situation occurs for a DB universe U over a DB skeleton g if the following relation is cyclic:

$$\{(M\,;D) \in \text{dom}(g)\times\text{dom}(g) \mid \exists h \in g(M) \tilde{\twoheadrightarrow} g(D) : \\ h \text{ connects } M \text{ permanently with } D \text{ in } U\},$$

or, in words, the set of all pairs of indices $(M\,;D)$ such that M is connected permanently with D in U by some attribute transformation h.

EXERCISES

3.16. Describe the conditions C14, C15, and C16 in Example 3.6.

3.17. Is the DB state v2 from Example 3.2 an element of UBP from Example 3.6?

3.18. Describe briefly, for $v \in$ UBP, the differences between the following tables.

(a) v(BOM) ⋈ v(PROD);

(b) v(BOM) ⋈ (v(PROD) ∞ h5);

(c) v(BOM) ⋈ v(PROD) ⋈ (v(PROD) ∞ h5).

3.19. Explain why UBP is not in 3NF.

3.20. Add to your solutions of the exercises 3.1, 3.3, 3.9, and 3.15 the definition of a corresponding DB universe.

□

3.5 Summary

In the construction of a DB universe over a given DB skeleton we have distinguished four phases. In each phase, we define one or more sets of values. The relations between those separate "modules" in this modular construction of the definition of a DB universe U can be represented by the scheme shown in Figure 3.4,

where $T_i \subseteq \Pi(F_i)$ and
$W_i \subseteq \mathbf{P}(T_i)$ and
$H = \{(E_1\,;W_1), (E_2\,;W_2), \ldots, (E_n\,;W_n)\}$ and
$U \subseteq \Pi(H)$ and

where $\boxed{A} \rightarrow \boxed{B}$ stands for: A is used in the definition of B.

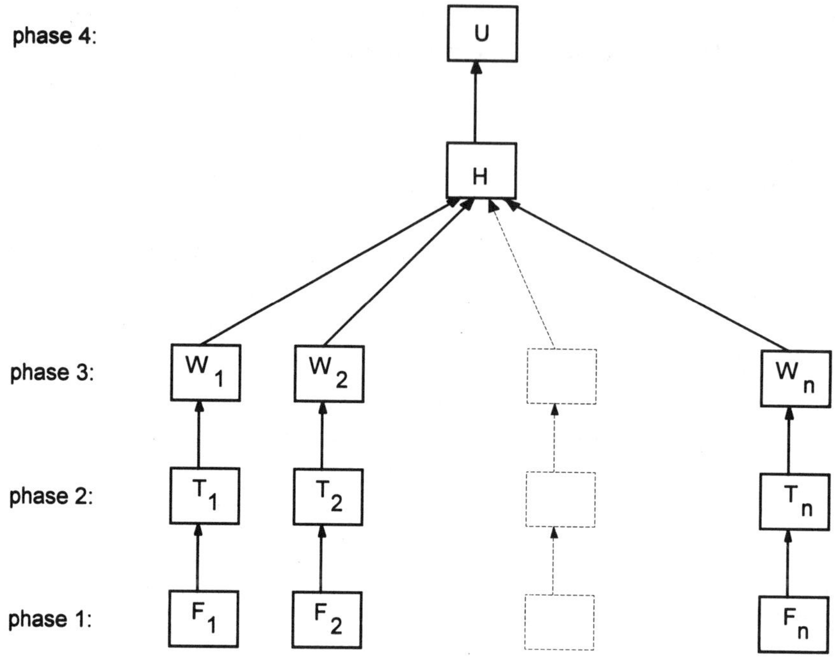

Figure 3.4: Modular definition of a DB universe

The definitions of the object characterizations F_1 through F_n are possibly preceded by the definitions of some auxiliary notions (such as constants, sets, or functions), as is the case in the examples 2.13 and 3.6 and in §4.2. Unfortunately, it is common practice in the field of databases to use the term "domain" for an auxiliary set serving as a set of values for attributes. This could cause confusion, however, because the traditional meaning of the word "domain" is the domain of a function, or the domain of a relation in general (see page 4).

We point out that this hierarchy of definitions can be represented in (at least) two different orders:

(A) Working per *table index*, that is, presenting per table index the results of the phases 1, 2, and 3 immediately one after the other. (Pattern: $(F\,;T\,;W)^*$.)

(B) Working per *phase*, that is, first presenting all the definitions from phase 1, then those from phase 2, and finally all definitions from phase 3. (Pattern: $F^*\,;T^*\,;W^*$.)

Both cases are followed by the definitions of the DB characterization H and (last but not least) the DB universe U.

We used order (A) in Example 2.13 and §4.2. Order (B) was used in Example 1.3, in the overview at the end of §2.4 (in fact for the same definitions as in Example 2.13), and in the present chapter. In Chapter 8 we will even sometimes present the definitions "backwards" (in this context also known as *top-down*): there we will sometimes first give the definitions of the DB universe, then the definition of the database characterization mentioned in it, then the definitions of the sets of tables mentioned in it, and so on.

Similar observations concerning the order of presentation apply to auxiliary concepts to be defined: in Example 2.13 and in §2.4 each auxiliary concept immediately precedes the (first) object characterization in which it is used, and in Example 3.6 and in §4.2 all auxiliary concepts are presented right at the beginning.

We will show that the construction described above always results in a DB universe, namely over the DB skeleton g defined by
$g = \{(E_1\,;\text{dom}(F_1)), (E_2\,;\text{dom}(F_2)), \ldots, (E_n\,;\text{dom}(F_n))\}$:

> We begin by noting that F_i is a set function.
> Therefore, not only $\Pi(F_i)$ but also every subset T_i of $\Pi(F_i)$ is a table over $\text{dom}(F_i)$, and consequently, over $g(E_i)$.
> But then not only $\mathbf{P}(T_i)$ but also every subset W_i of $\mathbf{P}(T_i)$ is a set of tables over $g(E_i)$.
> It now follows from the description of H given earlier that each element v of $\Pi(H)$ is a function over $\text{dom}(g)$, such that for each E_i in $\text{dom}(g)$ we have that $v(E_i)$ belongs to W_i.
> It follows from the last two conclusions that $v(E_i)$ is a table over $g(E_i)$.
> As a result, by Definition 1.3, we have that $\Pi(H)$, and therefore also every subset U of $\Pi(H)$, is a DB universe over g.

We have thus shown that, by using the procedure described above, we always obtain a DB universe. (This procedure also works in the case of an arbitrary number of table indices and not just for a finite number of indices, as might be suggested above.) In Exercise 3.23 it is asked (implicitly) to prove that, conversely, every DB universe can be described in this manner.

An essential question to be asked after defining a DB universe, is the question whether the just defined DB universe is *consistent*, i.e., whether it contains any elements at all; c.f. Exercise 1.5. After all, the definition - often quite extensive in practice - could well contain internal conflicts without one realizing this. The question above could be answered (affirmatively) by giving a concrete example of a state and showing that this example indeed satisfies all the conditions mentioned in the definition.

In most cases it is sensible to have "the empty state" over the set of table indices of the DB universe over g to be defined. This state, formally described as $\lambda E \in \text{dom}(g) : \varnothing$, could well serve as an "initial state". If it is proven that the empty state is an element of the DB universe just defined, then the question mentioned in the preceding paragraph is of course also answered (affirmatively).

Knowing that some DB universe U is consistent, still leaves us with the question whether each table index E of U is *consistent in* U, that is, whether it is ever possible for the E-table to contain any elements! (According to the terminology introduced in Exercise 1.5 this amounts to the question whether U is *regular*.) Usually, this question can be answered affirmatively by giving a state in which each table is non-empty, and showing that this example indeed satisfies all conditions posed in the definition. (It appears from one of the exercises in Chapter 1 that this solution is sufficient, yet not always possible for regular DB universes.)

EXERCISES

3.21. Give a "smallest possible" element of UBP from Example 3.6 in which each table is non-empty.

3.22. Let U be a DB universe over a set function g.

(a) Is there a "smallest" database characterization for U?
If so, which one is it, and in what sense is this database characterization the smallest one?

(b) Is there for each table index E of U a "smallest" characterizing set of tuples?
If so, define this set of tuples.

(c) Is there for each table index E of U a "smallest" object characterization?
If so, which one is it, and in what sense is this object characterization the smallest one?

3.23. If U is a DB universe over a set function g, then for each table index E of U there exists a set function F_E such that $U \subseteq \Pi(\lambda E \in \text{He}(U) : \mathbf{P}(\Pi(F_E)))$. Prove this.

□

CHAPTER 4

A Nontrivial Example of a Database Universe

In this chapter we present a nontrivial case of a DB universe. This example is meant to provide some insight into the practical problems that can arise during the design and use of *complex* databases, i.e., databases which contain many tables, attributes, references, and other constraints. In practice, databases may contain dozens of tables, hundreds of attributes, dozens of referential integrity constraints, and numerous other constraints as well. Complexity and *volume* (i.e., many tuples in the actual database state, say thousands or even millions of tuples) are two of the main problem areas in real-life databases.

Our example, which is a variant of the examples found in [Re 82] and [Br 84], extended with some ideas from [GOV 84], describes a (hypothetical) county hospital. In our hospital case, there are 19 tables and a total number of 128 attributes. It also contains many kinds of constraints (including so-called "business rules") that we gathered from various application areas in the course of time. The case also includes a few dozen of relevant DB functions.

The considerations underlying the filling in of details in our case were more of a didactic than of a medical nature. It was our purpose to represent, within one familiar case, most of the types of static constraints that we encountered in practice. Constraints from a wide range of application areas were "translated" to our hypothetical hospital application. The resulting case, therefore, is not to be considered as a "most suitable" database structure for a(ny) hospital, but rather as a representative "summary" of various real-life application areas.

Also, we did not strive for an "optimal" example from a database design point of view; the DB universe is not in third normal form, for instance. In such a way, the current case can also serve to illustrate the consequences of certain design decisions (e.g., the presence of redundant data) in the context of a complex database.

The case introduced here has already been used several times as a "functional benchmark" in order to test existing database management systems with respect to their data definition capabilities, for example, in Holland and (in cooperation with Codd & Date Ltd) in Great Britain and Germany; see [NGI 87/88] and [IDT 88/89/90].

§4.1 contains an informal description and §4.2 the formal definition of our hospital case. In order to indicate the relationship between the two sections more easily, we numbered some of the attribute constraints as well as *all* tuple, table, and database constraints (R01, R02, etcetera). The informal descriptions of the requirements will not always be sufficiently clear to be able to derive the precise formal definitions for them. However, this is representative for the situation in practice. Often, you have to return to the experts of the application area in order to "elicit" the precise formulation of a requirement.

In §4.3, we define some examples of DB functions over the DB universe defined in §4.2.

4.1 Informal Description

We start the informal description of our hospital case with an enumeration of the table indices used, and per table index a brief description of the objects represented by the tuples of the corresponding table:

[1] PAT : registered patients
[2] SM : staff members (generalization of [3] and [4])
[3] SP : specialists (including former ones)
[4] EMP : employees (generalization of [5] and [6])
[5] MP : medical personnel
[6] NMP : nonmedical personnel
[7] CE : compulsorily insured employees (differentiation of [4])
[8] GP : general practitioners in the region
[9] MUN : municipalities in the region
[10] DPT : departments
[11] RM : rooms (including former and planned rooms)
[12] ADM : admissions (including former ones)
[13] DIS : discharges
[14] REA : reassignments (including former ones)
[15] TRF : transfers (including former ones)
[16] TTP : treatment types
[17] PT : patient treatments (including former ones)
[18] MED : medicines
[19] MDP : medicine prescriptions (including former ones)

The two generalizations mentioned above constitute a subdivision of staff members into specialists and employees and, subsequently, a subdivision of employees into medical and nonmedical personnel. Moreover, the differentiation mentioned above indicates that some of the employees are compulsorily insured. Figure 4.1 illustrates this situation schematically.

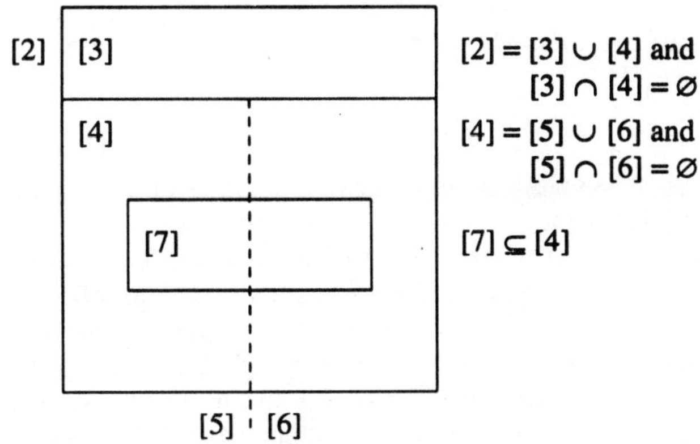

Figure 4.1: Two generalizations and a differentiation

We note that these equalities and inclusions only hold for the sets of *objects* to be represented but not, as we will see in a while, for the corresponding sets of *tuples*!

Each of the 19 tables will now be explained in a separate paragraph.

For each **registered patient**, the following data is relevant: patient number, NAZC-data (i.e., name, address, zip code, and city), place of birth, date of birth, registration date, blood group, rhesus factor, sex, identification number of the family doctor, NAZC-data of (the practice of) the family doctor, the dentist, and the dispensary of the patient, for each of the children of the patient the first name, date of birth, and sex, and, finally, a "comments" column (for annotations). Every registered patient is uniquely identified by his (or her) patient number [R01], and per patient every child is uniquely identified by his or her first name [R02]. A patient number is a 6-digit number [R03] and must be divisible by 9 [R04]. The first digit of each patient number can be considered as a check digit (in view of possible mistakes, such as typing errors). Such *error detecting codes* are often used in practice, though they usually are of a more subtle nature, e.g., the 11-test for bank account numbers mentioned in §3.1. Our hospital started on the first of April 1960 and therefore all dates concerning medical events (such as registration dates) have to be later than March 31, 1960 [R05]. At the opening of our hospital in 1960, a date of birth could go back as far as 1850 [R06]. A registration date is not allowed to be earlier than the date of birth of the patient [R07]. Only patients living in the region of our hospital can be registered [R08]. Finally, the family doctor of the patient has to be a so-called "regional doctor" [R09]. (The notion of a regional doctor will be explained later.)

The following attributes apply to *each* **staff member**: identification number (a number consisting of 3 or 4 digits), NAZC-data, department number, internal phone number (4 digits), kind of staff member (specialist, medical personnel, or nonmedical personnel), and a "comments" column. The identification number uniquely determines the staff member [R10]. Each staff member is formally assigned to a department of our hospital [R11]. Staff members with the same internal phone number have to work in the same department [R12].

Besides the general staff member data, the following additional attributes apply specifically to **specialists**: identification number of the locum tenens of the specialist, type of employment, specialisms (every specialist must have one or more specialisms), telephone number at home (consisting of an area code and a subscriber code), contractual number of work hours per week (with a maximum of 50 hours), fee per hour (with a legal minimum of 80 guilders), and number of formally available beds for the specialist; since we also want to keep track of all former specialists, we need to know whether or not an individual specialist is still in service. As a further explanation of the number of formally available beds, we note that every specialist can claim, in principle, a certain number of nursing beds; for each specialist, this number will be recorded in a contract. (Since such a contract does not lead to an actual reservation of physical beds, we speak of "paper beds" in this case). However, the total number of beds promised to specialists may not exceed the actual number of nursing beds by more than 10% [R13]. For specialists who do not work at our hospital any more, the number of formally available beds is zero, just as the contractual number of work hours per week [R14]. The identification number of a specialist consists of 3 digits. Every specialist, being a staff member, has his own unique identification number [R15]. For each staff member, the attribute "kind of staff member" indicates exactly whether this staff member is a specialist or not [R16]. The locum tenens of a specialist has to be another [R17] specialist (previously) associated with our hospital [R18]. (The information analysts of the hospital seemingly did not notice the plausible constraint that the locum tenens of a specialist who is still in service has to be in service as well; however, another reason might be that guarding this requirement was not considered important enough to capture it formally in a constraint.)

We note that the constraints R15 and R16 have to be stated explicitly (in combination with the constraints R25 and R19 below) in order to capture formally the first generalization mentioned at the beginning of §4.1.

By an **employee** we mean (by definition) a staff member who is not a specialist [R19]. For this category of staff members, the following additional attributes are relevant: identification number of the group leader, the number of half workdays per week (since part-time jobs are possible), monthly salary, and the number of days the employee did not work this year due to illness. Because of the weekends and holidays, the total sick leave of an employee cannot exceed 290 days. The salary cannot exceed the official civil maximum salary, which at the moment is 10720 guilders per month [R20]. For a (part-time) job, the salary cannot exceed (a proportional part of) this civil maximum salary [R21]. On the other hand, the salary may not be less than (the proportional part of) the civil minimum salary [R22], which is 975 guilders per month now [R23]. We do not keep track of former employees; hence, we only have historical data on specialists, and not on employees. All employees have to live in the region [R24]. The identification number of an employee consists of 4 digits. Every employee, being a staff member, has his own unique identification number [R25]. Every group leader is an employee who, in addition, is his own group leader [R26]. Group leaders are not allowed to have a part-time job [R27].

Our **medical personnel** consists (by definition) of those staff members who are registered as such [R28]. (As a consequence, specialists do not belong to our medical personnel; only employees can belong to the medical personnel). Besides the staff member data and the employee data, the following data are also relevant to medical personnel: the telephone number at home and the code of the (highest) education that that member of the medical personnel has attained. Every member of our medical personnel, being a staff member, has his own unique identification number [R29].

Our **nonmedical personnel** consists by definition of those staff members who are registered as such [R30]. Besides the staff member data and the employee data, the following data are also relevant to nonmedical personnel: function code, monthly allowance (although a member of the nonmedical personnel can have several allowances and other expenses, here we are only interested in the total amount), and the number of holidays entitled to this member of our nonmedical personnel. The monthly allowance should not exceed the monthly salary [R31]. Every member of the nonmedical personnel, being a staff member, has his own unique identification number [R32]. The constraints R32 and R30 in combination with the constraints R29 and R28 serve as an explicit expression of the second generalization mentioned at the beginning of §4.1.

Of each **compulsorily insured employee** we have to know the following additional data: medical insurance number (8 digits), identification number of the GP, and NAZC-data of the dispensary. Each compulsorily insured employee has to be registered as an employee as well [R33]. Because every employee has to live in the region, his GP has to be a so-called region doctor [R34]. Each compulsorily insured employee can be uniquely identified in two different ways: by his identification number [R35] or by his medical insurance number [R36]. The constraints R33 and R35 are necessary in order to formalize the differentiation mentioned at the beginning of §4.1.

Since our regional hospital has to accomplish certain registration tasks concerning the region, we have to record the following data of each **region doctor**, i.e., each GP whose practice lies within the area of the hospital: registration number, name, address of the practice, which has to be within the region [R37], telephone number, both private and practice, data concerning consulting hours, the number of patients on last New Year (the yearly reference date), the increase of the number of patients during the past year, and the expected increase in the current year. (A decrease will be denoted as a negative increase.) A region doctor can be uniquely identified by his registration number [R38], but also by the combination of his name and practice address [R39]. Of course, the *increase* in the number of patients during the past year cannot exceed the number of patients on last New Year [R40]. In case of an expected *decrease* for the current year, this decrease cannot be more than the number of patients on last New Year [R41].

In view of the regional registration tasks of our hospital, we also have to record some data for each **municipality in the region**, namely the name of that municipality, which has to be unique within the region [R42], the number of inhabitants (in thousands), the number of GPs, dispensaries, and dentists who are practising in that municipality, name and practice address of the GP and the dispensary who will be on duty for that municipality next weekend, and, finally, the identification number of our contact person for that municipality. A contact person is always a member of the nonmedical personnel [R43], often a social worker who knows the local situation very well. In municipalities in which at least four GPs have their practice, the service for the weekend always has to be performed by one of those very GPs [R44]. In any case, the weekend GP in each municipality has to be one of the region doctors [R45].

For each **department** in our hospital we have to know the department number, the department name, the identification number of the manager and of the assistant manager of that department, and the type of department. We distinguish five types of departments: medical, administrative, laboratory, service (such as the central technical service and the department for building affairs), and "others" [R46]. Each department has its own unique number [R47] as well as its own unique name [R48]. The assistant manager of a department must be a staff member of that department [R49]. The manager of a department must also be a staff member [R50], but not necessarily of the same department. (Hence, in principle, someone can be a manager of several departments at the same time). Within each department, the manager and the assistant manager must be different persons [R51]. It is, however, possible to be both the assistant manager of one department and the manager of another department. Finally, only group leaders can be assistant managers [R52].

For each current, former, and planned **room** of an existing department, the following data are of interest: room number (consisting of a code of at most nine characters), department number, floor space (in square meters), status (current, planned, or former), type of room, and number of beds. We distinguish five types of rooms: treatment rooms, nursing rooms, receptions, stores, and "various" [R53]. All former, current, and planned rooms within our hospital can be uniquely identified by their room number [R54]. (Indeed, room numbers of former rooms cannot be re-used in the course of time.) Each room may contain at most 15 beds. In each room, the floor space per bed must be at least four square metres [R55]. Only current treatment rooms and current nursing rooms can have beds [R56]. In our hospital, departments never cease to exist and therefore all former, current, and planned rooms always belong to an existing department [R57].

We have to keep track of all **admissions** in our hospital, both current and former admissions. (By an admission we mean a continuous stay of a patient in our hospital.) The following attributes apply to *all* admissions: patient number of the admitted patient, admission date, initial room number, identification number of the initially responsible person, initial reason of admission, name and (practice) address of the family doctor of the patient at the time of admission, dietary data, initial nursing comments, and discharge date (i.e., the *planned* discharge date for current stays and the *actual* discharge date for terminated stays). With respect to room number and nursing comments, we mean by the predicate *initial*: until a possible transfer to another room. With respect to responsible person and reason of admission, we mean by *initial(ly)*: until a possible reassignment to another responsible person. Explanation: During a stay in our hospital, a patient might be transferred to another room one or more times and, in principle independently of these transfers, the patient might also be reassigned to another responsible person once or more. We will return to transfers and reassignments in the following paragraphs.

We conclude our enumeration of the attributes that apply to all admissions by noting that we have to know whether that admission has already terminated and whether the patient has died during that stay in the hospital. If a patient dies, the admission will be considered as terminated [R58]. Admissions last, in principle, for at least one night, but the early death of a patient might cause an exception to this rule [R59]. A patient may be admitted only once a day [R60]. Different admissions of the same patient cannot overlap in time (although the discharge date of one admission might be the starting date of the next admission) [R61]. For each patient there can be at most one current admission, which must then be the admission with the most recent starting date [R62]. Of course, an admission can only be followed by another admission of the same patient if that patient did not die during the previous admission [R63]. An admitted patient must be registered [R64] and an admission can only take (or have taken) place in one of the current or former *nursing* rooms [R65]. The (initially) responsible person for an admission must always be a specialist of our hospital [R66].

Each **discharge** from the hospital has two additional relevant attributes (besides the ones that already apply to each admission), namely invoice amount (in cents) and instructions for aftercare. (An invoice will be made for each discharge from the hospital; to us, only the total invoice amount is relevant.) Each invoice amount must be at least 240 guilders. These two additional attributes apply to each discharge (terminated stay) and to none of the current stays [R67]. There can be several discharges per patient, but each discharge is uniquely identified by the combination of patient number and admission date [R68]. The constraints R67 and R68 explicitly express that the set of discharges, i.e., terminated admissions) is a differentiation of the set of all admissions.

As mentioned earlier, during an admission it is possible to reassign the responsibility for that admission from one specialist to another. Often this is due to a renewed reason for admission. For each such **reassignment** we want to record the number of the patient concerned, the date of reassignment, the identification number of the newly responsible person, and the (possibly renewed) reason for admission. From an administrative point of view, a patient can be reassigned only once a day [R69] (the reason being that only the last reassignment of the day is relevant). A reassignment can only take place *during* an admission of that patient which lasted at least one night at the moment of reassignment [R70]. The newly responsible person must always be one of our specialists [R71].

It is also possible that a patient will be transferred from one room to another while staying in our hospital. For each such **transfer** we want to record the number of the patient who is being moved, the date of transfer, the new room number, and the additional nursing comments during the stay in that room. Again, from an administrative point of view, a patient can be transferred only once a day [R72]. Just as with a reassignment, a transfer can only take place *during* an admission of that patient which lasted at least one night at the moment of transfer [R73]. The new room must be an existing or former *nursing* room [R74].

Of all **treatment types** that can be carried out in our hospital (our "assortment", so to say), the following data are relevant: treatment code, treatment name, kind of treatment, rate, minimally and maximally expected duration, and the estimated number of times this treatment has to be carried out during this year. This forecast has to be specified per month. A treatment type can be uniquely identified by its code [R75], but also by its name [R76]. Of course, the maximally expected duration must be at least as long as the minimally expected duration [R77].

For each **patient treatment** (i.e., for each application of a treatment type from our "assortment" to a patient) we have to know the following: the number of the treated patient, the code of the applied treatment, the identification number of the treating specialist (also called the main specialist of the treatment), the identification number of the assistant specialist (if there is no assistant, we register the identification number of the main specialist himself), the room number, the treatment date, the actual duration, the invoice amount, and a serial number. This serial number is used in order to distinguish different applications of the same treatment type to the same patient [R78]. The different applications of the same treatment type to the same patient are numbered consecutively and chronologically, starting with 1 [R79]. The main specialist must be one of our own specialists [R80]; the same holds for the assistant specialist [R81]. The treated patient has to be registered [R82] and the applied treatment type has to occur in our assortment [R83]. Finally, we note that a patient treatment can only take (or have taken) place in an existing or former *treatment* room [R84].

On behalf of our medical staff (i.e., specialists and medical personnel) and the dispensary of our hospital, some data concerning **medicines** have to be recorded, namely the code, name, and type of the medicine, the danger code (ranging from 1 to 20), the possible side effects, the number of units in stock, the price per unit and the kind of unit.

Depending on the medicine, the kind of unit is indicated by GR for grams, MG for milligrams, ML for millilitres (or CC for cubic centimetres), and PC if the medicine unit is number of pieces. Each medicine has a unique code [R85] as well as a unique name [R86].

The dispensary of our hospital can supply patients with medicines on the basis of a prescription of a specialist. For each **medicine prescription**, the following attributes are of interest: patient number, medicine code, starting date, identification number of the prescribing specialist, prescribed duration (with a maximum of 90 days), frequency per day (with a maximum of 6), prescribed number of units at a time, invoice amount (with a legal minimum of 250 cents), and a serial number. This serial number is used to distinguish different medicine prescriptions concerning the same patient [R87]. Per patient, the individual dispensings are numbered consecutively and chronologically, starting with 1 [R88]. The prescribing specialist has (or had) to be one of our own specialists [R89], the patient must be registered [R90], and the prescribed medicine must be known by our dispensary [R91]. We end with the constraint that our dispensary should not supply a patient with the same medicine more than once a day [R92].

The formal definitions will be given in §4.2. That section has the following (modular) structure:

- The first page starts with the definitions of some "auxiliary constants" and "auxiliary domains" (MINSAL up to and including PROGSET).
- Subsequently, we present for each of the 19 "entities":
  - An *object characterization* (FPAT, FSM, FSP, ..., FMED, FMDP); here, we only encounter *attribute constraints*.
  - Possibly an explicitly mentioned set of allowed tuples (TPAT, TSP, ..., TADM, TTP), namely for those (nine) entities for which there exist *tuple constraints*.
  - The set of allowed tables for that entity (WPAT, WSM, WSP, ..., WMED, WMDP); here, we encounter the *table constraints*.
- The last page but one contains the *database characterization* FHPT, which introduces the 19 table indices and assigns the corresponding set of allowed tables.
- Last but not least, the last page contains the definition of our *database universe* UHPT; here, we encounter all *database constraints*.

4.2 Formal Definition

Definitions	*Explanation*
MINSAL = 975;	see R23
MAXSAL = 10720;	see R20
DTBSET = [18500101 .. 19991231];	see R06
DATSET = [600401 .. 991231];	see R05
RMSET = { 'TRM', 'NRS', 'RCPT', 'STR', 'VAR'};	see R53
TYPSET = { 'MED', 'ADM', 'LAB', 'SERV', 'VAR'};	see R46
PNRSET = $\{k \mid k \in$ Snn(6) and	see R03
k mod 9 = 0};	see R04
TELSET = Π({(AREA; [10 .. 9999]),	area code (without leading zero)
(SUBS ; [100 .. 9999999])});	subscriber number
NAZCSET = Π({(NM ; Chs(20)),	name
(ADDR; Chs(20)),	address
(ZIP ; Chs(7)),	zip code
(CTY ; Chs(15))});	city
CHDSET = Π({(FNM ; Chs(14)),	first name
(DTB ; DTBSET),	date of birth
(SEX ; { 'M', 'F'})});	sex
PROGSET = $\{T \mid T \subseteq$ CHDSET and	
{FNM} is u.i. in T};	see R02
	REGISTERED PATIENTS:
FPAT = {(PNR ; PNRSET),	patient number
(NAZC ; NAZCSET),	NAZC-data
(PLB ; Chs(15)),	place of birth
(DTB ; DTBSET),	date of birth
(REGD ; DATSET),	registration date
(BLGR ; { 'O', 'A', 'B', 'AB'}),	blood group
(RHF ; { '+', '–'}),	rhesus factor
(SEX ; { 'M', 'F'}),	sex
(PROG ; PROGSET),	child data
(GPID ; [1 .. 9999]),	identification number of the family doctor
(NAGP ; NAZCSET),	NAZC-data of the practice of the family doctor
(NADT ; NAZCSET),	NAZC-data of the practice of the dentist
(NADP ; NAZCSET),	NAZC-data of the dispensary
(COMM ; Chs(800))};	comments
TPAT = $\{t \mid t \in$ Π (FPAT) and	
t(DTB) ≤ t(REGD) + 19000000};	see R07
WPAT = $\{T \mid T \subseteq$ TPAT and	
{PNR} is u.i. in T};	see R01

	STAFF MEMBERS:
FSM = {(IDNR ; Snn(3) ∪ Snn(4)),	identification number
(NAZC ; NAZCSET),	NAZC-data
(DNR ; [1 .. 100]),	department number
(ITEL ; Snn(4)),	internal phone number
(KDSM ; { 'SP', 'MP', 'NMP'}),	kind of staff member
(COMM; Chs(1000))};	comments
WSM = {*T* | *T* ⊆ Π(FSM) and	
{IDNR} is u.i. in *T* and	see R10
{ITEL} → {DNR} in *T*};	see R12
	SPECIALISTS:
FSP = {(IDNR ; Snn(3)),	identification number
(LOC ; Snn(3)),	id. no. of the locum tenens
(TOE ; Chs(15)),	type of employment
(SPEC ; **P**(Chs(15)) − {∅}),	specialisms
(TELH ; TELSET),	phone number at home
(FEEH ; [8000 ..)),	fee per hour (in cents)
(HPW ; [0 .. 50]),	number of hours per week
(NBD ; ℕ),	number of promised beds
(INS ; { 'YES', 'NO'})};	still in service?
TSP = {*t* | *t* ∈ Π (FSP) and	
t (LOC) ≠ *t* (IDNR) and	see R17
if *t* (INS) = 'NO'	see R14
then (*t* (NBD) = 0 and *t* (HPW) = 0)};	"
WSP = {*T* | *T* ⊆ TSP and	
{IDNR} is u.i. in *T* and	see R15
{(LOC; IDNR)} connects *T* with *T*};	see R18
	EMPLOYEES:
FEMP = {(IDNR ; Snn(4)),	identification number
(GLNR ; Snn(4)),	id. no. of the group leader
(NHD ; [1 .. 10]),	number of half workdays per week
(SAL ; [0 .. MAXSAL]),	monthly salary (in guilders)
(TSL ; [0 .. 290])};	total sick leave this year (in days)
TEMP = {*t* | *t* ∈ Π (FEMP) and	
t (SAL) ≥ (MINSAL * *t* (NHD)) div 10 and	see R22
t (SAL) ≤ (MAXSAL * *t* (NHD)) div 10 and	see R21
if *t* (IDNR) = *t* (GLNR) then *t* (NHD) = 10};	see R27
WEMP = {*T* | *T* ⊆ TEMP and	
{IDNR} is u.i. in *T* and	see R25
{(GLNR; IDNR)} connects *T*	see R26
with {*t* ∈ *T* | *t* (GLNR) = *t* (IDNR)}};	"

	MEDICAL PERSONNEL:
FMP = {(IDNR ; Snn(4)),	identification number
(TELH ; TELSET),	phone number at home
(EDUC ; Chs(8))};	(highest) education code
WMP = $\{T \mid T \subseteq \Pi$ (FMP) and	
{IDNR} is u.i. in $T\}$;	see R29

	NONMEDICAL PERSONNEL:
FNMP = {(IDNR ; Snn(4)),	identification number
(FCD ; Chs(10)),	function code
(ENH ; [15 .. 30]),	entitled number of holidays per year
(MALL ; $\mathbb{N}$)};	monthly allowance (in guilders)
WNMP = $\{T \mid T \subseteq \Pi$ (FNMP) and	
{IDNR} is u.i. in $T\}$;	see R32

	COMPULSORILY INSURED EMPLOYEES:
FCE = {(IDNR ; Snn(4)),	identification number
(MINR ; Snn(8)),	medical insurance number
(GPID ; [1 .. 9999]),	identification number of the GP
(NADP ; NAZCSET)};	NAZC-data of the dispensary
WCE = $\{T \mid T \subseteq \Pi$ (FCE) and	
{IDNR} is u.i. in T and	see R35
{MINR} is u.i. in $T\}$;	see R36

	GENERAL PRACTITIONERS IN THE REGION:
FGP = {(GPID ; [1 .. 9999]),	registration number of the GP
(NAGP ; NAZCSET),	NAZC-data of the practice
(TELP ; TELSET),	phone number of the practice
(TELH ; TELSET),	phone number at home
(CONH ; Chs(25)),	consulting hours
(PAT ; $\mathbb{N}$),	number of patients on last New Year
(INCR ; $\mathbb{Z}$),	increase of the number of patients last year
(EXPI ; $\mathbb{Z}$)};	expected increase this year
TGP = $\{t \mid t \in \Pi$ (FGP) and	
t(PAT) - t (INCR) ≥ 0 and	see R40
t(PAT) + t (EXPI) $\geq 0\}$;	see R41
WGP = $\{T \mid T \subseteq$ TGP and	
{GPID} is u.i. in T and	see R38
{NAGP} is u.i. in $T\}$;	see R39

	MUNICIPALITIES IN THE REGION:
FMUN = {(CTY ; Chs(15)),	name of the municipality
(INHA ; [0 .. 1000]),	number of inhabitants (in thousands)
(CPRS ; Snn(4)),	id. no. of the contact person
(GPOD ; NAZCSET),	GP on duty next weekend
(DPOD ; NAZCSET),	dispensary on duty next weekend
(NGP ; $\mathbb{N}$),	number of resident general practitioners
(NDP ; $\mathbb{N}$),	number of resident dispensaries
(NDT ; $\mathbb{N}$)};	number of resident dentists
TMUN = $\{t \mid t \in \Pi$ (FMUN) and	
if t (NGP) ≥ 4	see R44
then t (GPOD) (CTY) = t (CTY)};	,,
WMUN = $\{T \mid T \subseteq$ TMUN and	
{CTY} is u.i. in T};	see R42
	DEPARTMENTS:
FDPT = {(DNR ; [1 .. 100]),	department number
(DNM ; Chs(20)),	department name
(MNNR ; Snn(4) $\cup$ Snn(3)),	id. no. of the manager
(AMNR ; Snn(4)),	id. no. of the assistant manager
(TYPE ; TYPSET)};	type of department
TDPT = $\{t \mid t \in \Pi$ (FDPT) and	
t(MNNR) $\neq$ t (AMNR)};	see R51
WDPT = $\{T \mid T \subseteq$ TDPT and	
{DNR} is u.i. in T and	see R47
{DNM} is u.i. in T};	see R48
	ROOMS:
FRM = {(RNR ; Chs(9)),	room number
(DNR ; [1 .. 100]),	department number
(FLSP ; $\mathbb{N}$),	floor space (in square metres)
(STAT ; { 'CURR', 'PLAN', 'FORM'}),	status
(TPRM ; RMSET),	type of room
(NBD ; [0 .. 15])};	number of beds
TRM = $\{t \mid t \in \Pi$ (FRM) and	
t (FLSP) $\geq 4 * t$ (NBD) and	see R55
if t (NBD) $\neq 0$	see R56
then t (STAT) = 'CURR' and	,,
t (TPRM) $\in$ { 'TRM', 'NRS'}};	,,
WRM = $\{T \mid T \subseteq$ TRM and	
{RNR} is u.i. in T};	see R54

	ADMISSIONS:
FADM = {(PNR ; PNRSET),	patient number
(ADMD ; DATSET),	admission date
(RNR ; Chs(9)),	(initial) room number
(IDNR ; Snn(3)),	id. no. of the (initially) responsible specialist
(ADMR ; Chs(40)),	(initial) reason for admission
(NAGP ; NAZCSET),	family doctor (at admission time)
(DIET ; Chs(240)),	dietary data
(NCOM ; Chs(1200)),	nursing comments
(DISD ; DATSET),	(planned) discharge date
(DISC ; { 'YES', 'NO'}),	discharged?
(DCSD ; { 'YES', 'NO'})};	deceased?
TADM = {t | $t \in \Pi$ (FADM) and t(ADMD) $\leq$ t(DISD) and	see R59
(if t(ADMD) = t(DISD)	"
then t(DCSD) = 'YES') and	"
(if t(DCSD) = 'YES' then t(DISC) = 'YES')};	see R58
WADM = {T | $T \subseteq$ TADM and {PNR, ADMD} is u.i. in T and	see R60
$\forall t \in T$: $\forall t' \in T$: if t (PNR) = t'(PNR) and	
t (ADMD) < t'(ADMD)	
then t (DISD) $\leq$ t' (ADMD) and	see R61
t (DISC) = 'YES' and	see R62
t (DCSD) = 'NO'};	see R63
	DISCHARGES:
FDIS = {(PNR ; PNRSET),	patient number
(ADMD ; DATSET),	admission date
(INVA ; [24000 ..)),	invoice amount (in cents)
(AFTC ; Chs(160))};	instructions for aftercare
WDIS = {T | $T \subseteq \Pi$ (FDIS) and {PNR, ADMD} is u.i. in T};	see R68
	REASSIGNMENTS:
FREA = {(PNR ; PNRSET),	patient number
(BDAT ; DATSET),	date of reassignment
(IDNR ; Snn(3)),	id. no. of the newly responsible specialist
(ADMR ; Chs(40))};	(renewed) reason for admission
WREA = {T | $T \subseteq \Pi$ (FREA) and {PNR, BDAT} is u.i. in T};	see R69
	TRANSFERS:
FTRF = {(PNR ; PNRSET),	patient number
(BDAT ; DATSET),	date of transfer
(RNR ; Chs(9)),	new room number
(NCOM; Chs(400))};	additional nursing comments
WTRF = {T | $T \subseteq \Pi$ (FTRF) and	
{ PNR, BDAT} is u.i. in T};	see R72

	TREATMENT TYPES:
FTTP = {(TCD ; Chs(4)),	treatment code
(TNM ; Chs(50)),	treatment name
(TKND ; Chs(3)),	kind of treatment
(TAR ; [10 ..)),	rate (in guilders)
(MIND ; [1 ..)),	min. expected duration (in minutes)
(MAXD; [1 ..)),	max. expected duration (in minutes)
(FMD ; $[1 .. 12] \twoheadrightarrow \mathbb{N}$)};	forecast of monthly demand
TTTP = $\{t \mid t \in \Pi$ (FTTP) and t (MIND) $\leq t$(MAXD)};	see R77
WTTP = $\{T \mid T \subseteq$ TTTP and	
{TCD} is u.i. in T and	see R75
{TNM} is u.i. in T};	see R76
	PATIENT TREATMENTS:
FPT = {(PNR ; PNRSET),	patient number
(TCD ; Chs(4)),	treatment code
(SNR ; [1 ..)),	serial number
(IDNR ; Snn(3)),	id. no. of the treating specialist
(ASNR ; Snn(3)),	id. no. of the assistant specialist
(RNR ; Chs(9)),	room number
(BDAT ; DATSET),	date of treatment
(DUR ; [1 ..)),	actual duration (in minutes)
(INVA ; [1000 ..))};	invoice amount (in cents)
WPT = $\{T \mid T \subseteq \Pi$ (FPT) and	
{ PNR, TCD, SNR} is u.i. in T and	see R78
$\forall t \in T$: if t(SNR) $\neq 1$	see R79
then $\exists t' \in T : t' \restriction$ {PNR, TCD} $= t \restriction$ {PNR, TCD}	”
and t' (SNR) $= t$ (SNR) $- 1$	”
and t' (BDAT) $\leq t$ (BDAT)};	”
	MEDICINES:
FMED = {(MCD ; Chs(6)),	medicine code
(MNM ; Chs(20)),	medicine name
(MTYP ; Chs(4)),	type of medicine
(DCD ; [1 .. 20]),	danger code
(SDEF ; **P** (Chs(15))),	possible side effects
(NST ; $\mathbb{N}$),	number of units in stock
(UNIT ; { ‘GR’, ‘MG’, ‘ML’, ‘CC’, ‘PC’}),	kind of unit
(PRCU ; $\mathbb{N}$)};	price per unit (in cents)
WMED = $\{T \mid T \subseteq \Pi$ (FMED) and	
{MCD} is u.i. in T and	see R85
{MNM} is u.i. in T};	see R86

	MEDICINE DISPENSINGS:
FMDP = {(PNR ; PNRSET),	patient number
(MCD ; Chs(6)),	medicine code
(DAT ; DATSET),	starting date
(SNR ; [1 ..)),	serial number
(IDNR ; Snn(3)),	id. no. of the prescribing specialist
(DUR ; [1 .. 90]),	prescribed duration (in days)
(FREQ ; [1 .. 6]),	frequency per day
(NUT ; [1 ..)),	number of units at a time
(INVA ; [250 ..))};	invoice amount (in cents)
WMDP = {T | $T \in \Pi$ (FMDP) and	
{ PNR, MCD, DAT} is u.i. in T and	see R92
{ PNR, SNR} is u.i. in T and	see R87
$\forall t \in T$: if t (SNR) $\neq$ 1	see R88
then $\exists t' \in T$: t' (PNR) = t (PNR) and	"
t' (SNR) = t (SNR) − 1 and	"
t' (DAT) $\leq$ t (DAT)};	"

	DATABASE CHARACTERIZATION:
FHPT = {(PAT ; WPAT),	registered patients
(SM ; WSM),	staff members
(SP ; WSP),	specialists (including former ones)
(EMP ; WEMP),	employees
(MP ; WMP),	medical personnel
(NMP ; WNMP),	nonmedical personnel
(CE ; WCE),	compulsorily insured employees
(GP ; WGP),	general practitioners in the region
(MUN ; WMUN),	municipalities in the region
(DPT ; WDPT),	departments
(RM ; WRM),	rooms (including former and planned ones)
(ADM ; WADM),	admissions (including former ones)
(DIS ; WDIS),	discharges
(REA ; WREA),	reassignments (including former ones)
(TRF ; WTRF),	transfers (including former ones)
(TTP ; WTTP),	treatment types
(PT ; WPT),	patient treatments (including former ones)
(MED ; WMED),	medicines
(MDP ; WMDP)};	medicine dispensings (including former ones)

UHPT = {v | $v \in \Pi$ (FHPT) and					
id({PNR})	connects v(ADM)	with v(PAT)	and		see R64
id({PNR})	connects v(PT)	with v(PAT)	and		see R82
id({PNR})	connects v(MDP)	with v(PAT)	and		see R90
{(AMNR; IDNR), (DNR; DNR)}	connects v(DPT)	with v(SM)	and		see R49
{(MNNR; IDNR)}	connects v(DPT)	with v(SM)	and		see R50
{(ASNR; IDNR)}	connects v(PT)	with v(SP)	and		see R81
id({IDNR})	connects v(PT)	with v(SP)	and		see R80
id({IDNR})	connects v(ADM)	with v(SP)	and		see R66
id({IDNR})	connects v(REA)	with v(SP)	and		see R71
id({IDNR})	connects v(MDP)	with v(SP)	and		see R89
id({IDNR})	connects v(CE)	with v(EMP)	and		see R33
{(AMNR; GLNR)}	connects v(DPT)	with v(EMP)	and		see R52
{(CPRS; IDNR)}	connects v(MUN)	with v(NMP)	and		see R43
{(GPOD; NAGP)}	connects v(MUN)	with v(GP)	and		see R45
id({GPID, NAGP})	connects v(PAT)	with v(GP)	and		see R09
id({GPID})	connects v(CE)	with v(GP)	and		see R34
id({DNR})	connects v(SM)	with v(DPT)	and		see R11
id({DNR})	connects v(RM)	with v(DPT)	and		see R57
id({TCD})	connects v(PT)	with v(TTP)	and		see R83
id({MCD})	connects v(MDP)	with v(MED)	and		see R91

id({RNR}) connects

v(ADM) with {$t \in v$(RM) | t(STAT) $\neq$ 'PLAN' and t(TPRM) = 'NRS'},	see R65
v(TRF) with {$t \in v$(RM) | t(STAT) $\neq$ 'PLAN' and t(TPRM) = 'NRS'} and	see R74
v(PT) with {$t \in v$(RM) | t(STAT) $\neq$ 'PLAN' and t(TPRM) = 'TRM'}, and	see R84
id({CTY}) connects	
{t(NAZC) | $t \in v$(SM) and t(KDSM) $\neq$ 'SP'} with v(MUN),	see R24
{t(NAZC) | $t \in v$(PAT)} with v(MUN) and	see R08
{t(NAGP) | $t \in v$(GP)} with v(MUN), and	see R37
id({IDNR}) connects	
v(SP) bilaterally with {$t \in v$(SM) | t(KDSM) = 'SP'},	see R16
v(EMP) bilaterally with {$t \in v$(SM) | t(KDSM) $\neq$ 'SP'},	see R19
v(MP) bilaterally with {$t \in v$(SM) | t(KDSM) = 'MP'} and	see R28
v(NMP) bilaterally with {$t \in v$(SM) | t(KDSM) = 'NMP'}, and	see R30
id({PNR, ADMD}) connects	
v(DIS) bilaterally with {$t \in v$(ADM) | t(DISC) = 'YES'} and	see R67
($\sum t \in v$(SP) : t(NBD)) $\leq$	see R13
(11/10) * ($\sum t \in v$(RM) and t(TPRM) = 'NRS' : t(NBD)) and	"
($\forall t \in v$(NMP) $\bowtie$ v(EMP) : t(MALL) $\leq$ t(SAL)) and	see R31
($\forall t \in v$(REA) $\cup$ v(TRF) : $\exists t' \in v$(ADM) :	see R70
(t'(PNR) = t(PNR) and t'(ADMD) < t(BDAT) and	and
if t'(DISC) = 'YES' then t(BDAT) $\leq$ t'(DISD)))}.	R73

EXERCISES

4.1. (a) Is "the empty state" allowed? (I.e., ($\lambda E \in$ He (UHPT): $\varnothing$) $\in$ UHPT?)

(b) Let UHPT2 be the DB universe defined by substituting the "≤"-symbol in R13 in the definition of UHPT by the "<"-symbol. Is "the empty state" allowed in UHPT2?

4.2. Let GHPT be the DB skeleton over which the DB universe UHPT is defined.

(a) Explicitly determine dom (GHPT).

(b) Explicitly determine GHPT (SM).

4.3. Test for each of the following statements its validity (or even its meaninglessness) in UHPT. Mention for each valid statement the constraint(s) from which this statement follows. For each (sometimes) unvalid or meaningless statement, briefly indicate what changes in the definition of the DB universe are required to satisfy the statement.

(a) No patient can undergo the same treatment more than once a day.
(b) The treatment type KNO has a fixed rate of 40 guilders.
(c) Each treatment type has its own fixed rate.
(d) Department 9 has at least twenty staff members.
(e) Department 1 has at least twenty female staff members.
(f) Department 7 has at least twenty female employees.
(g) The neurology department has at least five female employees.
(h) A specialist may belong to more than one department.
(i) A specialist for zero hours per week is no longer in service.
(j) A specialist with available beds is still in service.
(k) A patient can be admitted for more than one reason.
(l) Only "current" admissions are kept track of.
(m) A patient is someone who has undergone an admission, a treatment, or a medicine dispensing.
(n) The rate of a treatment is determined by the combination of the treatment code and the treating specialist.
(o) The rate of a treatment is determined by the combination of the type of treatment and the treating specialist.
(p) It can be checked whether a specialist has been active.
(q) A staff member can also be a patient.
(r) Per medicine dispensing the total amount of supplied medicine is fixed.
(s) Each treatment occurs during an admission.
(t) Nobody is a contact person for two or more municipalities at the same time.
(u) Each contact person for a municipality in the region lives in that municipality.
(v) A specialist can be a group leader as well.

(w) Nobody can be the manager of more than one department.
(x) For each patient treatment, the treating specialist and the assistant specialist belong to the same department.
(y) A patient treatment always occurs in the department of the treating specialist.
(z) In each nursing room the number of current admissions does not exceed the number of beds in that room.

4.4. Is $\{\nu(\text{PAT}) \mid \nu \in \text{UHPT}\}$ in BCNF or in 3NF?
(You may assume that Mk $(\{\nu(\text{PAT}) \mid \nu \in \text{UHPT}\}) = \{\{\text{PNR}\}\}$.)

4.5. Does the addition of any specialist tuple t to "the empty state" return a "correct" DB state (i.e., an element of UHPT)?
If not, sketch the requirements on the other tuples that must at least be added to obtain a correct DB state.

4.6. Does the "union" of two "correct" states (w.r.t. UHPT) return another correct state? More formally:
$\forall \nu \in \text{UHPT} : \forall \nu' \in \text{UHPT} : (\lambda E \in \text{He(UHPT)} : \nu(E) \cup \nu'(E)) \in \text{UHPT}?$

□

4.3 Some Database Functions

In this section we will define 34 relevant DB functions over UHPT. In all cases but one the name of the DB function with respect to the ordered pair of table indices $(\alpha\,;\beta)$ is of the form "H $\alpha\beta$".

Hspsp $= \lambda v \in \text{UHPT}: \{(t\,;u) \in v(\text{SP}) \times v(\text{SP}) \mid t(\text{LOC}) = u(\text{IDNR})\}$

Hempemp $= \lambda v \in \text{UHPT}: \{(t\,;u) \in v(\text{EMP}) \times v(\text{EMP}) \mid t(\text{GLNR}) = u(\text{IDNR})\}$

Hadmpat $= \lambda v \in \text{UHPT}: \{(t\,;u) \in v(\text{ADM}) \times v(\text{PAT}) \mid t(\text{PNR}) = u(\text{PNR})\}$

Hptpat $= \lambda v \in \text{UHPT}: \{(t\,;u) \in v(\text{PT}) \times v(\text{PAT}) \mid t(\text{PNR}) = u(\text{PNR})\}$

Hmdppat $= \lambda v \in \text{UHPT}: \{(t\,;u) \in v(\text{MDP}) \times v(\text{PAT}) \mid t(\text{PNR}) = u(\text{PNR})\}$

Hdptsm $= \lambda v \in \text{UHPT}: \{(t\,;u) \in v(\text{DPT}) \times v(\text{SM}) \mid t(\text{MNNR}) = u(\text{IDNR})\}$

Hptsp $= \lambda v \in \text{UHPT}: \{(t\,;u) \in v(\text{PT}) \times v(\text{SP}) \mid t(\text{IDNR}) = u(\text{IDNR})\}$

Hptspa $= \lambda v \in \text{UHPT}: \{(t\,;u) \in v(\text{PT}) \times v(\text{SP}) \mid t(\text{ASNR}) = u(\text{IDNR})\}$

Hadmsp $= \lambda v \in \text{UHPT}: \{(t\,;u) \in v(\text{ADM}) \times v(\text{SP}) \mid t(\text{IDNR}) = u(\text{IDNR})\}$

Hreasp $= \lambda v \in \text{UHPT}: \{(t\,;u) \in v(\text{REA}) \times v(\text{SP}) \mid t(\text{IDNR}) = u(\text{IDNR})\}$

Hmdpsp $= \lambda v \in \text{UHPT}: \{(t\,;u) \in v(\text{MDP}) \times v(\text{SP}) \mid t(\text{IDNR}) = u(\text{IDNR})\}$

Hceemp $= \lambda v \in \text{UHPT}: \{(t\,;u) \in v(\text{CE}) \times v(\text{EMP}) \mid t(\text{IDNR}) = u(\text{IDNR})\}$

Hmunnmp $= \lambda v \in \text{UHPT}: \{(t\,;u) \in v(\text{MUN}) \times v(\text{NMP}) \mid t(\text{CPRS}) = u(\text{IDNR})\}$

Hmungp $= \lambda v \in \text{UHPT}: \{(t\,;u) \in v(\text{MUN}) \times v(\text{GP}) \mid t(\text{GPOD}) = u(\text{NAGP})\}$

Hpatgp $= \lambda v \in \text{UHPT}: \{(t\,;u) \in v(\text{PAT}) \times v(\text{GP}) \mid t(\text{GPID}) = u(\text{GPID})\}$

Hcegp $= \lambda v \in \text{UHPT}: \{(t\,;u) \in v(\text{CE}) \times v(\text{GP}) \mid t(\text{GPID}) = u(\text{GPID})\}$

Hsmdpt $= \lambda v \in \text{UHPT}: \{(t\,;u) \in v(\text{SM}) \times v(\text{DPT}) \mid t(\text{DNR}) = u(\text{DNR})\}$

Hrmdpt $= \lambda v \in \text{UHPT}: \{(t\,;u) \in v(\text{RM}) \times v(\text{DPT}) \mid t(\text{DNR}) = u(\text{DNR})\}$

Hptttp $= \lambda v \in \text{UHPT}: \{(t\,;u) \in v(\text{PT}) \times v(\text{TTP}) \mid t(\text{TCD}) = u(\text{TCD})\}$

Hmdpmed $= \lambda v \in \text{UHPT}: \{(t\,;u) \in v(\text{MDP}) \times v(\text{MED}) \mid t(\text{MCD}) = u(\text{MCD})\}$

Hadmrm $= \lambda v \in \text{UHPT}: \{(t\,;u) \in v(\text{ADM}) \times v(\text{RM}) \mid t(\text{RNR}) = u(\text{RNR})\}$

Htrfrm $= \lambda v \in \text{UHPT}: \{(t\,;u) \in v(\text{TRF}) \times v(\text{RM}) \mid t(\text{RNR}) = u(\text{RNR})\}$

Hptrm $= \lambda v \in \text{UHPT}: \{(t\,;u) \in v(\text{PT}) \times v(\text{RM}) \mid t(\text{RNR}) = u(\text{RNR})\}$

Hspsm $= \lambda v \in \text{UHPT}: \{(t\,;u) \in v(\text{SP}) \times v(\text{SM}) \mid t(\text{IDNR}) = u(\text{IDNR})\}$

Hempsm $= \lambda v \in \text{UHPT}: \{(t\,;u) \in v(\text{EMP}) \times v(\text{SM}) \mid t(\text{IDNR}) = u(\text{IDNR})\}$

Hmpemp $= \lambda v \in \text{UHPT}: \{(t\,;u) \in v(\text{MP}) \times v(\text{EMP}) \mid t(\text{IDNR}) = u(\text{IDNR})\}$

Hnmpemp $= \lambda v \in \text{UHPT}: \{(t\,;u) \in v(\text{NMP}) \times v(\text{EMP}) \mid t(\text{IDNR}) = u(\text{IDNR})\}$

Hdptemp $= \lambda v \in \text{UHPT}: \{(t\,;u) \in v(\text{DPT}) \times v(\text{EMP}) \mid t(\text{AMNR}) = u(\text{IDNR})\}$

Hdisadm $= \lambda v \in \text{UHPT}: \{(t\,;u) \in v(\text{DIS}) \times v(\text{ADM}) \mid t \upharpoonright \{\text{PNR, ADMD}\} = u \upharpoonright \{\text{PNR,ADMD}\}\}$

Hpatmun $= \lambda v \in \text{UHPT}: \{(t\,;u) \in v(\text{PAT}) \times v(\text{MUN}) \mid t(\text{NAZC})\,(\text{CTY}) = u(\text{CTY})\}$

Hgpmun $= \lambda v \in \text{UHPT}: \{(t\,;u) \in v(\text{GP}) \times v(\text{MUN}) \mid t(\text{NAGP})\,(\text{CTY}) = u(\text{CTY})\}$

Hempmun $= \lambda v \in \text{UHPT}: \{(t\,;u) \in v(\text{EMP}) \times v(\text{MUN}) \mid \exists m \in v(\text{SM}): m(\text{IDNR}) = t(\text{IDNR})$ and $m(\text{NAZC})\,(\text{CTY}) = u(\text{CTY})\}$

Hreaadm $= \lambda v \in \text{UHPT}: \{(t\,;u) \in v(\text{REA}) \times v(\text{ADM}) \mid t(\text{PNR}) = u(\text{PNR})$ and
$u(\text{ADMD}) < t(\text{BDAT})$ and
if $u(\text{DISC}) =$ 'YES'
then $t(\text{BDAT}) \leq u(\text{DISD})\}$

Htrfadm $= \lambda v \in \text{UHPT}: \{(t\,;u) \in v(\text{TRF}) \times v(\text{ADM}) \mid t(\text{PNR}) = u(\text{PNR})$ and
$u(\text{ADMD}) < t(\text{BDAT})$ and
if $u(\text{DISC}) =$ 'YES'
then $t(\text{BDAT}) \leq u(\text{DISD})\}$

The following figure shows for each of the DB functions H defined above, from where to where the function $H(v)$ "runs" in state v. In view of the systematic naming of these DB functions, this figure (as opposed to Figure 2.11) does not contain the names of the DB functions concerned, but the most important constraints for the existence of those functions instead. The injective functions mentioned in Exercise 4.9 have been represented by a bold arrow.

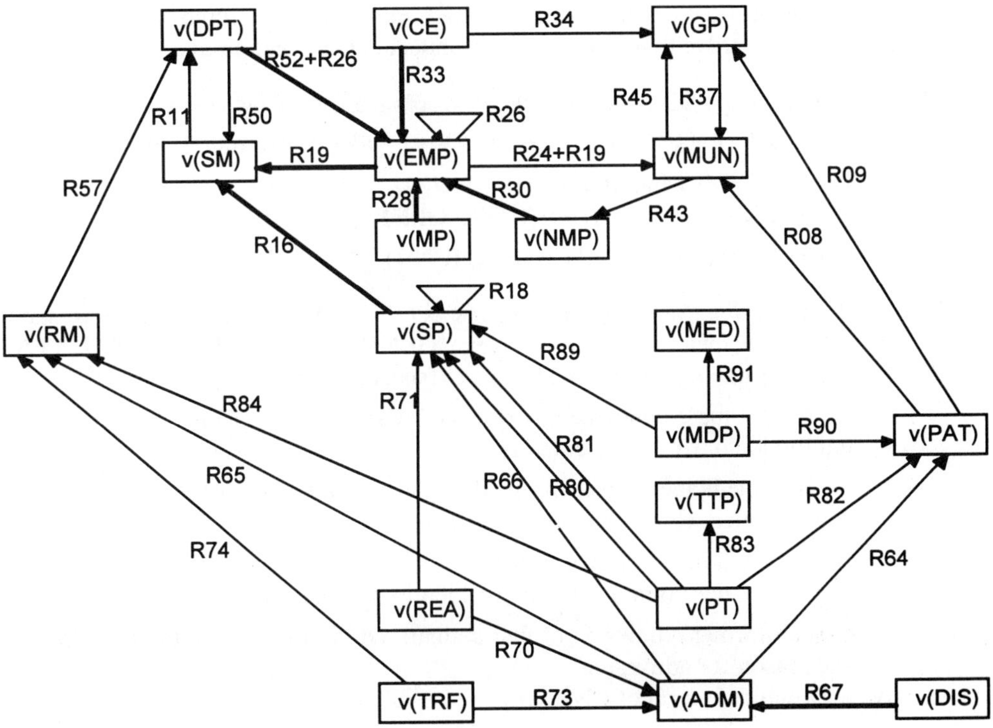

Figure 4.2: The constraints that induce our 34 DB functions

EXERCISES

4.7. Prove that the functions defined above are indeed DB functions over UHPT. (We note that we divided these 34 functions by means of empty lines into six groups, on the basis of the argumentations to be given here.)

4.8. Let Hpatgp2 = $\lambda\, v \in$ UHPT: $\{(t\,;u) \in v(\text{PAT}) \times v(\text{GP}) \mid t(\text{NAGP}) = u(\text{NAGP})\}$.
Prove that Hpatgp2 = Hpatgp.

4.9. Prove that for each $v \in$ UHPT the following functions are injective:
Hdptemp(v), Hmpemp(v), Hnmpemp(v), Hdisadm(v), Hspsm(v), Hceemp(v), Hempsm(v).

4.10. Give a formal definition of the DB function over UHPT that in each state assigns to each tuple of a compulsorily insured employee the tuple of his or her residence, and prove that this function is indeed a DB function over UHPT.

4.11. Let $v \in$ UHPT be a DB state; describe in words the following sets:

(a) $(((v(\text{PT}) \upharpoonright \{\text{PNR, BDAT}\}) \bowtie v(\text{TRF})) \upharpoonright \{\text{PNR}\}) \bowtie \text{rng}(\text{Hmdppat}(v))$.

(b) $\{t \mid t \in v(\text{EMP}) \text{ and } t(\text{GLNR}) = t(\text{IDNR})\} \upharpoonright \{\text{IDNR}\}$
$\quad - (v(\text{EMP}) \bowtie v(\text{CE})) \infty \{(\text{IDNR; GLNR})\}$.

(c) $((v(\text{PT}) \infty \{(\text{LOC; ASNR}), (\text{IDNR; IDNR})\}) \bowtie v(\text{SP})) \upharpoonright \{\text{IDNR}\}$.

4.12. By CNR(v,t), *the (concise) nursing report* of a patient tuple t in DB state $v \in$ UHPT, we mean a function over {GENDATA, MDPDATA, PTDATA, ADMDATA} having the following values (successively):

- the patient tuple concerned, "extended" with the (two) phone numbers of the family doctor of the patient,
- of each medicine dispensing to that patient: medicine code, starting date, daily frequency, and the number of units at a time,
- of each treatment of that patient: treatment code, treatment name, serial number, date of treatment, and the identity number of the treating specialist,
- of each former admission of that patient: admission date, date of discharge, and reason for admission.

Give a formal definition of CNR(v,t).

□

CHAPTER 5

Dynamic Constraints

5.1 Transition Relations

By defining a DB universe U, we establish which *states* are formally allowed in an organization. In general, however, not all state *transitions* between those (in itself) allowed states are admissible in that organization. We can establish the set of admissible transitions by means of a subset R of $U \times U$, having the following intuitive meaning:

$(v\,;\,v') \in R \iff$ the direct transition from state v to state v' is allowed.

If $(v\,;\,v') \notin R$ then it might still be possible that v' is *indirectly* reachable from v, namely if $(v\,;\,v') \in \text{Tcl}(R)$, that is, if v' is reachable from v via a number of allowed intermediate steps (cf. Definition 23 on page 16).

An element of $U \times U$ is called a *transition within U*. A set of admissible transitions for the DB universe U is called a *transition relation on U*. In more general terms:

DEFINITION 5.1:
If U is a set, then:

(a) p is a **transition within** U $\quad \overset{D}{\iff} p \in U \times U$;

(b) R is a **transition relation on** U $\quad \overset{D}{\iff} R \subseteq U \times U$.

Usually, the transition from each state $v \in U$ to v itself should be allowed. Such a "trivial" transition might arise when we try to delete a tuple that appears not to occur in v. In short, usually we want such a transition relation R to be *reflexive on U*, i.e. $\forall v \in U : (v\,;v) \in R$.

EXAMPLE 5.1:

Suppose that in the organization with the DB universe EXU from Example 1.3, also described below, the following requirements should hold:

(DC1) Existing department numbers must not expire (although, for example, the name of a department is allowed to change).

(DC2) An employee must always remain within the same department.

(DC3) Salaries of employees must not decrease.

In order to formalize the constraints (DC2) and (DC3), we will assume that "in the course of time" an employee retains the same identity number. These constraints can be formally represented by the transition relation EXR on EXU, as defined below. (For sake of completeness we will also repeat the definition of the DB universe EXU.)

$$\begin{aligned}\text{FE} = \{&(\text{NO} \ ; \mathbb{N}),\\ &(\text{NAME} \ ; \text{Chs}(40)),\\ &(\text{SAL} \ ; \mathbb{N}),\\ &(\text{SEX} \ ; \{\text{'M'}, \text{'F'}\}),\\ &(\text{DEPNO}; [1 \,..\, 99])\};\end{aligned}$$

$$\begin{aligned}\text{FD} = \{&(\text{DNO} \ ; \mathbb{N}),\\ &(\text{NAME} \ ; \text{Chs}(45)),\\ &(\text{MANNO} \ ; \mathbb{N})\};\end{aligned}$$

$$\text{WE} = \{T \mid T \subseteq \Pi(\text{FE}) \text{ and } \{\text{NO}\} \text{ is u.i. in } T\};$$

$$\text{WD} = \{T \mid T \subseteq \Pi(\text{FD}) \text{ and } \{\text{DNO}\} \text{ is u.i. in } T \text{ and } \{\text{NAME}\} \text{ is u.i. in } T\};$$

$$\begin{aligned}\text{HF} = \{&(\text{EMPL} \ ; \text{WE}),\\ &(\text{DEP} \ ; \text{WD})\};\end{aligned}$$

$$\begin{aligned}\text{EXU} = \{v \mid\ & v \in \Pi(\text{HF}) \text{ and}\\ & \{(\text{DEPNO}; \text{DNO})\} \text{ connects } v(\text{EMPL}) \text{ with } v(\text{DEP}) \text{ and}\\ & \{(\text{MANNO}; \text{NO})\} \text{ connects } v(\text{DEP}) \text{ with } v(\text{EMPL})\};\end{aligned}$$

$$\begin{aligned}\text{EXR} = \{(v\,;v') \mid\ & (v\,;v') \in \text{EXU} \times \text{EXU} \text{ and}\\ & v(\text{DEP}) \Vdash \{\text{DNO}\} \subseteq v'(\text{DEP}) \Vdash \{\text{DNO}\} \text{ and} && \text{(DC1)}\\ & \forall t \in v(\text{EMPL}) \text{: } \forall t' \in v'(\text{EMPL})\text{:}\\ & [\text{if } t(\text{NO}) = t'(\text{NO}) \text{ then } (t(\text{DEPNO}) = t'(\text{DEPNO}) && \text{(DC2)}\\ & \qquad \text{and } t(\text{SAL}) \leq t'(\text{SAL}))]\} && \text{(DC3)}\end{aligned}$$

□ Example 5.1.

The requirements on the *states* in an organization are called *static constraints*, and the requirements on the *transitions* are called *dynamic constraints*.

We note that it is sometimes inconvenient to treat dynamic constraints as "ironclad rules". After all, the situation might arise that in the end a certain transaction appeared to be erroneous or unintentional, yet cannot be undone because of the dynamic constraints. If for example department numbers (or order numbers) that are already present must not expire at any time, then the erroneous addition of a department (or an order) cannot be undone. We say in this case that the transition is *irreversible*:

DEFINITION 5.2:
If $(x\,;y)$ is an ordered pair and R is a set of ordered pairs, then:

(a) $(x\,;y)$ is **reversible in R** $\overset{D}{\Longleftrightarrow}$ $(y\,;x) \in \text{Tcl}(R)$;

(b) $(x\,;y)$ is **irreversible in R** $\overset{D}{\Longleftrightarrow}$ $(y\,;x) \notin \text{Tcl}(R)$.

If R contains only reversible elements, then R itself is also called reversible:

DEFINITION 5.3:
If R is a set of ordered pairs, then:
R is **reversible** $\overset{D}{\Longleftrightarrow} \forall p \in R : p$ is reversible in R.

In many cases of non-reversible transition relations, a dynamic constraint is not used as a "law", but rather as a warning ("Do you *really* want this?") or as a condition pertaining to special authorization required to carry out the modification. In these cases this means that these dynamic constraints cannot be used as genuine transition invariants.

In the following example we discuss some general forms of dynamic constraints. Each general form will be illustrated by EXU or EXR (cf. Example 5.1).

EXAMPLE 5.2:

We begin with a DB skeleton g, a DB universe U over g, $E \in \text{dom}(g)$, $S \subseteq g(E)$, $B \subseteq g(E)$, $C \subseteq g(E)$, and $a \in g(E)$, where the a-values for E are numbers. We will express each form of constraint in terms of an arbitrary transition $(v\,;v')$ within U.

(V1) The E-table is *cumulative*, i.e., no E-data will be deleted or modified. In brief, no E-tuples must expire:

$$v(E) \subseteq v'(E).$$

It is interesting to note that this dynamic constraint can also be regarded as a connection requirement concerning two different "points in time":

id (g(E)) connects $v(E)$ with $v'(E)$.

This would be quite a severe demand for E = DEP in EXU, implying that a department (number) must not expire, that the corresponding department name must not be altered, and also that the manager of that department must not be replaced. In fact the insertion of completely new departments is the

only allowed modification of the department-table.
If the E-table is intended for logging activities for example, then this severe demand of cumulativity can be realistic, however.

(V2) No single combination of values of *primary* attributes - i.e. attributes belonging to a minimal key (see the definitions 2.13 and 2.19) - may expire in the E-table:

id(Prim (E, U)) connects $v(E)$ with $v'(E)$.

For E = DEP in EXU this means:

{DNO, NAME} connects v(DEP) with v'(DEP).

In other words, a department number should not expire and the corresponding department name may not change; however, the manager can be replaced (and new departments can also be added).

Note that the requirement (V1) implies the requirement (V2).

(V3) The E-table is *cumulative with respect to S*, that is, no S-values are allowed to expire:

$v(E) \mathbin{\|\!\upharpoonright} S \subseteq v'(E) \mathbin{\|\!\upharpoonright} S$.

Again, this can be rephrased as a connection requirement:

id(S) connects $v(E)$ with $v'(E)$.

An example of a dynamic constraint of this form is the requirement (DC1) from Example 5.1.

If S contains only primary attributes, e.g., if S is a minimal key of E in U, then $S \subseteq \text{Prim}(E, U)$; in that case the requirement (V2) implies the requirement (V3).

(V4) For each B-value remaining in the E-table, the corresponding C-values must remain constant:

$\forall t \in v(E) : \forall t' \in v'(E)$: if $t \upharpoonright B = t' \upharpoonright B$ then $t \upharpoonright C = t' \upharpoonright C$.

The requirement (DC2) from Example 5.1 is a special case of this form. (Take U = EXU, E = EMPL, B = {NO} and C = {DEPNO}.)

If B is a key of E in U and $S = B \cup C$ in (V3), then that requirement (V3) implies the requirement (V4).

(V5) The a-value of each E-tuple in the new state must be greater than or equal to the a-value of each E-tuple with the same S-value in the old state:

$\forall t \in v(E) : \forall t' \in v'(E)$: if $t \upharpoonright S = t' \upharpoonright S$ then $t(a) \leq t'(a)$.

In this form, S is usually a key of E in U, as is for example the case in the requirement (DC3) in Example 5.1.

If $B = S$ and $C = \{a\}$ in (V4), then that requirement (V4) implies the requirement (V5).

(V6) The number of E-tuples is not allowed to decrease:

$| v(E) | \leq | v'(E) |$.

For E = DEP in EXU this would mean that departments cannot expire all of a sudden, although they can apparently be replaced by other departments.

If S in (V3) is a key of E in U, then the requirement (V3) implies the requirement (V6).

□ Example 5.2.

We noticed in examples 5.1 and 5.2 that sometimes one of the minimal keys of E in U plays a special role. The intuition behind this is that in the course of time the values for that special key continue to correspond one-to-one to the "real world" objects they intend to represent. Such a special minimal key is sometimes called a *primary key*. The other minimal keys are called *alternate keys* in this regard. Although in the literature the distinction between primary keys and alternate keys is usually made on the basis of other (often vague) criteria, the reason just mentioned is in our view the most significant argument for such a distinction. This topic is discussed in more depth in for example Chapter 3 of [Da 86].

We also noticed in Example 5.2 that the concept of a connection is useful not only for the formulation of static constraints, but for the formulation of dynamic constraints as well. In those cases the connecting attribute transformation is obviously an identity function.

For the class of dynamic constraints encountered in (V4) of Example 5.2, we shall introduce special names and notations. In the case below we will therefore call *C transition dependent on B at* $(T\,;T')$, by analogy to momentary dependency.

DEFINITION 5.4:
If A, B, and C are sets and T and T' are tables over A, then:
$B \overset{\sim}{\rightarrow} C$ **at** $(T\,;T') \overset{D}{\Longleftrightarrow} \forall t \in T : \forall t' \in T'$: if $t \upharpoonright B = t' \upharpoonright B$ then $t \upharpoonright C = t' \upharpoonright C$.

The requirement (V4) in Example 5.2 can now be written as: $B \tilde{\rightarrow} C$ at $(v(E)\,;\,v'(E))$.

The following lemma, the analogon to Lemma 2.7, describes some basic properties of transition dependency.

LEMMA 5.1:

If A is a set and T and T' are tables over A, and $B \subseteq A$ and $C \subseteq A$ and $D \subseteq A$, then:

(a) if $C \subseteq B$ then $B \tilde{\rightarrow} C$ at $(T\,;\,T')$;

(b) if $B \tilde{\rightarrow} C$ at $(T\,;\,T')$ and $C \tilde{\rightarrow} D$ at $(T\,;\,T')$ then $B \tilde{\rightarrow} D$ at $(T\,;\,T')$;

(c) $B \tilde{\rightarrow} C$ at $(T\,;\,T')$ iff $\forall c \in C : B \tilde{\rightarrow} \{c\}$ at $(T\,;\,T')$.

Lemma 5.2 relates transition dependency to momentary dependency (and in (c) to itself).

LEMMA 5.2:

If A is a set and T and T' are tables over A, and $B \subseteq A$ and $C \subseteq A$, then:

(a) $B \rightarrow C$ in T $\iff$ $B \tilde{\rightarrow} C$ at $(T\,;\,T)$;

(b) $B \rightarrow C$ in $T \cup T'$ $\iff$ $B \tilde{\rightarrow} C$ at $(T\,;\,T')$ and $B \rightarrow C$ in T and $B \rightarrow C$ in T';

(c) $B \tilde{\rightarrow} C$ at $(T\,;\,T')$ $\iff$ $B \tilde{\rightarrow} C$ at $(T'\,;\,T)$.

The proofs of these lemmas are left to the reader (see the exercises below). To illustrate part (b) of Lemma 5.2, we note that in Example 5.1 the dynamic constraint DC2 together with the uniqueness condition in the definition of WE are equivalent to the *dynamic* constraint that $\{\text{NO}\} \rightarrow \{\text{DEPNO}\}$ in $v(\text{EMPL}) \cup v'(\text{EMPL})$.

We would like to define the concept of transition dependency also (and particularly) at the level of transition relations: In the case below we will call *C constantly dependent on B in E at R*.

DEFINITION 5.5:

If g is a set function and U is a DB universe over g, and $E \in \text{dom}(g)$ and B and C are sets and $R \subseteq U \times U$, then:

$B \tilde{\rightarrow} C$ **in** E **at** R $\overset{D}{\Longleftrightarrow} \forall (v\,;\,v') \in R : B \tilde{\rightarrow} C$ at $(v(E)\,;\,v'(E))$.

A straightforward yet important observation is that for reflexive transition relations constant dependency implies permanent dependency:

THEOREM 5.1:

If g is a set function and U is a DB universe over g, and $E \in \text{dom}(g)$ and $B \subseteq g(E)$ and $C \subseteq g(E)$ and $R \subseteq U \times U$, then:

if $B \tilde{\rightarrow} C$ in E at R and R is reflexive on U then $B \hat{\rightarrow} C$ in E of U.

Proof:
We have to prove that $\forall v \in U : B \rightarrow C$ in $v(E)$;

$B \tilde{\rightarrow} C$ in E at R	
$\Leftrightarrow \forall (v\,;v') \in R : B \tilde{\rightarrow} C$ at $(v(E)\,;v'(E))$	(by Definition 5.5)
$\Rightarrow \forall v \in U : B \tilde{\rightarrow} C$ at $(v(E)\,;v(E))$	(since R is reflexive on U)
$\Leftrightarrow \forall v \in U : B \rightarrow C$ in $v(E)$	(by Lemma 5.2 (a))

□

EXERCISES

5.1. Is EXR reflexive on EXU in Example 5.1?

5.2. Consider the addition of the ordered pair (ST; {'U', 'M', 'D', 'W'}) to FE in Example 5.1, where ST stands for status, 'U' for unmarried, 'M' for married, 'D' for divorced and 'W' for widow or widower. Describe in formal terms the requirements that should be added to the definition of EXU.

5.3. Describe in formal terms the following dynamic constraints for a transition $(v\,;v')$ within EXU in Example 5.1.

(a) The number of employees of a department must not increase by more than five persons at a time.

(b) The number of employees of an existing department must not increase by more than five persons at a time.

(c) The number of employees of a manager must not increase by more than five persons at a time.

(d) The number of employees under a newly appointed manager must not exceed five persons.

5.4. (a) Explain why EXR from Example 5.1 is not reversible.

(b) Give (nevertheless) a reversible element $(v\,;v')$ of EXR such that $v \neq v'$.

(c) Does a salary increase of an employee lead to an irreversible transition in EXR?

5.5. In Example 5.2, (V2) through (V6) all end with an implication. Prove those five implications.

5.6. Indicate for each of the six constraint forms (V1) to (V6) in Example 5.2 under which additional conditions (if any) a transition $(v\,;v)$ with $v \in$ EXU satisfies that constraint form.

5.7. Replace the word "expire" by the words "be added" in the descriptions of the requirements in (V1), (V2), and (V3) of Example 5.2, and reformulate these three new requirements using the connection concept.

5.8. Is the requirement (V2) of Example 5.2 equivalent to the statement that no value of a minimal key is allowed to expire?
Give a proof or a counterexample for each of the two implications.

5.9. Prove Lemma 5.1.

5.10. Formulate and prove the analogue of Lemma 2.8.

5.11. If A is a set and T and T' are tables over A and $B \subseteq A$ and $C \subseteq A$, then:

(a) $B \stackrel{\sim}{\rightarrow} C$ at $(\varnothing ; T')$;

(b) $B \stackrel{\sim}{\rightarrow} \varnothing$ at $(T ; T')$;

(c) $\varnothing \stackrel{\sim}{\rightarrow} C$ at $(T ; T')$ iff $T = \varnothing$ or $T' = \varnothing$ or $| T \upharpoonright C \cup T' \upharpoonright C | \leq 1$.

Prove this analogue of Lemma 2.9.

5.12. Prove Lemma 5.2. Also show that it does not necessarily follow from $B \stackrel{\sim}{\rightarrow} C$ at $(T ; T')$ that $B \rightarrow C$ in $T \cup T'$.

5.13. If A is a set and T and T' are tables over A, and $B \subseteq A$ and $C \subseteq A$, then:

(a) if $B \stackrel{\sim}{\rightarrow} C$ at $(T ; T')$, then $B \rightarrow C$ in $(T \bowtie T' \upharpoonright B) \cup (T' \bowtie T \upharpoonright B)$;

(b) if B is u.i. in T and B is u.i. in T', then:
$(B \stackrel{\sim}{\rightarrow} C$ at $(T ; T')$ and $T \upharpoonright B \subseteq T' \upharpoonright B) \Longleftrightarrow T \upharpoonright (B \cup C) \subseteq T' \upharpoonright (B \cup C)$.

Prove this.

5.14. We call a set R of ordered pairs *symmetric* iff $\forall (x ; y) \in R : (y ; x) \in R$.
Now prove the following statement.
If R is a set of ordered pairs, then:

(a) If R is symmetric, then R is reversible.

(b) The following three statements are equivalent:
  (b1) R is reversible;
  (b2) Tcl(R) is reversible;
  (b3) Tcl(R) is symmetric.

(c) If R is reversible, then $\forall p \in$ Tcl(R): p is reversible in R.

□

5.2 A Nontrivial Example of a Transition Relation

To give an impression of the possible (subtle) forms of dynamic constraints appearing in the context of a database universe that is already complex in its own right, we will define in this section a nontrivial transition relation on the database universe UHPT from Chapter 4.

We will start with an informal description of the dynamic constraints, continue with a "semi-formal" intermediate form of some of the more subtle constraints (as an analysis aid), and finish by offering the formal definition of the transition relation RHPT on UHPT. As in Chapter 4 (and in general), it holds for transition relations that an informal description is usually too poor a basis for the unambiguous derivation of the formal definition.

We begin with an informal description of the dynamic constraints for the medical part and the associated administration, immediately followed by those for personnel affairs.

(C00) A department (number) must not expire; the name or the manager or the assistant manager of a department are allowed to change, however.

(C01) All data on medicine prescriptions must remain unaltered in the database.

(C02) All data on patient treatments must also remain unaltered in the database.

(C03) After introduction, the following data on each admission must remain unaltered in the database: patient number, admission date, room number, identity number of the initially responsible specialist, and the data concerning the family doctor of the patient at admission time.

(C04) The other admission data of each completed admission must also remain unaltered in the database, as is the case with the corresponding discharge data.

(C05) Almost all reassignment data must remain unaltered in the database: only the reason for admission may be altered.

(C06) Almost all transfer data must remain unaltered in the database: only *additions* to the nursing comments are allowed. (Already present comments must be neither changed nor removed.) In view of the formalization of this requirement, we refer to the second last paragraph before Definition 22 on page 15.

(C07) A medicine (code) will always remain of the same type.

(C08) A treatment will always remain of the same kind.

(C09) For each patient whose data remain present, the following data must not be altered at any time: place of birth, date of birth, registration date, blood group, and rhesus factor.

(C10) For male patients, the name is never altered.

(C11) The salary, per half workday a week, of an employee must not decrease.

(C12) The sick leave of an employee cannot decrease, with the exception of the moments at which the sick leave is reduced to 0 for *all* employees.

(C13) The unions have achieved that it is not allowed to reduce the number of holidays per year (on the basis of a full-time job) of any nonmedical staff member who is compulsorily insured.

(C14) After changing the data on the number of patients, the previous increase in the number of patients, or the expected increase in the number of patients of a general practitioner, the new "increase in the number of patients during the last year" must be equal to the difference between the new number of patients and the old number of patients of that general practitioner. (Contrary to the situation for the intended yearly modifications mentioned in C12, to be carried out for all employees simultaneously, it must be possible to carry out the alterations referred to in C14 separately for each general practitioner.)

(C15) In order to safeguard the continuity of departments, the management of a department, that is, the manager together with the assistant manager of that department, must not be replaced by two entirely "new" persons in one go. (It is still possible, however, that the manager leaves and that at the same time the assistant manager becomes the new manager of that department.)

As far as the "life cycle" of a room in our hospital is concerned, the following rules and conditions apply.

(C16) All "former" rooms in the new state must already be known in the old state, but not have the status "planned". (A room cannot expire without previously being known, and the data of a planned room that eventually will not occur are simply removed.)

(C17) Each room number having the status "current" never ceases to exist, always retains the same floor space, and never regains the status "planned".

(C18) The type of each current treatment room and nursing room will never be altered. (The types of receptions, stores, and "various" rooms can change, however; they can even become nursing rooms or treatment rooms. On the other hand, if a certain nursing room or treatment room is going to be used for other purposes, it will become a "former" room in our administration, and continue to exist under another room number in our hospital. We note that such administrative constructions are not unusual in practice.)

(C19) The data on all former rooms must continue to exist in the new state, without any modifications.

The only admissible status transitions for a room number (by C16 through C19) can also be represented schematically by Figure 5.1 (where "~" indicates the situation that the room number does not occur in the room-table):

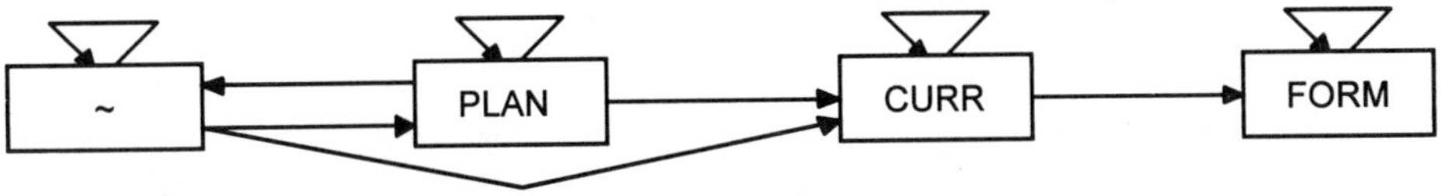

Figure 5.1: The allowed status transitions for a room (number)

The same information can also be represented by the matrix shown in Figure 5.2.

old \ new	~	PLAN	CURR	FORM
~	+	+	+	-
PLAN	+	+	+	-
CURR	-	-	+	+
FORM	-	-	-	+

Figure 5.2: The allowed status transitions represented by a matrix

The reasons for not allowing certain status transitions as well as the conditions on status transitions that *are* allowed are shown in Figure 5.3 by giving the C-numbers concerned. The rectangles in that picture indicate to which cases the mentioned constraints apply. (Here $t \in v(\text{RM})$, $t' \in v'(\text{RM})$ and $t(\text{RNR}) = t'(\text{RNR})$.)

old \ new	~	PLAN	CURR	FORM	
~	+	+	+	-	C16
PLAN	+	+	+	-	
CURR	-	-	+	+	C17 and C18
FORM	-	-	-	+	C19

Figure 5.3: The relevant constraints

Ad C17: $t(\text{FLSP}) = t'(\text{FLSP})$
Ad C18: if $t(\text{TPRM}) \in$ { 'TRM', 'NRS'} then $t(\text{TPRM}) = t'(\text{TPRM})$
Ad C19: $t = t'$.

Such schematic representations could turn out to be useful when constructing dynamic constraints, as an aid to obtain the eventually sought formulation.

In our hospital, the following rules and conditions apply to the careers of specialists.

(C20) Each specialist occurring in the new state as being not in service, already occurs in the old state having the same locum tenens, the same type of employment, the same specialisms, the same fee per hour, the same department number, and the same internal phone number. (The reason for this is that on leaving the service or while being out of service, these specialist data are no longer to be changed.)

(C21) The data of a specialist remain in the database forever, containing at least the same specialisms as before. (This requirement makes sense, because in data concerning medical actions, in particular concerning admissions, reassignments, patient treatments, and medicine prescriptions, many references are often made to the specialists involved at that time.)

(C22) Since a specialist is always in service on the basis of a contract with a department, a specialist being and remaining in service will always retain the same department number, type of employment, contractual number of hours per week, and number of formally available beds in the new state; furthermore, the fee per hour must not decrease.

(C23) For a transition, the identification numbers for new specialists are the numbers starting from 100 plus the number of specialists *already* known to the database up to (but excluding) 100 plus the *new* number of specialists known to the database.

The dynamic constraints for specialists, C20 through C23, will be represented in the same manner as those for rooms in our hospital. We will begin with a "transition diagram" on the basis of being or not being in service. In Figure 5.4 five cases are distinguished:

(1) entering the service,
(2) remaining in service,
(3) leaving the service,
(4) remaining out of service, and
(5) re-entering the service.

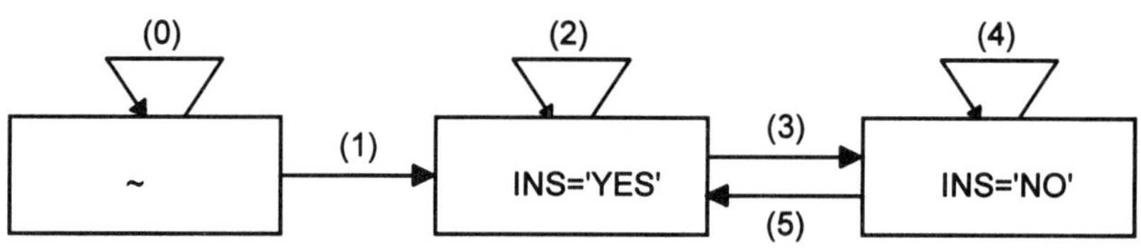

Figure 5.4: The "life cycle" of a specialist

In the matrix representation below, we will use the same numbering as in the preceding diagram. Since the data on a specialist have been spread over two tables, namely the SP-table and the SM-table, we will take $t \in v(\mathrm{SP}) \bowtie v(\mathrm{SM})$, $t' \in v'(\mathrm{SP}) \bowtie v'(\mathrm{SM})$, and $t(\mathrm{IDNR}) = t'(\mathrm{IDNR})$.

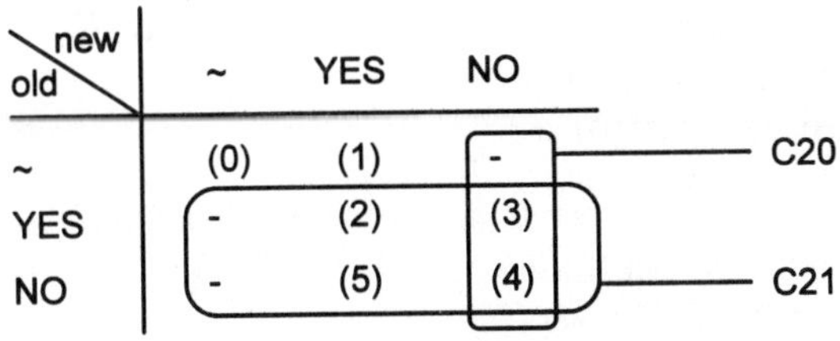

Figure 5.5: The relevant constraints

Ad C20: $t \equiv t'$ on {LOC, TOE, SPEC, FEEH, DNR, ITEL};
see Definition 16 on page 11.
Ad C21: $t(\mathrm{SPEC}) \subseteq t'(\mathrm{SPEC})$.
Ad (2), C22: $t \equiv t'$ on {TOE, HPW, NBD, DNR} and $t(\mathrm{FEEH}) \leq t'(\mathrm{FEEH})$.

Requirement C23, referring to case (1) exclusively, is of a somewhat different nature and can be phrased in terms of intervals as follows:

$$\{t'(\mathrm{IDNR}) \mid t' \in v'(\mathrm{SP})\} - \{t(\mathrm{IDNR}) \mid t \in v(\mathrm{SP})\} \subseteq [100 + |v(\mathrm{SP})| \;..\; 100 + |v'(\mathrm{SP})|)$$

We conclude this section with the formal definition of the transition relation RHPT on UHPT, which is determined by the preceding dynamic constraints.

RHPT =
$\{(v\,;v') \mid (v\,;v') \in$ UHPT $\times$ UHPT and
$v(\text{DPT}) \upharpoonright \{\text{DNR}\} \subseteq v'(\text{DPT}) \upharpoonright \{\text{DNR}\}$ and C00
$v(\text{MDP}) \subseteq v'(\text{MDP})$ and C01
$v(\text{PT}) \subseteq v'(\text{PT})$ and C02
id({PNR, ADMD, RNR, IDNR, NAGP}) connects $v(\text{ADM})$ with $v'(\text{ADM})$ and C03
$v(\text{ADM}) \bowtie v(\text{DIS}) \subseteq v'(\text{ADM}) \bowtie v'(\text{DIS})$ and C04
$v(\text{REA}) \ddagger \{\text{ADMR}\} \subseteq v'(\text{REA}) \ddagger \{\text{ADMR}\}$ and C05
$[\forall t \in v(\text{TRF})$: C06
  $\exists t' \in v'(\text{TRF})$: $(t \dagger \{\text{NCOM}\} = t' \dagger \{\text{NCOM}\}$ and $t(\text{NCOM}) \subseteq t'(\text{NCOM}))]$ and "
$\{\text{MCD}\} \overset{\sim}{\rightarrow} \{\text{MTYP}\}$ at $(v(\text{MED}); v'(\text{MED}))$ and C07
$\{\text{TCD}\} \overset{\sim}{\rightarrow} \{\text{TKND}\}$ at $(v(\text{TTP}); v'(\text{TTP}))$ and C08
$\{\text{PNR}\} \overset{\sim}{\rightarrow} \{\text{PLB, DTB, REGD, BLGR, RHF}\}$ at $(v(\text{PAT}); v'(\text{PAT}))$ and C09
$[\forall t \in v(\text{PAT}): \forall t' \in v'(\text{PAT})$: if $t(\text{PNR}) = t'(\text{PNR})$ and $t(\text{SEX}) =$ 'M' C10
  then $t(\text{NAZC})(\text{NM}) = t'(\text{NAZC})(\text{NM})]$ and "
$[\forall t \in v(\text{EMP}): \forall t' \in v'(\text{EMP})$: if $t(\text{IDNR}) = t'(\text{IDNR})$ C11
  then $t(\text{SAL})/t(\text{NHD}) \leq t'(\text{SAL})/t'(\text{NHD})]$ and "
$[(\forall t \in v(\text{EMP}): \forall t' \in v'(\text{EMP})$: if $t(\text{IDNR}) = t'(\text{IDNR})$ then $t(\text{TSL}) \leq t'(\text{TSL}))$ C12
  or $(\forall t' \in v'(\text{EMP}): t'(\text{TSL}) = 0)]$ and "
$[\forall t \in v(\text{NMP}) \bowtie v(\text{CE}): \forall t' \in v'(\text{NMP})$: if $t(\text{IDNR}) = t'(\text{IDNR})$ C13
  then $t(\text{ENH}) \leq t'(\text{ENH})]$ and "
$[\forall t \in v(\text{GP}): \forall t' \in v'(\text{GP})$: if $t(\text{GPID}) = t'(\text{GPID})$ and C14
  t and t' do not match on {PAT, INCR, EXPI} "
  then $t'(\text{INCR}) = t'(\text{PAT}) - t(\text{PAT})]$ and "
$[\forall t \in v(\text{DPT}): \forall t' \in v'(\text{DPT})$: if $t(\text{DNR}) = t'(\text{DNR})$ C15
  then $\{t(\text{MNNR}), t(\text{AMNR})\} \cap$ "
  $\{t'(\text{MNNR}), t'(\text{AMNR})\} \neq \varnothing]$ and "
id({RNR}) connects C16
  $\{t' \in v'(\text{RM}) \mid t'(\text{STAT}) =$ 'FORM'$\}$ with $\{t \in v(\text{RM}) \mid t(\text{STAT}) \neq$ 'PLAN'$\}$ and "
id({RNR, FLSP}) connects C17
  $\{t \in v(\text{RM}) \mid t(\text{STAT}) =$ 'CURR'$\}$ with $\{t' \in v'(\text{RM}) \mid t'(\text{STAT}) \neq$ 'PLAN'$\}$ and "
id({RNR, TPRM}) connects C18
  $\{t \in v(\text{RM}) \mid t(\text{STAT}) =$ 'CURR' and $t(\text{TPRM}) \in \{$ 'TRM', 'NRS'$\}\}$ with $v'(\text{RM})$ and "
  $\{t \in v(\text{RM}) \mid t(\text{STAT}) =$ 'FORM'$\} \subseteq v'(\text{RM})$ and C19
id({IDNR, LOC, TOE, SPEC, FEEH, DNR, ITEL}) connects C20
  $\{t' \in v'(\text{SP}) \bowtie v'(\text{SM}) \mid t'(\text{INS}) =$ 'NO'$\}$ with $v(\text{SP}) \bowtie v(\text{SM})$ and "
$[\forall t \in v(\text{SP}) \bowtie v(\text{SM}): \exists t' \in v'(\text{SP}) \bowtie v'(\text{SM})$:
  $(t(\text{IDNR}) = t'(\text{IDNR})$ and $t(\text{SPEC}) \subseteq t'(\text{SPEC})$ and C21
  if $t(\text{INS}) = t'(\text{INS}) =$ 'YES' C22
  then $(t(\text{FEEH}) \leq t'(\text{FEEH})$ and "
    t and t' match on {TOE, HPW, NBD, DNR}))] and "
$\{t'(\text{IDNR}) \mid t' \in v'(\text{SP})\} - \{t(\text{IDNR}) \mid t \in v(\text{SP})\}$ C23
  $\subseteq [100 + |v(\text{SP})| \,..\, 100 + |v'(\text{SP})|)\}$. "

EXERCISES

5.15. (a) Is RHPT reflexive on UHPT?
(b) Is RHPT reversible?
Explain your answers.

5.16. In the case of RHPT, does all SP-data of specialists who during a transition are and remain out of service, remain unaltered? If so, mention the constraints from which this follows; if not, mention *all* SP-attributes whose values are liable to change in that case.

5.17. Check truth or falsity in UHPT or RHPT for each of the following statements. Mention for each true statement the constraint(s) from which this statement follows; indicate for each other statement whether it is a static or dynamic constraint, and give its formal representation.

(a) A specialist is never permitted to change his or her department.

(b) As long as an employee is compulsorily insured, this person is not allowed to change to another type of department.

(c) Patients ever having undergone an admission, a treatment, or a medicine dispensing, will never be removed from the database.

(d) Treatments that have ever been carried out, and medicines that have ever been prescribed, do not expire.

(e) The number of staff members in service does not increase.

(f) Only in the case of the latest reassignment of a patient, can the reason for admission still be adapted.

(g) Only in the case of the latest reassignment of a still admitted patient, can the reason for admission still be adapted.

5.18. Contrive some other dynamic constraints over UHPT and represent them both formally and informally.

5.19. Prove that $\{t'(\text{IDNR}) \mid t' \in v'(\text{SP})\} = [100 \,..\, 100 + \mid v'(\text{SP}) \mid)$ for each $v' \in$ UHPT, that according to RHPT is reachable from the empty state, i.e., for each $v' \in$ UHPT for which $(\lambda E \in \text{dom(GHPT)}: \varnothing \,;\, v') \in$ Tcl(RHPT).
(Hint: use mathematical induction.)

□

CHAPTER 6

Retrieval

By retrieval, i.e. querying a database, we mean, informally speaking, requesting for data of any (DB) state of the (DB) universe concerned. More specifically, a query can be conceived of as a function that assigns to each state of the universe concerned an "answer", for example a table, a number or a yes/no-answer.

We distinguish between *formulating*, *posing*, and *executing* a query.

- The *formulation* of a query amounts to the specification of a function over the universe under consideration, that is, a function that assigns to each state that which is requested.
- *Posing* a query q to a database in state v boils down to the application of the function q to the argument v. We call $q(v)$ the *answer* to query q in state v.
- By the *computation* of the answer to the query q in state v we mean the determination of the "simplest" representation of the answer $q(v)$.

In an automated environment, the task of *formulating* queries is typically performed by designers, the application builders and the more experienced users, whereas *posing* queries is mainly the responsibility of the end-users, and the *computation* of queries should be taken care of by the (database management) system in question.

In this chapter we will mainly concentrate on the *formulation* of queries.

6.1 Queries

In the introduction we already informally described what we mean by a query. We will now give a formal definition of this concept. In that definition, the universe can be any set.

DEFINITION 6.1:
If U is a set, then:
q is a **query over** $U \overset{D}{\Longleftrightarrow} q$ is a function over U.

EXAMPLE 6.1:

We give two examples of queries, one over a set of tables, the other over a DB universe.

1. The query "Give the number of persons not living in their place of birth" over the set of tables WP from Example 2.8 can be formally represented as follows:

$$\lambda T \in \text{WP} : \mid \{t \in T \mid t(\text{TOWN}) \neq t(\text{BPL})\} \mid$$

The answer to this query in the state depicted in Figure 2.7 is clearly 3.

2. The analogous query "Give the number of patients not living in their place of birth" over the DB universe UHPT from Chapter 4 can be formally represented as follows:

$$\lambda v \in \text{UHPT} : \mid \{t \in v(\text{PAT}) \mid t(\text{NAZC})\,(\text{CTY}) \neq t(\text{PLB})\} \mid$$

□ Example 6.1.

Using the concepts and notations introduced so far, we are in fact capable of specifying a large variety of queries. To give an impression, we will treat several illustrative classes of queries in the following examples (K1, K2, etc.). Under (A) the general form will be given, under (B) a specific example (within the context of the semantically rich DB universe UHPT from Chapter 4), and possibly under (C) a few remarks. (Nevertheless, the informal description under (B) does not always suggest that a query of the form under (A) is meant.) Some queries under (B) and in the exercises are variations of queries originally posed in Chapter 8 of [Re 82]. It can be quite convenient in practice to be able to fall back on different formal representations of the same query, for example because a certain (in itself correct) solution is not directly expressible in the query language of the DBMS at hand, or because another formulation could well lead to a significantly shorter response time. We will therefore sometimes give more than one solution under (A). Under (B) we will always use only one of these numbered variants for the specific UHPT-example.

In the general forms of the examples as mentioned under (A), we start with a DB universe U over a DB skeleton g, table indices E and E' such that $\{a,b,c,d,e\} \subseteq g(E)$, $A \subseteq g(E)$ and $d' \in g(E')$, $B \subseteq g(E) \cap g(E')$, a DB function H over U w.r.t. $(E\,;E')$, and a DB function G over U w.r.t. $(E'\,;E)$.

Each of the queries in Example 6.2 concerns only one table.

EXAMPLE 6.2:

K1: (A) Give all of the data from the *E*-table.

(1) $\lambda v \in U : v(E)$

(B) Give the data of all municipalities in the region.

(1) $\lambda v \in \text{UHPT} : v(\text{MUN})$

(C) Apparently, the answer results in a table.

K2: (A) Give the *A*-values of all *E*-tuples.

(1) $\lambda v \in U : v(E) \Vert\!\upharpoonright A$

(2) $\lambda v \in U : \{t \upharpoonright A \mid t \in v(E)\}$

(B) Give code, name, and number of units in stock of each medicine.

(1) $\lambda v \in \text{UHPT} : v(\text{MED}) \Vert\!\upharpoonright \{\text{MCD, MNM, NST}\}$

(C) If the set of attributes *A* in (A) is not a key of *E* in *U*, then in some states *v* the number of tuples in the answer might be smaller than the number of tuples in the table *v*(*E*) itself. For instance, in case of the query "Give each type of medicine", *A* equals {MTYP}, and {MTYP} is not a key of MED in UHPT. In a state *v* in which there are different medicine-tuples having the same type of medicine, the answer will therefore contain a smaller number of tuples than *v*(MED) itself.

K3: (A) Give the *A*-values of each *E*-tuple of which the *a*-value is equal to *x* or the *b*-value is not equal to *y*.

(1) $\lambda v \in U : \{t \in v(E) \mid t(a) = x \text{ or } t(b) \neq y\} \Vert\!\upharpoonright A$

(2) $\lambda v \in U : \{t \upharpoonright A \mid t \in v(E) \text{ and } (t(a) = x \text{ or } t(b) \neq y)\}$

(3) $\lambda v \in U : \{t \upharpoonright A \mid t \in v(E) \text{ and (if } t(b) = y \text{ then } t(a) = x)\}$

(4) $\lambda v \in U : (\{t \in v(E) \mid t(a) = x\} \cup \{t \in v(E) \mid t(b) \neq y\}) \Vert\!\upharpoonright A$

(5) $\lambda v \in U : (\{t \in v(E) \mid t(a) = x\} \Vert\!\upharpoonright A) \cup$
$(\{t \in v(E) \mid t(b) \neq y\} \Vert\!\upharpoonright A)$

(6) $\lambda v \in U : \{t \upharpoonright A \mid t \in v(E) \text{ and } t(a) = x\} \cup$
$\{t \upharpoonright A \mid t \in v(E) \text{ and } t(b) \neq y\}$

(B) Give patient number, blood group, and rhesus factor of all female patients and of all patients having children.

(6) $\lambda v \in \text{UHPT}$:
$\{t \upharpoonright \{\text{PNR, BLGR, RHF}\} \mid t \in v(\text{PAT}) \text{ and } t(\text{SEX}) = \text{'F'}\} \cup$
$\{t \upharpoonright \{\text{PNR, BLGR, RHF}\} \mid t \in v(\text{PAT}) \text{ and } t(\text{PROG}) \neq \varnothing\}$

(C) The solution below, in which *t* is a function over *A*, is only correct if $\{a,b\} \subseteq A$.

(7) $\lambda v \in U : \{t \in v(E) \Vert\!\upharpoonright A \mid t(a) = x \text{ or } t(b) \neq y\}$

As indicated, we gave in (B) a solution in accordance with variant (6) under (A).

K4: (A) Give the number of E-tuples of which the a-value does not occur as b-value in the E-table.

(1) $\lambda v \in U : | \{t \in v(E) \mid t(a) \notin \{t'(b) \mid t' \in v(E)\}\} |$

(2) $\lambda v \in U : | \{t \in v(E) \mid \forall t' \in v(E) : t'(b) \neq t(a)\} |$

(3) $\lambda v \in U : | \{t \in v(E) \mid 0 = | \{t' \in v(E) \mid t'(b) = t(a)\} | \} |$

(B) Give the number of specialists who are not a locum tenens.

(2) $\lambda v \in \text{UHPT} : | \{t \in v(\text{SP}) \mid \forall t' \in v(\text{SP}) : t'(\text{LOC}) \neq t(\text{IDNR})\} |$

(C) If $\{a\}$ is a key of E in U (as is the case in (B), for example), then the following variants are correct as well:

(4) $\lambda v \in U : | \{t(a) \mid t \in v(E) \text{ and } t(a) \notin \{t'(b) \mid t' \in v(E)\}\} |$

(5) $\lambda v \in U : | \{t(a) \mid t \in v(E)\} - \{t'(b) \mid t' \in v(E)\} |$

K5: (A) Give the sum of the product of the a-value and the b-value of all E-tuples whose c-value equals x, y, or z.

(1) $\lambda v \in U : (\Sigma t \in v(E) \text{ and } t(c) \in \{x, y, z\} : t(a) * t(b))$

(B) Give the total price of all medicines of type 'K', 'N' or 'O'.

(1) $\lambda v \in \text{UHPT}$:
$(\Sigma t \in v(\text{MED}) \text{ and } t(\text{MTYP}) \in \{\text{'K'}, \text{'N'}, \text{'O'}\} : t(\text{NST}) * t(\text{PRCU}))$

(C) Just as is the case of the preceding form, the outcome will always result in one single number.

K6: (A) Indicate by 'YES' or 'NO' whether there are more than 1000 E-tuples.

(1) $\{(v; \text{'YES'}) \mid v \in U \text{ and } | v(E) | > 1000\} \cup$
$\{(v; \text{'NO'}) \mid v \in U \text{ and } | v(E) | \leq 1000\}$

(2) $(\lambda v \in U \text{ and } | v(E) | > 1000 : \text{'YES'}) \cup$
$(\lambda v \in U \text{ and } | v(E) | \leq 1000 : \text{'NO'})$

(3) $(\lambda v \in U : \text{'NO'}) \ \theta$
$(\lambda v \in U \text{ and } | v(E) | > 1000 : \text{'YES'})$

(4) $(\lambda v \in U : \text{'YES'}) \ \theta \ (\lambda v \in U \text{ and } | v(E) | \leq 1000 : \text{'NO'})$

(B) Indicate by 'YES' or 'NO' whether there are more than 1000 general practitioners in the region.

(3) $(\lambda v \in \text{UHPT} : \text{'NO'}) \ \theta$
$(\lambda v \in \text{UHPT and } | v(\text{GP}) | > 1000 : \text{'YES'})$

(C) This is an example of a yes/no-question.

K7: (A) Give of each E-tuple the a-value, the b-value, and (under the name α) the product of the c-, d-, and e-value.

(1) $\lambda v \in U : \{ t \restriction \{a, b\} \cup \{(\alpha; t(c) * t(d) * t(e))\} \mid t \in v(E)\}$

(2) $\lambda v \in U : \{\{(a\,;t(a)),\,(b\,;t(b)),\,(\alpha;t(c)*t(d)*t(e))\} \mid t \in v(E)\}$

(B) For all medicine prescriptions give the patient number, the medicine code, and (under the name AM) the prescribed amount.

(1) $\lambda v \in \text{UHPT}:$
$\{t \upharpoonright \{\text{PNR, MCD}\} \cup \{(\text{AM}; t(\text{NUT}) * t(\text{FREQ}) * t(\text{DUR}))\}$
$\mid t \in v(\text{MDP})\}$

(C) For the choice of α we impose the condition that $\alpha \notin \{a\,,b\}$.
Under (A) the answer is in each state a table over $\{a\,,b\,,\alpha\}$.
If $\{a\,,b\}$ is not a key of E in U (as is the case in the example under (B)), then the solutions indicate for each $(a\,;b)$-combination *which* α-values occur, but not *how many times* they occur.

K8: (A) Give each A-combination occurring in the E-table, and (under the name β) the number of times that this combination occurs.

(1) $\lambda v \in U : \{w \cup \{(\beta;\mid \{t \in v(E) \mid t \upharpoonright A = w\} \mid)\} \mid w \in v(E) \Vert\!\upharpoonright A\}$

(B) Give for each treated patient the patient number and (under the name NUMTR) the number of treatments up till now.

(1) $\lambda v \in \text{UHPT} : \{w \cup \{(\text{NUMTR}\,;\mid \{t \in v(\text{PT}) \mid t \upharpoonright \{\text{PNR}\} = w\} \mid)\}$
$\mid w \in v(\text{PT}) \Vert\!\upharpoonright \{\text{PNR}\}\}$

(C) Under (A) we require for the choice of β that $\beta \notin A$; in each state the answer constitutes a table over $A \cup \{\beta\}$.
Suppose that we are also interested in the patients that have never been treated, then w should not "vary over" $v(\text{PT}) \Vert\!\upharpoonright \{\text{PNR}\}$, but over $v(\text{PAT}) \Vert\!\upharpoonright \{\text{PNR}\}$ instead. In that case, the query concerns more than one table.

□ Example 6.2.

As for the queries in Example 6.3, the data each time originates from only one table, yet on the basis of information to be found in other tables.

EXAMPLE 6.3:

K1: (A) Give the A-value of each E-tuple whose a-value is greater than or equal to m and less than n, provided that there is also an E'-tuple having the same B-value.

(1) $\lambda v \in U : \{t \upharpoonright A \mid t \in v(E) \text{ and } m \leq t(a) \text{ and } t(a) < n \text{ and}$
$\exists t' \in v(E') : t' \upharpoonright B = t \upharpoonright B\}$

(2) $\lambda v \in U : \{t \upharpoonright A \mid t \in v(E) \text{ and } t(a) \geq m \text{ and } t(a) < n \text{ and}$
$0 < \mid \{t' \in v(E') \mid t' \upharpoonright B = t \upharpoonright B\} \mid\}$

(3) $\lambda v \in U : (\{t \in v(E) \mid t(a) \in [m\,..\,n)\} \Vert\!\upharpoonright A) \cap$
$(\{t \in v(E) \mid \{t' \in v(E') \mid t' \upharpoonright B = t \upharpoonright B\} \neq \varnothing\} \Vert\!\upharpoonright A)$

(4) $\lambda v \in U : \{t \upharpoonright A \mid t \in v(E) \text{ and } t(a) \in [m \,..\, n) \text{ and}$
$t \upharpoonright B \in v(E') \Vert\!\upharpoonright B\}$

(5) $\lambda v \in U : ((v(E') \Vert\!\upharpoonright B) \bowtie \{t \in v(E) \mid t(a) \in [m \,..\, n)\}) \Vert\!\upharpoonright A$

(6) $\lambda v \in U : \{t \upharpoonright A \mid t \in v(E) \bowtie (v(E') \Vert\!\upharpoonright B) \text{ and } t(a) \in [m \,..\, n)\}$

(B) Give the patient number, date of birth, registration date, and NAZC-data of all admitted or formerly admitted patients born in 1989.

(5) $\lambda v \in$ UHPT : ((v(ADM) $\Vert\!\upharpoonright$ {PNR}) $\bowtie$ {$t \in v$(PAT) | t(DTB) $\in$
[19890101 .. 19900101)}) $\Vert\!\upharpoonright$ {PNR, DTB, REGD, NAZC}

K2: (A) Give under the names α, β, and γ the *a*-, *b*- and *c*-value respectively of each *E*-tuple such that the d'-value of the corresponding E'-tuple is greater than w according to the DB function H.

(1) $\lambda v \in U : \{\{(\alpha ; t(a)), (\beta ; t(b)), (\gamma ; t(c))\}$
$\mid t \in v(E) \text{ and } H(v)\,(t)\,(d') > w\}$

(B) Give under the names PATIENT, DATE and LOCATION the patient number, the date of transfer, and the new room number respectively, of each transfer during an admission that started later than June 10, 1989.

(1) $\lambda v \in$ UHPT : {{(PATIENT ; t(PNR)),
(DATE ; t(BDAT)),
(LOCATION; t(RNR))}
| $t \in v$(TRF) and
Htrfadm(v) (t) (ADMD) > 890610}

(C) Note that we showed here how to "polish up" the heading of the resulting table.
After writing out the definition of the DB function Htrfadm, given in §4.3, we can give the following alternative formulation:

$\lambda v \in$ UHPT : {{(PATIENT ; t(PNR)),
(DATE ; t(BDAT)),
(LOCATION; t(RNR))}
| $t \in v$(TRF) and
$\exists u \in v$(ADM): (t(PNR) = u(PNR) and
t(BDAT) > u(ADMD) and
u(ADMD) > 890610 and
if u(DISC) = 'YES'
then t(BDAT) $\leq$ u(DISD))}

This example makes clear why DB functions are useful when formulating queries. But this should not come as a surprise, considering the fact that DB functions formalize intuitive relationships assumed between tables.

K3: (A) Give the E-tuples that, according to the generalized composition $G \odot H$, refer to themselves (that is, via the E'-table).

(1) $\lambda v \in U : \{t \in v(E) \mid (G \odot H)(v)(t) = t\}$

(2) $\lambda v \in U : \{t \in v(E) \mid (G(v) \circ H(v))(t) = t\}$

(3) $\lambda v \in U : \{t \in v(E) \mid G(v)(H(v)(t)) = t\}$

(B) Give the data of each department whose manager is a staff member of the same department.

(1) $\lambda v \in \text{UHPT} : \{t \in v(\text{DPT}) \mid (\text{Hsmdpt} \odot \text{Hdptsm})(v)(t) = t\}$

(C) Thus, under (A) we ask for the *fixed points* of the function $(G \odot H)(v)$, for each state v.
We give for (B) also a solution without the use of DB functions:

$$\lambda v \in \text{UHPT} : \{t \in v(\text{DPT}) \mid \exists t' \in v(\text{SM}) : (t'(\text{IDNR}) = t(\text{MNNR}) \text{ and } t'(\text{DNR}) = t(\text{DNR}))\}$$

□ Example 6.3.

In the following example we will treat several queries departing from the situation that a DB function G over U with respect to the pair of table indices $(E' ; E)$ is given. Often the queries in Example 6.4 are slight variations of each other. We will show how it is possible that some solutions are and some others are not suitable for straightforward adjustments under such slight variations. Such problems of adaptation in the case of minor alterations serve as an illustration of similar problems that might arise in the use of languages such as SQL.

For the reader who is familiar with CODASYL (see for example [CO 71], [Ol 78], or [Re 82]), we note that in a conventional CODASYL-environment the DB function G can be implemented by way of a (AUTOMATIC MANDATORY) "DBTG set", provided that this is done in a controlled and disciplined manner. It is required, however, that in every state $v \in U$ for each $t' \in v(E')$ the E-tuple $G(v)(t')$ is chosen to be the "owner" of t'. In that case, the set of tuples $G(v)$ inv t represents, for $t \in v(E)$, the set of "members" of t. In such a third-generation-environment, our formal queries could serve as the *formal specifications* of the (COBOL-)programs to be written.

In Example 6.4, we give under (C) some additional solutions in the case that

$$\forall v \in U : \forall t \in v(E) : \forall t' \in v(E') : (G(v)(t') = t \Longleftrightarrow t' \text{ and } t \text{ are joinable}), \qquad (**)$$

which is not uncommon in practice. For example, Exercise 2.86 offers sufficient conditions for (**). We also note that t' and t are joinable iff $t' \upharpoonright g(E) = t \upharpoonright g(E')$.

EXAMPLE 6.4:

K1: (A) Give all E-tuples to which, according to G, there corresponds an E'-tuple.

(1) $\lambda v \in U : \{t \in v(E) \mid \exists t' \in v(E') : G(v)(t') = t\}$

(2) $\lambda v \in U : \{t \in v(E) \mid \{t' \in v(E') \mid G(v)(t') = t\} \neq \varnothing\}$

(3) $\lambda v \in U : \{t \in v(E) \mid (G(v) \text{ inv } t) \neq \varnothing\}$

(4) $\lambda v \in U : \{t \in v(E) \mid \ \mid G(v) \text{ inv } t \mid \neq 0\}$

(5) $\lambda v \in U : \{t \in v(E) \mid \ \mid G(v) \text{ inv } t \mid \geq 1\}$

(B) Give all patients who have ever been treated.

(3) $\lambda v \in \text{UHPT} : \{t \in v(\text{PAT}) \mid (\text{Hptpat}(v) \text{ inv } t) \neq \varnothing\}$

(C) If (**) holds, then the following solutions are also correct:

(6) $\lambda v \in U : \{t \in v(E) \mid \exists t' \in v(E') : t' \restriction g(E) = t \restriction g(E')\}$

(7) $\lambda v \in U : (v(E) \bowtie v(E')) \Vert\!\restriction g(E)$

(8) $\lambda v \in U : v(E) \bowtie (v(E') \Vert\!\restriction g(E))$

Elaboration of solution (6) for the query under (B) results in:

(6) $\lambda v \in \text{UHPT} : \{t \in v(\text{PAT}) \mid \exists t' \in v(\text{PT}) : t'(\text{PNR}) = t(\text{PNR})\}$

We observe that the first five solutions stress the *functional relationships* between the tables, solution (6) is written in the style of the *relational calculus*, and the solutions (7) and (8) belong to the realm of *relational algebra*. The reader is referred to [Sh 81] and [Co 72b] for further explanation of these three terms.

K2: (A) Give all E-tuples to which, according to G, there corresponds no E'-tuple.

(1) $\lambda v \in U : \{t \in v(E) \mid \forall t' \in v(E') : G(v)(t') \neq t\}$

(2) $\lambda v \in U : \{t \in v(E) \mid \{t' \in v(E') \mid G(v)(t') = t\} = \varnothing\}$

(3) $\lambda v \in U : \{t \in v(E) \mid (G(v) \text{ inv } t) = \varnothing\}$

(4) $\lambda v \in U : \{t \in v(E) \mid \ \mid G(v) \text{ inv } t \mid = 0\}$

(5) $\lambda v \in U : \{t \in v(E) \mid \ \mid G(v) \text{ inv } t \mid < 1\}$

(B) Give all treatments that have never been carried out.

(4) $\lambda v \in \text{UHPT} : \{t \in v(\text{TTP}) \mid \ \mid \text{Hpttp}(v) \text{ inv } t \mid = 0\}$

(C) The following solutions are also correct, provided that (**) holds:

(6) $\lambda v \in U : \{t \in v(E) \mid \forall t' \in v(E') : t' \restriction g(E) \neq t \restriction g(E')\}$

(7) $\lambda v \in U : v(E) - (v(E) \bowtie v(E')) \Vert\!\restriction g(E)$

(8) $\lambda v \in U : v(E) - (v(E) \bowtie (v(E') \Vert\!\restriction g(E)))$

K3: (A) Give all E-tuples to which, according to G, there correspond at least three E'-tuples.

(1) $\lambda v \in U : \{t \in v(E) \mid \exists t' \in v(E') : \exists t'' \in v(E') : \exists t''' \in v(E') :$
$G(v)(t') = t \text{ and } G(v)(t'') = t$
$\text{and } G(v)(t''') = t$
$\text{and } t' \neq t'' \text{ and } t' \neq t''' \text{ and } t'' \neq t'''\}$

(2) $\lambda v \in U : \{t \in v(E) \mid \ \mid G(v) \text{ inv } t \mid \geq 3\}$

(B) Give the data of all departments having at least three staff members.

(2) $\lambda v \in \text{UHPT} : \{t \in v(\text{DPT}) \mid \ \mid \text{Hsmdpt}(v) \text{ inv } t \mid \geq 3\}$

(C) The counterpart of solution (6) under K1, in case (**) holds, is left to the reader (in Exercise 6.3).
The solutions (7) and (8) under K1 are not suitable for immediate adaptation to the query posed in K3.

K4: (A) Give all E-tuples to which, according to G, there corresponds an E'-tuple having d'-value w'.

(1) $\lambda v \in U : \{t \in v(E) \mid \exists t' \in (G(v) \text{ inv } t) : t'(d') = w'\}$

(2) $\lambda v \in U : \{t \in v(E) \mid \{t' \in (G(v) \text{ inv } t) \mid t'(d') = w'\} \neq \varnothing\}$

(3) $\lambda v \in U : \{t \in v(E) \mid \ \mid \{t' \in (G(v) \text{ inv } t) \mid t'(d') = w'\} \mid \ \geq 1\}$

(4) $\lambda v \in U : \{t \in v(E) \mid w' \in \{t'(d') \mid t' \in (G(v) \text{ inv } t)\}\}$

(B) Give the data of all admissions during which a reassignment to specialist 129 took place.

(1) $\lambda v \in \text{UHPT} :$
$\{t \in v(\text{ADM}) \mid \exists t' \in (\text{Hreaadm}(v) \text{ inv } t) : t'(\text{IDNR}) = 129\}$

(C) If (**) holds then, for example, the following solutions are also correct:

(5) $\lambda v \in U : \{t \in v(E) \mid \exists t' \in v(E') : (t' \upharpoonright g(E) = t \upharpoonright g(E') \text{ and } t'(d') = w')\}$

(6) $\lambda v \in U : (v(E) \bowtie \{t' \in v(E') \mid t'(d') = w'\}) \Vert\!\upharpoonright g(E)$

(7) $\lambda v \in U : \{t' \in v(E) \bowtie v(E') \mid t'(d') = w'\} \Vert\!\upharpoonright g(E)$

The condition (**) does not hold for the DB function Hreaadm in our example under (B). Elaboration of this DB function gives the following result (see the definition in §4.3):

$$\lambda v \in \text{UHPT} : \{t \in v(\text{ADM}) \mid \exists t' \in v(\text{REA}) : (t'(\text{IDNR}) = 129 \text{ and } t'(\text{PNR}) = t(\text{PNR}) \text{ and } t(\text{ADMD}) < t'(\text{BDAT}) \text{ and if } t(\text{DISC}) = \text{'YES' then } t'(\text{BDAT}) \leq t(\text{DISD}))\}$$

K5: (A) Give all E-tuples to which, according to G, there corresponds an E'-tuple having a d'-value other than w'.

(1) $\lambda v \in U : \{t \in v(E) \mid \exists t' \in (G(v) \text{ inv } t) : t'(d') \neq w'\}$

(2) $\lambda v \in U : \{t \in v(E) \mid \{t' \in (G(v) \text{ inv } t) \mid t'(d') \neq w'\} \neq \varnothing\}$

(3) $\lambda v \in U : \{t \in v(E) \mid (\{t'(d') \mid t' \in (G(v) \text{ inv } t)\} - \{w'\}) \neq \varnothing\}$

(B) Give the SP-data of each specialist who has ever prescribed something other than a medicine coded 'ASPRO'.

(2) $\lambda v \in \text{UHPT} : \{t \in v(\text{SP}) \mid \{t' \in (\text{Hmdpsp}(v) \text{ inv } t) \mid t'(\text{MCD}) \neq \text{'ASPRO'}\} \neq \varnothing\}$

(C) If (**) holds then, for example, the following solutions are also correct:

(4) $\lambda v \in U : (v(E) \bowtie \{t' \in v(E') \mid t'(d') \neq w'\}) \upharpoonright g(E)$

(5) $\lambda v \in U : \{t' \in v(E) \bowtie v(E') \mid t'(d') \neq w'\} \upharpoonright g(E)$

Experience has taught us that the query "Give all E-tuples to which, according to G, there corresponds no E'-tuple such that d' has the value w'" is often (mistakenly) answered by giving a solution belonging to the class K5. We will return to this matter in Exercise 6.4.

K6: (A) Give all E-tuples to which, according to G, there correspond in the E'-table the d'-values x , x', and x'', but not the d'- values y and y'.

(1) $\lambda v \in U : \{t \in v(E) \mid \{t'(d') \mid t' \in (G(v) \text{ inv } t)\} \cap \{x, x', x'', y, y'\} = \{x, x', x''\} \}$

(B) Give the data of each patient who has undergone the treatments K1, K3, and K5, but not the treatments K2 and K4.

(1) $\lambda v \in \text{UHPT} : \{t \in v(\text{PAT}) \mid \{t'(\text{TCD}) \mid t' \in (\text{Hptpat}(v) \text{ inv } t)\} \cap \{\text{'K1'}, \text{'K2'}, \text{'K3'}, \text{'K4'}, \text{'K5'}\} = \{\text{'K1'}, \text{'K3'}, \text{'K5'}\}\}$

□ Example 6.4.

The queries in Example 6.5 ask for data from different tables at the same time. Considering the ad hoc nature of such queries, we will not give general query forms in Example 6.5, but restrict ourselves to specific queries concerning UHPT (V1, V2, et cetera).

EXAMPLE 6.5:

V1: Give all of the persons-data concerning compulsorily insured members of the nonmedical personnel. (By "all persons-data" we mean in this case all SM-, EMP-, NMP- and CE-data.)

(1) $\lambda v \in \text{UHPT} : v(\text{SM}) \bowtie v(\text{EMP}) \bowtie v(\text{NMP}) \bowtie v(\text{CE})$

Differentiation and *generalization* - see Chapter 3 - usually cause the data of one "object" to distribute over several tables. Reconstruction of all this distributed object data can usually be realized by means of joins (as is illustrated in this example).

V2: Consider all treatments on November 10, 1986, in which neither the specialist nor the assistant specialist belongs to the department in which the treatment took place. Give for each such treatment the treatment code and the identification number of the specialist, and for the involved patient the number, the NAZC-data, and the date of birth.

(1) $\lambda v \in$ UHPT :

$\{t \upharpoonright \{TCD, SNR\} \cup Hptpat(v)(t) \upharpoonright \{PNR, DTB, NAZC\}$
$\mid t \in v(PT)$ and $t(BDAT) = 861110$ and
$(Hspsm \odot Hptsp)(v)(t)(DNR) \neq Hptrm(v)(t)(DNR)$ and
$(Hspsm \odot Hptspa)(v)(t)(DNR) \neq Hptrm(v)(t)(DNR)\}$

(2) $\lambda v \in$ UHPT :

$\{t \upharpoonright \{TCD, SNR\} \cup t' \upharpoonright \{PNR, DTB, NAZC\}$
$\mid (t ; t') \in v(PT) \times v(PAT)$ and
$t(PNR) = t'(PNR)$ and $t(BDAT) = 861110$ and
$\exists r \in v(RM) : \exists m \in v(SM) : \exists m' \in v(SM) :$
$[r(RNR) = t(RNR)$ and $m(IDNR) = t(IDNR)$ and
$m'(IDNR) = t(ASNR)$ and $m(DNR) \neq r(DNR)$ and
$m'(DNR) \neq r(DNR)]\}$

(3) $\lambda v \in$ UHPT :

$\{t \mid t \in v(PT) \bowtie v(PAT)$ and $t(BDAT) = 861110$ and
$\forall r \in v(RM) : \forall m \in v(SM) : \forall m' \in v(SM) :$
[if $r(RNR) = t(RNR)$ and $m(IDNR) = t(IDNR)$ and
$m'(IDNR) = t(ASNR)$
then $m(DNR) \neq r(DNR)$ and $m'(DNR) \neq r(DNR)$]
$\} \Vert\!\upharpoonright \{TCD, SNR, PNR, DTB, NAZC\}$

The concise solution (1) uses the DB functions defined in §4.3, whereas solution (2) is closer to a possible solution in SQL.

The "∃-solution" under (2) and the "∀-solution" under (3) are equivalent since {RNR} and {IDNR} are keys (in UHPT) of RM and SM, respectively!

V3: Give under the names BEGIN, ID, NAME, and NDEP, for all admissions that finished in June 1989: the starting date, the (identification) number and the name of the patient concerned, and the number of different departments in which that patient resided during that admission.

(1) $\lambda v \in$ UHPT :

$\{\{(BEGIN ; t(ADMD)),$
$(ID ; t(PNR)),$
$(NAME ; Hadmpat(v)(t)(NAZC)(NM)),$
$(NDEP ; \mid \{Hadmrm(v)(t)(DNR)\} \cup$
$\{Htrfrm(v)(u)(DNR) \mid u \in Htrfadm(v) \text{ inv } t\} \mid)\}$
$\mid t \in v(ADM)$ and $t(DISD)$ div $100 = 8906$ and $t(DISC) =$ 'YES'$\}$

(2) $\lambda v \in$ UHPT :

$\{\{(BEGIN ; t(ADMD)),$
$(ID ; t(PNR)),$
$(NAME ; t'(NAZC)(NM)),$

$$(\text{NDEP} \quad ; \mid \{r(\text{DNR}) \mid r \in v(\text{RM}) \text{ and } [t(\text{RNR}) = r(\text{RNR}) \text{ or } \exists u \in (\text{Htrfadm}(v) \text{ inv } t) : u(\text{RNR}) = r(\text{RNR})]\} \mid)\}$$
$$\mid (t \,;\, t') \in v(\text{ADM}) \times v(\text{PAT}) \text{ and } t(\text{PNR}) = t'(\text{PNR}) \text{ and } 890601 \leq t(\text{DISD}) \text{ and } t(\text{DISD}) < 890701 \text{ and } t(\text{DISC}) = \text{'YES'}\}$$

Just as in the case of solution (3) for the query V2, a solution using a join is possible (instead of a Cartesian product). Furthermore, the DB function Htrfadm in solution (2) could be removed. For this matter the reader is referred to Exercise 6.8.

V4: Give the so-called nursing report of the admission of patient 123210 starting on July 10, 1989. (By the *nursing report* of an admission we mean, in our hospital of Chapter 4, a table over {FROM, COMMENTS}, recording for each period in which the admission is divided by possible transfers, the starting date and the nursing comments during that period.)

(1) $\lambda v \in \text{UHPT}:$

$$\{\{(\text{FROM}; t(\text{ADMD})), (\text{COMMENTS}; t(\text{NCOM}))\} \mid t \in v(\text{ADM}) \text{ and } t(\text{PNR}) = 123210 \text{ and } t(\text{ADMD}) = 890710\} \cup$$
$$\{\{(\text{FROM}; t(\text{BDAT})), (\text{COMMENTS}; t(\text{NCOM}))\} \mid t \in v(\text{TRF}) \text{ and } t(\text{PNR}) = 123210 \text{ and } \text{Htrfadm}(v)\,(t)\,(\text{ADMD}) = 890710\}$$

Should the above admission not exist in state v, then by the preceding definition the nursing report must be the empty table (regardless of the question whether a patient with number 123210 actually exists). If such an admission does indeed exist and there are n transfers (where $n \geq 0$), then apparently the number of tuples in the nursing report must be $n + 1$.

V5: In our hospital we call a patient treatment (tuple) x a *direct source* of possible infections for a patient treatment (tuple) y if and only if x takes place before or on the same day as y, and x and y concern the same patient or have someone in common from the treatment team (consisting of the treating specialist plus the assistant specialist, if any). In particular, each patient treatment tuple is one of its own direct sources.
We will now define for each $v \in \text{UHPT}$ the relation DS_v as the set of ordered pairs $(x \,;\, y)$ for which, in state v, x is a direct source for y:

$$\text{DS}_v = \{(x \,;\, y) \mid (x \,;\, y) \in v(\text{PT}) \times v(\text{PT}) \text{ and } x(\text{BDAT}) \leq y(\text{BDAT}) \text{ and } [x(\text{PNR}) = y(\text{PNR}) \text{ or } \{x(\text{IDNR}), x(\text{ASNR})\} \cap \{y(\text{IDNR}), y(\text{ASNR})\} \neq \varnothing]\}$$

Note that DS_v is *reflexive*, that is, $\text{id}(v(\text{PT})) \subseteq \text{DS}_v$.

Because of a minor accident on September 8, 1988, all specialists of department 9 may have been infected. Therefore, for each patient who, as a consequence thereof, could have been infected directly or indirectly via a treatment, we want to know, besides the patient number, the NAZC-data, and the blood group, also the identification number and the name of the contact of the city of that patient.

This query over UHPT, which is of a *recursive* nature, can be formally represented as follows:

$$\begin{aligned}
&\lambda v \in \text{UHPT}: \\
&\qquad \{t \upharpoonright \{\text{PNR, NAZC, BLGR}\} \cup \\
&\qquad\ \{(\text{CPRS}\,;\, t'(\text{IDNR})),\, (\text{NAME}\,;\, t'(\text{NAZC})\,(\text{NM}))\} \\
&\qquad \mid (t\,;\,t') \in v(\text{PAT}) \times v(\text{SM}) \text{ and} \\
&\qquad\ t'(\text{IDNR}) = \text{Hpatmun}(v)\,(t)\,(\text{CPRS}) \text{ and} \\
&\qquad\ \exists (x\,;\,y) \in \text{Tcl}(\text{DS}_v) : (y(\text{PNR}) = t(\text{PNR}) \text{ and } x(\text{BDAT}) \geq 880908 \text{ and} \\
&\qquad \{x(\text{IDNR}),\, x(\text{ASNR})\} \cap \\
&\qquad \{m(\text{IDNR}) \mid m \in v(\text{SM}) \text{ and } m(\text{DNR}) = 9\} \neq \varnothing)\}
\end{aligned}$$

In this recursive query we used $\text{Tcl}(\text{DS}_v)$, i.e., the transitive closure of the relation DS_v; see Definition 23(a) on page 16.

□ Example 6.5.

In Example 6.6 we will deal with queries whose answers usually consist of more than one single table. Such queries are typically encountered in the area of (weekly) surveys, (monthly and annual) reports, dossiers, and database dumps, for instance. Also a so-called *external schema* or *subschema* can be treated formally in this way.

EXAMPLE 6.6:

In K2 we will make use of the concept of a "subskeleton". We call g' a *subskeleton* of the DB skeleton g iff g' is a set function and $\text{dom}(g') \subseteq \text{dom}(g)$ and $\forall E \in \text{dom}(g') : g'(E) \subseteq g(E)$. Hence, a subskeleton of g is a DB skeleton in which each table index is a table index of g as well, such that all attributes of that table index according to the subskeleton are also attributes of that table index according to g.

To give one example, we define for the personnel department the subskeleton PDS of the DB skeleton GHPT, used in Chapter 4, as follows:

$$\begin{aligned}
\text{PDS} = \text{GHPT} &\upharpoonright \{\text{SM, EMP, MP, NMP, CE}\} \\
&\cup \{(\text{SP};\, \text{GHPT}(\text{SP}) - \{\text{LOC, NBD}\})\}
\end{aligned}$$

Thus, the subskeleton PDS consists of the table indices SM, EMP, MP, NMP, CE, and SP, together with almost all corresponding attributes; merely the attributes LOC and NBD of the table index SP take no part in PDS.

K1: (A) Give the entire database state. (This is also known as a *dump* of the database.)

(1) $\lambda v \in U : v$

(2) $\mathrm{id}(U)$

(B) Give all data in our hospital database.

(2) $\mathrm{id}(\mathrm{UHPT})$

(C) This rather trivial query does indeed serve a practical purpose: think of "back-ups" for instance.

K2: (A) Give all data according to the subskeleton g', the so-called *subschema* according to g'.

(1) $\lambda v \in U : (\lambda E \in \mathrm{dom}(g') : v(E) \upharpoonleft\!\upharpoonleft g'(E))$

(B) Give all data according to the subskeleton PDS.

$$\lambda v \in \mathrm{UHPT} : v \upharpoonleft \{\mathrm{SM, EMP, MP, NMP, CE}\} \cup \{(\mathrm{SP}; v(\mathrm{SP}) \not\upharpoonleft\!\upharpoonleft \{\mathrm{LOC, NBD}\})\}$$

(C) If $g'(E) = g(E)$ for all E in $\mathrm{dom}(g')$, then the solution under (A) can be simplified to

(2) $\lambda v \in U : v \upharpoonleft \mathrm{dom}(g')$

Our solution under (B) is also based on the property above.

K3: (A) Give for all table indices containing the attribute a, all tuples whose a-value is equal to w (excluding that a-column itself).

(1) $\lambda v \in U : \{(E ; \{t \not\upharpoonleft \{a\} \mid t \in v(E) \text{ and } t(a) = w\}) \mid E \in \mathrm{dom}(g) \text{ and } a \in g(E)\}$

(2) $\lambda v \in U : (\lambda E \in \mathrm{dom}(g) \text{ and } a \in g(E) : \{t \in v(E) \mid t(a) = w\} \not\upharpoonleft\!\upharpoonleft \{a\})$

(B) Give all persons- and medical data of the patient 177912 (excluding the patient number itself).

(1) $\lambda v \in \mathrm{UHPT} : \{(E ; \{t \not\upharpoonleft \{\mathrm{PNR}\} \mid t \in v(E) \text{ and } t(\mathrm{PNR}) = 177912\}) \mid E \in \{\mathrm{PAT, MDP, PT, ADM, DIS, REA, TRF}\}\}$

(C) Note that the answer in K3 always results in a DB state over the subskeleton

$$\{(E ; g(E) - \{a\}) \mid E \in \mathrm{dom}(g) \text{ and } a \in g(E)\}.$$

In spite of this, K3 is not a special case of K2, because in K2 all tuples participate, while in K3 also a selection takes place.

K4: (A) Give in a table over {ENTITY, NUMBER} an overview of all table indices together with their corresponding number of elements.

(1) $\lambda v \in U : \{\{(\text{ENTITY} ; E), (\text{NUMBER} ; | v(E) |)\} \mid E \in \text{dom}(g)\}$

(B) Give in a table over {ENTITY, NUMBER} an overview of all table indices together with the corresponding number of elements in our hospital database.

(1) $\lambda v \in \text{UHPT} : \{\{(\text{ENTITY} ; E), (\text{NUMBER} ; | v(E) |)\} \mid E \in \text{dom(GHPT)}\}$

(C) Note that this query refers partly to the DB skeleton (the "structure") and partly to the DB state (the "contents").

□ Example 6.6.

The preceding selection of examples offers an impression of the variety of queries that can be posed, and of the way(s) in which these queries can be formally specified.

Our examples may suggest - and in practice it is usually the case to a much larger extent - that even a detailed formulation of the query in natural language does not convey the precise meaning of the query. It is not even unusual that on closer examination a query turns out to be ambiguous. Moreover, the care taken in formulating the query often leaves much to be desired. In those cases further consultation of the person responsible for the original query is essential.

EXERCISES

6.1. Give formal specifications of the following queries over the DB universe UHPT from Chapter 4.

(a) Give number and name of each department in which in 1987 no female patients from Amsterdam were treated.

(b) Are there any departments in which in 1987 no female patients from Amsterdam were treated?

(c) Is it true that there are more nonmedical personnel than medical personnel?

(d) Give number and name of all specialists who are managers of the department to which they are formally attached, and also have performed at most three different *kinds* of treatments (as treating specialist or as assistant specialist).

(e) Give all persons-data of all contact persons representing at least two municipalities inhabited by at least 100 registered patients. (By "all persons-data" we mean here all SM-, EMP-, and NMP-data plus (if applicable) CE-data.) Hint: use the outer join, defined in Exercise 2.93.

(f) Give the total number of prognosticated treatments for the current year.

(g) Give the total number of admitted days in October 1987. (The number of *admitted days* of an admission is the number of days that this admission lasted, including the day of admission and the day of discharge.)

(h) Give for each childless female patient born and living in Sellafield the concise nursing report (as defined in Exercise 4.12).
Hint: use the expression CNR, introduced in Exercise 4.12, for the concise nursing report.

(i) Give in a tuple over {ADMISSIONS, TREATMENTS, MEDICINES} the total of all invoice amounts of all female patients from Eindhoven registered in 1989, split up into admissions, patient treatments and medicine prescriptions.

(j) Give the total of *all* invoice amounts over all female patients from Eindhoven registered in 1989.

(k) Give in a table over {SEX, TREATMENTS} for both sexes the total patient treatment costs (= invoice amounts) of all patients from Eindhoven registered in 1989.

6.2. Describe the following queries over UHPT informally as questions or orders.

(a) $\lambda v \in \text{UHPT} : \{t \in v(\text{MDP}) \mid t(\text{PNR}) = 256896\} \upharpoonright \{\text{MCD}, \text{DAT}\}$

(b) $(\lambda v \in \text{UHPT} : \text{'YES'})\ \theta$
$(\lambda v \in \text{UHPT and } v(\text{DPT}) \upharpoonright \{\text{DNR}\} \subseteq v(\text{RM}) \upharpoonright \{\text{DNR}\} : \text{'NO'})$

(c) $\lambda v \in \text{UHPT} : \{t \in v(\text{SP}) \mid \forall t' \in (\text{Hptsp}(v) \text{ inv } t) :$
$\quad \mid \{u \in (\text{Hptsp}(v) \text{ inv } t) \mid u(\text{TCD}) = t'(\text{TCD})\} \mid \leq 5\}$

(d) $\lambda v \in \text{UHPT} : (\Sigma t \in v(\text{MED}) : (t(\text{NST}) * t(\text{PRCU})) \text{ div } 100)$

6.3. Give for the query in K3 of Example 6.4 the analogue of solution (6) in K1, provided that (**) holds.

6.4. Give a formal specification of the query "Give all E-tuples to which, according to G, there corresponds no E'-tuple that has w' as d'-value". (For the context of the query see class K5 of Example 6.4.)

6.5. Give a formal specification of the query "Give all E-tuples for which according to G in the E'-table no d'-value occurs more than five times".

6.6. Give a formal specification of the following query, taking the same situation as in Example 6.4 as starting point.
Give all E-tuples that, according to G, have in the E'-table at least all d'-values that the E-tuple t_0 (if it exists) also has.

6.7. This exercise concerns an extension of K4 from Example 6.6. Not only do we ask for an overview of all table indices and the corresponding number of elements, but we also want (in a table over {ENTITY, ATTRIBUTE, NUMBER}) an overview of all attributes together with the number of different values occurring for that attribute in the table concerned. The total answer is to be conceived of as a (table-valued) function over {ENTITIES, ATTRIBUTES}.

6.8. Give for the query V3 in Example 6.5 a solution, by replacing the Cartesian product in the solution (2) by a join and removing the DB function Htrfadm (using the definition in §4.3).

6.9. (a) Give for $p \in \mathbb{N}$ and $d \in$ DATSET a formal definition of the function NRP(p,d) over UHPT that assigns to each $v \in$ UHPT the ***nursing report*** of the admission (if existing) on date d of the patient having patient number p. (See query V4 of Example 6.5 for a description of nursing reports.)

(b) Give for $p \in \mathbb{N}$ a formal definition of the function NRPS(p) over UHPT that assigns to each $v \in$ UHPT a table over {ADMDAT, REPORT} containing the admission date and the nursing report of each admission of the patient p (if existing). Make use of the function NRP(p,d) above.

6.10. In the hospital of Chapter 4, *the dossier of an admission* stands for a function over {ADMDATA, READATA, PTDATA} having the following successive values: the admission tuple in question, the set of all reassignment tuples belonging to that admission, and, finally, the set of all treatment tuples during that admission of the patient concerned (excluding treatments on dates of admission or discharge). Give a formal specification of the following query over UHPT:

Give all admission dossiers of patient 123453.

6.11. The management of the hospital of Chapter 4 wants an overview for each month in the years 1960 to 1988, of the total sum of invoice amounts of the discharges that took place in that month - this sum being approximated to the nearest pound. Some people in the management want the answer to look like a table (having 30 attributes and 12 elements) as depicted in Figure 6.1(a), while some others want as an answer a table (having 13 attributes and 29 elements) as depicted in Figure 6.1(b).

MONTH	60	61	...	87	88
1 ⋮ 12					

(a)

YEAR	1	2	...	11	12
60 ⋮ 88					

(b)

Figure 6.1

Represent either possibility as a query over UHPT.

□

6.2 Views

Certain queries might be used repeatedly in an organization. Should that be the case for a particular query, then it makes sense to provide it with a name, and to refer to that query by using its name (instead of specifying the whole query each time). Such a "named query" is called a *view* (because it is, so to speak, a "view on the database"). Formally speaking, a view is an ordered pair whose second co-ordinate is a query:

DEFINITION 6.2:
If U is a set, then:
p is a **view on** U $\overset{D}{\Longleftrightarrow}$ p is an ordered pair and
$\pi_2(p)$ is a query over U.

If p is a view, say $p = (n\ ;\ q)$, then n is called *the name of p* and q *the definition of p*.

Since various queries in practice are not of an ad hoc nature but are used many times, we normally want to represent an entire *set* of queries as views. It is of course required that the names of the views are mutually distinct. In other words, such a set of queries must be a function. We call such a function, assigning to view names the corresponding queries over U, a *view system on U*:

DEFINITION 6.3:
If U is a set, then:
V is a **view system on** U $\overset{D}{\Longleftrightarrow}$ V is a function and
$\forall p \in V : p$ is a view on U.

An alternative description is that V is a view system on U iff V is a function and $\forall n \in \text{dom}(V) : V(n)$ is a query over U.

EXAMPLE 6.7:

We will now define a view system VS1 on the DB universe UHPT in Chapter 4. The view system consists of seven views. The view names are character strings, and the queries are partly extracted from the examples in §6.1.

The views have the following names and informal descriptions:

'STOCK OVERVIEW'	:	code, name, and stock level of all medicines (see Example 6.2, K2(B)).
'DEPARTMENTS'	:	the department data including the number of employees per department.
'PATIENT COSTS'	:	of each patient from Eindhoven registered in 1989: patient number, name, date of birth, sex, and total of invoice amounts, the latter split up into admissions, treatments, and medicine dispensings.

'QUARTERLY COSTS'	: the total amount of quarterly incomes to be paid (on the basis of the current amounts).
'PDVIEW'	: the subschema relevant to the personnel department (see Example 6.6, K2(B)).
'DBDUMP'	: the entire database state (see Example 6.6, K1).
'DBSIZE'	: overview of all table indices with the corresponding numbers of elements (see Example 6.6, K4).

The definition of our view system VS1 on UHPT now runs as follows:

$$
\begin{array}{l}
\text{VS1} = \{\ (\text{'STOCK OVERVIEW'};\\
\qquad \lambda v \in \text{UHPT} : v(\text{MED}) \Vert\!\upharpoonright \{\text{MCD, MNM, NST}\}),\\
\quad (\text{'DEPARTMENTS'};\\
\qquad \lambda v \in \text{UHPT} :\\
\qquad\quad \{\ a \cup \{(\text{NROFEMPS};\\
\qquad\qquad\qquad | \{m \in v(\text{SM}) \bowtie v(\text{EMP}) \mid m(\text{DNR}) = a(\text{DNR})\} |)\}\\
\qquad\quad \mid a \in v(\text{DPT})\}),\\
\quad (\text{'PATIENT COSTS'};\\
\qquad \lambda v \in \text{UHPT} :\\
\qquad\quad \{\{(\text{NUMBER} \ ; p(\text{PNR})),\\
\qquad\quad\ (\text{NAME} \ ; p(\text{NAZC})(\text{NM})),\\
\qquad\quad\ (\text{BIRTHDT} \ ; p(\text{DTB})),\\
\qquad\quad\ (\text{SEX} \ ; p(\text{SEX})),\\
\qquad\quad\ (\text{ADMAM} \ ; \Sigma t \in v(\text{DIS}) \text{ and } t(\text{PNR}) = p(\text{PNR}) : t(\text{INVA})),\\
\qquad\quad\ (\text{TTPAM} \ ; \Sigma t \in v(\text{PT}) \text{ and } t(\text{PNR}) = p(\text{PNR}) : t(\text{INVA})),\\
\qquad\quad\ (\text{MDPAM} \ ; \Sigma t \in v(\text{MDP}) \text{ and } t(\text{PNR}) = p(\text{PNR}) : t(\text{INVA}))\}\\
\qquad\quad \mid p \in v(\text{PAT}) \text{ and } p(\text{REGD}) \text{ div } 10000 = 89 \text{ and}\\
\qquad\quad\ p(\text{NAZC})(\text{CTY}) = \text{'Eindhoven'}\}),\\
\quad (\text{'QUARTERLY COSTS'};\\
\qquad \lambda v \in \text{UHPT} :\\
\qquad\quad 13 * (\Sigma t \in v(\text{SP}) \text{ and } t(\text{INS}) = \text{'YES'} : t(\text{FEEH}) * t(\text{HPW}))\\
\qquad\quad +3 * (\Sigma t \in v(\text{EMP}) : t(\text{SAL})) * 100\\
\qquad\quad +3 * (\Sigma t \in v(\text{NMP}) : t(\text{MALL})) * 100),\\
\quad (\text{'PDVIEW'};\\
\qquad \lambda v \in \text{UHPT} : v \upharpoonright \{\text{SM, EMP, MP, NMP, CE}\} \cup\\
\qquad\quad \{(\text{SP}; v(\text{SP}) \Vert\!\upharpoonright \{\text{LOC, NBD}\})\}),\\
\quad (\text{'DBDUMP'};\\
\qquad \text{id(UHPT)}),\\
\quad (\text{'DBSIZE'};\\
\qquad \lambda v \in \text{UHPT} : \{\{(\text{ENTITY}; E),\\
\qquad\qquad\qquad (\text{NUMBER} \ ; | v(E) |)\}\\
\qquad\qquad\qquad \mid E \in \text{dom(GHPT)}\})\ \}.
\end{array}
$$

Now that the view system VS1 is given, it can be used when formulating new queries. To take one example, we consider the question "Give number, name, and the sum of invoice amounts of each patient from Eindhoven registered in 1989 who has been provided with at least 250 guilders worth of medicines". Using VS1, the corresponding query is easily specified as follows:

$$\begin{aligned}\lambda v \in \text{UHPT} : \{\ & t \upharpoonright \{\text{NUMBER}, \text{NAME}\} \cup \\ & \{(\text{TOTAL}\ ;\ t(\text{ADMAM}) + t(\text{TTPAM}) + t(\text{MDPAM}))\} \\ & \mid t \in \text{VS1}(\text{'PATIENTCOSTS'})\,(v) \text{ and } t(\text{MDPAM}) > 25000\}\end{aligned}$$

Without any reference to VS1, the formulation of this query requires considerably more effort:

$$\begin{aligned}\lambda v \in \text{UHPT} : \{\ \{\ & (\text{NUMBER}\ ;\ p(\text{PNR}))\ , \\ & (\text{NAME}\ ;\ p(\text{NAZC})\,(\text{NM}))\ , \\ & (\text{TOTAL}\ ;\ \Sigma t \in v(\text{DIS}) \cup v(\text{PT}) \cup v(\text{MDP}) \text{ and} \\ & \qquad t(\text{PNR}) = p(\text{PNR}) : t(\text{INVA}))\} \\ \mid\ & p \in v(\text{PAT}) \text{ and } p(\text{REGD}) \text{ div } 10000 = 89 \text{ and} \\ & p(\text{NAZC})\,(\text{CTY}) = \text{'Eindhoven' and} \\ & (\Sigma t \in v(\text{MDP}) \text{ and } t(\text{PNR}) = p(\text{PNR}) : t(\text{INVA})) > 25000\}\end{aligned}$$

□ Example 6.7.

We note that the views called 'DBDUMP' and 'DBSIZE' in VS1 are of such a general nature that they should be (and often will be) delivered as "standard accessories" of a DBMS.

A view $(n\ ;\ q)$ can be interpreted as a "knowledge rule", where n is the "concept" to be defined, and q is the "definition" of that concept. A clear example of this is the view called 'QUARTERLY COSTS' in VS1 (meant for the salary administration), establishing accurately the detailed knowledge which ingredients (in which proportions) determine the total quarterly salary expenses. Using views, we are in this way capable of constructing an entire "library" of derivable concepts around a database universe. Since a database management system often allows more than one view system per defined database universe, e.g., one view system per user or user group, in most cases even different sorts of libraries can be constructed.

By means of our general concept of a view, we not only model *SQL views* ([SQL 92]), but we also model the ANSI/SPARC *external views* ([TK 78]). The view 'STOCK OVERVIEW' in VS1 is a typical example of the former, whereas the view 'PDVIEW' in VS1 is an instance of the latter.

Needless to say that it is often useful in practice to be able to define new views in terms of previously defined ones (see also the exercises below). Most database management systems do indeed offer this possibility. The interested reader is referred to for instance "Focal Point 6" in [IDT 90].

EXERCISES

6.12. Give formal specifications of the following questions over the DB universe UHPT in Chapter 4, give them a name, and cast them in a view system VS2 on UHPT. Although some of these questions already occurred in Exercise 6.1, you are now supposed to use the view system VS1 defined in Example 6.7.

(a) Construct a tuple over {ADMISSIONS, TREATMENTS, MEDICINES} concerning the total of invoice amounts over all female patients from Eindhoven registered in 1989, split up into admissions, patient treatments, and medicine dispensings.

(b) Give the total of *all* invoice amounts over all female patients from Eindhoven registered in 1989.

(c) Give in a table over {SEX, TREATMENTS} for both sexes the total of patient treatment costs of all patients from Eindhoven registered in 1989.

(d) Give the average *quarterly costs* per (employed) staff member, approximated to the nearest guilder.

6.13. Cast, using self-chosen names, the following questions over the DB universe UHPT in Chapter 4 as views in a view system VS3 on UHPT. Wherever possible, make use of the view systems VS1 in Example 6.7 and VS2 in the preceding exercise.

(a) Give in a table over {SEX, TREATMENTS} for both sexes the mutual percentages of the total patient treatment costs of all patients from Eindhoven registered in 1989 (approximated to tenths of percents).

(b) Give for each medical staff member the identity number, name, salary, and the difference with the average quarterly expenses per employed staff member (positive if the salary is greater than the average, otherwise negative).

(c) Give in a table over {1, 2} all pairs of patient treatments such that the first patient treatment is a direct source of possible infections for the second one (in the sense of Example 6.5, V5).
Hint: see also Exercise 1.13.

6.14. Cast the following questions over UHPT, based on query V5 of Example 6.5, as (recursive) views in a view system VS4 on UHPT. Use self-chosen names. You are permitted to use previously defined view systems.

(a) Give the patient data of all patients who have possibly been infected by specialist 109 via a treatment, whether directly or indirectly.

(b) Give the identity numbers of all specialists who, since July 3, 1989, have possibly been infected via a treatment, due to a seat of infection in treatment room 'XP4', whether directly or indirectly.

□

CHAPTER 7

Maintenance

7.1 Transactions

The state of an organization is usually liable to change: employees, customers, and products come and go, orders and invoices are received and handled, and salaries, stocks, and prices go up and down in the meantime. The administrative repercussions of such changes - in the field of databases referred to as *maintenance* - can be specified formally by means of functions that assign to each possible DB state the DB state reflecting the new situation. We call such functions *transactions*. The (very) general definition reads as follows:

DEFINITION 7.1:
If U is a set, then:
f is a **transaction on** $U \overset{D}{\Longleftrightarrow} f \in U \twoheadrightarrow U$.

EXAMPLE 7.1:

We illustrate the notion of a transaction by means of the DB universe EXU from Example 1.3 and the following tuple:

t4 = {(DNO; 3), (NAME; 'PURCHASE'), (MANNO; 7)}

We might well be tempted, at first sight, to describe the addition of the department tuple t4 by means of the following function f5:

f5 = $\lambda\, v \in$ EXU: {(EMPL; v(EMPL)),
(DEP ; v(DEP) $\cup$ {t4})}.

Yet, the function f5 turns out not to be a transaction on EXU! Indeed, f5 is a function *over* EXU, but not *into* EXU: for some v in EXU, f5(v) is not an element of EXU. This holds in particular if t4 $\notin$ v(DEP), while the department number 3 or the department name 'PURCHASE' does already occur in v(DEP), or the employee number 7 does not occur in v(EMPL). (See also in this regard the requirements (2), (3), and (5) in Example 1.3.) Should we want to leave the state unaltered in those special cases, then the description of such an insertion *attempt* could look like this:

$$\text{f6} = \lambda v \in \text{EXU}: \begin{cases} \text{f5}(v) & \text{if f5}(v) \in \text{EXU} \\ v & \text{otherwise} \end{cases}$$

The function f6 is indeed a transaction on EXU.

If, in addition, dynamic constraints have been established on EXU, then it must also be the case that (v; f5(v)) is an admissible transition. Suppose for instance that new departments can only be added in certain situations, e.g., if the number of employees is a tenfold or a tenfold plus one. (Reality often surpasses our imagination.) In that case we want to have the following transition relation:

$$\begin{aligned} R_0 = \{(v\,;v') \mid\ & (v\,;v') \in \text{EXU} \times \text{EXU and} \\ & \text{if } |\,v(\text{EMPL})\,| \bmod 10 \notin \{0,1\} \\ & \text{then id}(\{\text{DNO}\}) \text{ connects } v'(\text{DEP}) \text{ with } v(\text{DEP})\}. \end{aligned}$$

(Aside, we would like to note that this is also an example of a conditional connection.)

Again if we want to leave the state unaltered in the event of a non-allowed transition, then the intended transaction is

$$\text{f7} = \lambda v \in \text{EXU}: \begin{cases} \text{f5}(v) & \text{if } (v\,;\text{f5}(v)) \in R_0 \\ v & \text{otherwise} \end{cases}$$

Observing that $(v\,;\text{f5}(v)) \in \text{f5}$, the function f7 can be rewritten by means of Definition 17 on page 11 as follows:

$$\begin{aligned} \text{f7} &= \{(v\,;\text{f5}(v)) \mid v \in \text{EXU and } (v\,;\text{f5}(v)) \in R_0\} \cup \\ &\quad\ \{(v\,;v) \quad\ \mid v \in \text{EXU and } (v\,;\text{f5}(v)) \notin R_0\} \\ &= \text{id(EXU)}\ \theta\ (R_0 \cap \text{f5}). \end{aligned}$$

□ Example 7.1.

In Example 7.1 we put forward that a transaction should also satisfy all dynamic constraints and should therefore "fit" in the transition relation R_0. In that case we speak of a *transaction within* R_0. Formally:

DEFINITION 7.2:
If R is a relation, then:
f is a **transaction within** $R \overset{D}{\Longleftrightarrow} f$ is a function and $f \subseteq R$.

When we compare Definition 7.1 with Definition 7.2, we observe that each transaction *on* U is a transaction *within* $U \times U$ as well. The reverse does not need to hold, since the domain of a transaction within $U \times U$ is not necessarily equal to U (or, in other words, since the transaction is not necessarily defined in each state).

In Example 7.1
- f5 is not a transaction on EXU,
- f6 is a transaction on EXU, yet not a transaction within R_0, and
- f7 is a transaction within R_0.

The adjustments made in Example 7.1 to f5, resulting in the transaction f7 within the transition relation R_0, are of a more general interest. We therefore introduce the following concept:

DEFINITION 7.3:
If U is a set and $R \subseteq U \times U$ and f is a function, then:
$\text{Ad}(U, R, f) \overset{D}{=} \text{id}(U) \, \theta \, (R \cap f)$.

We call Ad(U, R, f) *the adaptation of f determined by U and R*. We speak of *the adaptation of f determined by U* if there are no dynamic constraints, in which case we are dealing with the transition relation $U \times U$, which is the most "liberal" transition relation on U. We will denote this adaptation (solely determined by the static constraints) by Adap(U, f):

DEFINITION 7.4:
If U is a set and f is a function, then:
$\text{Adap}(U, f) \overset{D}{=} \text{Ad}(U, U \times U, f)$.

Below we give the following alternative descriptions of the two concepts just introduced:

$$\text{Adap}(U, f) = \lambda v \in U : \begin{cases} f(v) & \text{if } v \in \text{dom}(f) \text{ and } f(v) \in U \\ v & \text{otherwise} \end{cases}$$

$$\text{Ad}(U, R, f) = \lambda v \in U : \begin{cases} f(v) & \text{if } v \in \text{dom}(f) \text{ and } (v\,; f(v)) \in R \\ v & \text{otherwise} \end{cases}$$

In the "otherwise"-case, which means so to speak that the alteration attempt is cancelled, we speak of a *rollback* of the alteration attempt.

Returning to Example 7.1, we observe that

Adap(EXU, f5) = f6 and
Ad(EXU, R_0, f5) = f7.

THEOREM 7.1:
If U is a set and $R \subseteq U \times U$ and f is a function, then:

(a) Adap(U, f) is a transaction on U;

(b) Ad(U, R, f) is a transaction on U;

(c) if R is reflexive on U, then Ad(U, R, f) is a transaction within R;

(d) if f is a transaction on U and within R, then Ad(U, R, f) = f;

(e) if R is reflexive on U, then Ad(U, R, Ad(U, R, f)) = Ad(U, R, f).

Proof:
Since f is a function, $R \cap f$, by Lemma 3(a) on page 6, is a function as well.
It is also given that $R \subseteq U \times U$, so $R \cap f \subseteq U \times U$.
From Definition 7.3 and Lemma 12(a) on page 11 it now follows that Ad(U, R, f) is a function over U, namely an element of $U \twoheadrightarrow U$.
This proves both (b) and the special case (a).

If R is reflexive on U, then id(U) $\subseteq R$;
it now follows from Definition 7.3 that Ad(U, R, f) $\subseteq R$.
This proves (c).

f is a transaction within R, so $f \subseteq R$. (1)
f is a transaction on U, hence dom(f) = U. (2)
Application of Definition 7.3, of (1), and of (2) above, results in the following:

$$\begin{aligned}\text{Ad}(U, R, f) &= \text{id}(U)\ \theta\ (R \cap f)\\ &= \text{id}(U)\ \theta\ f\\ &= f.\end{aligned}$$

This proves (d).

Finally, (e) follows immediately from (b), (c), and (d).

□

We also introduced the adaptation concepts above because they model well what an interaction between a user and a database management system could look like in general: for each function f, given by the user as a maintenance command (hence, as a special sort of "application"), the DBMS could *de facto* carry out the adaptation of f determined by the DB universe and the transition relation as known to the DBMS. Consequently, this means that every static and dynamic constraint that can be specified in the DBMS under consideration need not be "interwoven" in all those separate applications, but could be dealt with by the DBMS. As to the extent to which all sorts of refined constraints can be given as input to existing DBMSs when specifying DB universes and transition relations, we refer the reader to "Focal Point 4" in [IDT 90].

We do stress that the successive application of the adaptations of two functions f and g need not at all render the same result as the application of the adaptation of the composed function $g \circ f$ as one "atomic unit" (alias a *unit of work*). In other words, $\mathrm{Ad}(U, R, g) \circ \mathrm{Ad}(U, R, f)$ might well be another function than the transaction $\mathrm{Ad}(U, R, g \circ f)$! As a clarification we will elaborate on both functions and illustrate our statement by an example. We will even assume that $U \subseteq \mathrm{dom}(f) \cap \mathrm{dom}(g)$ and $\mathrm{rng}(f) \subseteq \mathrm{dom}(g)$, in other words, f and g are defined for every DB state of U, and g is in addition defined for every result of f, even if that is not a DB state consistent with U.

$$\mathrm{Ad}(U, R, g \circ f) = \lambda v \in U : \begin{cases} g(f(v)) & \text{if } (v\,; g(f(v))) \in R & \text{(A)} \\ v & \text{if } (v\,; g(f(v))) \notin R & \text{(B)} \end{cases}$$

$$\begin{aligned} &\mathrm{Ad}(U, R, g) \circ \mathrm{Ad}(U, R, f) \\ &= \lambda v \in U : \begin{cases} \mathrm{Ad}(U, R, g)\,(f(v)) & \text{if } (v\,; f(v)) \in R \\ \mathrm{Ad}(U, R, g)\,(v) & \text{if } (v\,; f(v)) \notin R \end{cases} \\ &= \lambda v \in U : \begin{cases} g(f(v)) & \text{if } (v\,; f(v)) \in R \text{ and } (f(v)\,; g(f(v))) \in R & (++) \\ f(v) & \text{if } (v\,; f(v)) \in R \text{ and } (f(v)\,; g(f(v))) \notin R & (+-) \\ g(v) & \text{if } (v\,; f(v)) \notin R \text{ and } (v\,; g(v)) \in R & (-+) \\ v & \text{if } (v\,; f(v)) \notin R \text{ and } (v\,; g(v)) \notin R & (--) \end{cases} \end{aligned}$$

All of the eight combinations (A++, A+−, A−+, A−−, B++, B+−, B−+, and B−−) are possible, in principle. However, only in the situations A++ and B−− are we sure that both functions render the same results.

Even if there are no dynamic constraints, we are still confronted with a number of differences:

$$\mathrm{Adap}(U, g \circ f) = \lambda v \in U : \begin{cases} g(f(v)) & \text{if } g(f(v)) \in U & \text{(A)} \\ v & \text{if } g(f(v)) \notin U & \text{(B)} \end{cases}$$

$$\mathrm{Adap}(U, g) \circ \mathrm{Adap}(U, f) = \lambda v \in U : \begin{cases} g(f(v)) & \text{if } f(v) \in U \text{ and } g(f(v)) \in U & (++) \\ f(v) & \text{if } f(v) \in U \text{ and } g(f(v)) \notin U & (+-) \\ g(v) & \text{if } f(v) \notin U \text{ and } g(v) \in U & (-+) \\ v & \text{if } f(v) \notin U \text{ and } g(v) \notin U & (--) \end{cases}$$

With the exception of A+− and B++, all of the other six situations may arise. Again, only in the situations A++ and B−− are we sure that both functions always render the same results.

EXAMPLE 7.2:

We define two functions f72 and g72 and sketch in Figure 7.1

(a) how *without* any dynamic constraints each of the situations A++, A−+, A−−, B+−, B−+, and B−− can actually occur, and

(b) how *with* dynamic constraints the situations sketched under (a) can still remain possible, and how, in addition, the situations A+− and B++ can also occur.

Again we will use the DB universe EXU in Example 1.3, and under (b) we will use the transition relation R_0 defined in Example 7.1.

The function f72 describes the addition to the database of a female employee called Fox, employed by department 2, earning a salary of 3300 pounds. The employee number is chosen to be the number of employees plus one (taking for granted, possibly erroneously, that employees are assigned numbers consecutively from 1 onwards).

The function g72 describes the addition of the department Marketing, having employee 2 as its manager. The department number is chosen to be the number of departments plus one (assuming that departments are also numbered consecutively from one onwards).

Note that the tuples to be added partly depend on the state to which they will be added. This dependency is described by the auxiliary functions f71 and g71, which we introduce first.

We aim at choosing the domains of the functions g71 and g72 so large that both EXU and rng(f72) are included, in order that our assumptions (mentioned just before our introduction to the case analysis) do hold. We choose to that end a DB universe EXU7 without any database constraints and without any tuple and table constraints for the table index EMPL.

The definitions now read as follows:

EXU7 = Π({(EMPL; **P**(Π(FE))),
(DEP ; WD)});

$$f71 = \lambda v \in \text{EXU} \;\; : \{(\text{NO}; \,|v(\text{EMPL})| + 1),\; (\text{DEPNO}; 2),\; (\text{NAME}; \text{`FOX'}),\; (\text{SAL}; 3300),\; (\text{SEX}; \text{`F'})\};$$
$$g71 = \lambda v \in \text{EXU7} : \{(\text{DNO}; \,|v(\text{DEP})| + 1),\; (\text{MANNO}; 2),\; (\text{NAME}; \text{`MARKETING'})\};$$

$$f72 = \lambda v \in \text{EXU} \;\; : v \,\theta\, \{(\text{EMPL}; v(\text{EMPL}) \cup \{f71(v)\})\};$$
$$g72 = \lambda v \in \text{EXU7} : v \,\theta\, \{(\text{DEP}\;\; ; v(\text{DEP}) \;\; \cup \{g71(v)\})\}.$$

In Figure 7.1 we mention for each of the possible situations which conditions must ("+") and which conditions must not ("−") be satisfied by a DB state in order to let this situation occur. The plus and minus symbols between brackets are not *extra* requirements, but they are *consequences* of the other requirements. Besides the demands indicated in Figure 7.1 we stipulate, for each of those DB states, the requirement that they did not yet contain the department Marketing ('MARKETING' $\notin \{t(\text{NAME}) \mid t \in v(\text{DEP})\}$).

All eight situations were characterized by the possibility or impossibility to apply the functions f72, g72, and g72 $\circ$ f72. The associated conditions have been repeated in Figure 7.1.

We use the following abbreviations in Figure 7.1:

$m_v \;= |\, v(\text{EMPL})\,| + 1$
$a_v \;\;= |v(\text{DEP})| + 1$
$M_v = \{t(\text{NO}) \mid t \in v(\text{EMPL})\}$
$A_v \;= \{t(\text{DNO}) \mid t \in v(\text{DEP})\}$

	A++	A−+	A−−	B+−	B−+	B−−
g72(f72(v)) ∈ EXU	+	+	+	−	−	−
f72(v) ∈ EXU	+	−	−	+	−	−
g72(v) ∈ EXU		+	−		+	−
$m_v \in M_v$?	−	−	−	−	+	+
$2 \in M_v$?	(+)	+	−		+	
$2 \in M_v \cup \{m_v\}$?	+	(+)	+		(+)	
$a_v \in A_v$?	−	−	−	+	−	+
$2 \in A_v$?	+	−	−	+		
$2 \in A_v \cup \{a_v\}$?	(+)	+	+	(+)		

(a) Possible situations *without* any dynamic constraints

	A++	A−+	A−−	B+−	B−+	B−−	A+−	B++
$(v;\ g72(f72(v))) \in R_0$	+	+	+	−	−	−	+	−
$(v;\ f72(v)) \in R_0$	+	−	−	+	−	−	+	+
$(v;\ g72(v)) \in R_0$		+	−		+	−		
$(f72(v);\ g72(f72(v))) \in R_0$	+			−			−	+
(a) $m_v \in M_v$?	−	−	−	−	+	+	−	−
$2 \in M_v$?	(+)	+	−		+			(+)
$2 \in M_v \cup \{m_v\}$?	+	(+)	+		(+)		+	+
$a_v \in A_v$?	−	−	−	+	−	+	−	−
$2 \in A_v$?	+	−	−	+			+	+
$2 \in A_v \cup \{a_v\}$?	(+)	+	+	(+)			(+)	(+)
(b) $\lvert v(\text{EMPL})\rvert$ mod 10?	0	0 or 1	0 or 1	0 or 1	0 or 1	0 or 1	1	9
$m_v = 2$?	(−)	(−)	(+)					(−)
$a_v = 2$?	(−)	(+)	(+)				(−)	(−)

(b) Possible situations *with* dynamic constraints

Figure 7.1: Sufficient conditions for characteristic examples

For each of the eight situations, we will give a DB state in EXU that satisfies all the necessary conditions for the occurrence of that situation. We use to that end Figure 7.2. This figure depicts a DEP-table with 3 tuples and an EMPL-table with 11 tuples, where the DEP-table still contains the "parameters" α and β, and the EMPL-table the "parameters" γ and δ.

	NO	DEPNO	NAME	SEX	SAL
	1	1	Arthur C. Clarke	M	3000
A−−					
	4	1	John Irving	M	3000
	5	1	M. Minco	F	3000
	6	1	Paul Erdman	M	3000
	7	1	M. van Keulen	F	3000
	8	1	Steven Schlosstein	M	3000
	9	1	Stephen King	M	3000
	γ	1	A.M.G. Schmidt	F	3000
	δ	1	G. Reve	M	3000
B++					
	14	1	R. Rubinstein	F	3000
A++					
	15	1	G. Krol	M	3000

(a) A template for some EMPL-tables

	DNO	NAME	MANNO
	1	PRODUCTION	1
A−+, A−−			
	α	SALES	4
	β	RESEARCH	5

(b) A template for some DEP-tables

Figure 7.2: A template for some DB states in EXU

On the basis of these "table templates", we describe in Figure 7.3 eight DB states in EXU, by first choosing appropriate numbers of DEP-tuples and EMPL-tuples, and subsequently choosing appropriate values for the parameters α, β, γ, and δ (when they apply). In those situations in which for a DB state less than three departments or less than eleven employees are needed, we leave out "the tuples below" (see the open spaces between the tuples in Figure 7.2). Hence, we will choose all three DEP-tuples and all eleven EMPL-tuples to acquire the situations B+−, B−+, B−−, and A+−; for the situation A++, we leave out employee 15; for B++, we leave out the two employees 14 and 15; for A−+, department 1 (and eleven employees) suffice; finally, for A−−, we restrict ourselves to department 1 and employee 1. (In Figure 7.3, "na" means "not applicable".)

		A++	A−+	A−−	B+−	B−+	B−−	A+−	B++
g72 ∘ f72 applicable?		+	+	+	−	−	−	+	−
f72 applicable?		+	−	−	+	−	−	+	+
g72 applicable?		+	+	−	−	+	−	−	+
|ν(DEP)|		3	1	1	3	3	3	3	3
|ν(EMPL)|		10	11	1	11	11	11	11	9
DEP:	α	2	na	na	2	2	3	2	2
	β	3	na	na	4	3	4	3	3
EMPL:	γ	2	2	3	3	2	3	2	2
	δ	13	13	13	13	12	12	13	13

Figure 7.3: Eight characteristic DB states in EXU, based on Figure 7.2

□ Example 7.2.

EXERCISES

7.1. In this exercise we refer to the functions f5 and f6 introduced in Example 7.1. We define f8 = Ad(EXU, EXR, f5), where EXR is the transition relation defined in Example 5.1.
Prove that f8 = f6.

7.2. If U is a set and $R \subseteq U \times U$ and f is a function, then $\text{Ad}(U, R, f)$ is a transaction within $R \cup \text{id}(U)$. Prove this.

7.3. Give a reason for each of the twelve occurrences of minus symbols in Figure 7.3.

□

7.2 Some Common Classes of Transactions

To give an impression of the common sorts of transaction possibilities supported by actual DBMSs, and by the SQL2-standard for example (see [SQL 92]), we will introduce some special classes of transactions that together cover the largest part of the actual transaction possibilities, and in some respects even go far beyond that. This largest part of the current transaction possibilities in practice is characterized by the fact that changes are confined to one table index at a time. To be somewhat more precise: the available transactions all have the form $\text{Ad}(U, R, f)$, where f is a function over the DB universe U such that for exactly one given table index E_0 of U the value $f(v)$ for each $v \in U$ is a function over the set $\text{He}(U)$ of table indices with the property that $f(v) \not\restriction \{E_0\} = v \not\restriction \{E_0\}$. This means essentially that in those cases only the changes for the E_0-table have to be specified. We therefore introduce the following auxiliary concept:

DEFINITION 7.5:
If U is a DB universe and $R \subseteq U \times U$ and $E \in \text{He}(U)$ and τ is a function over U, then:
$\text{Main}(U, R, E, \tau) \stackrel{D}{=} \text{Ad}(U, R, \lambda v \in U : v \,\theta\, \{(E\,; \tau(v))\})$.

So, $\text{Main}(U, R, E, \tau)$ is the function over U that assigns to each DB state v of U the state in which the E-table has the value $\tau(v)$ and the other table indices retain their "old" value, provided that this transition is admissible; if not, then v is assigned to v itself. We call $\text{Main}(U, R, E, \tau)$ *the maintenance of E according to* τ (within R on U). By way of illustration we note that the function f7 from Example 7.1 can be written as $\text{Main}(\text{EXU}, \text{R}_0, \text{DEP}, \lambda v \in \text{EXU} : v(\text{DEP}) \cup \{\text{t4}\})$.

Using this special class of "one-table-transactions", introduced in Definition 7.5, common SQL-like transactions are now easy to define.

We start with an elementary "insert operation", namely the addition of one given tuple t to the E-table (provided that all static and dynamic constraints remain satisfied):

DEFINITION 7.6:
If U is a DB universe and $R \subseteq U \times U$ and $E \in \text{He}(U)$ and t is a function, then:
$\text{Inst}(U, R, E, t) \stackrel{D}{=} \text{Main}(U, R, E, \lambda v \in U : v(E) \cup \{t\})$.

The function f7 from Example 7.1 is an example of this form, and can be written as $\text{Inst}(\text{EXU}, \text{R}_0, \text{DEP}, \text{t4})$. Note that this is a concise and correct specification of the addition (attempt) of the tuple t4 to the DEP-table within the transition relation R_0 on the DB universe EXU.

We continue with the second common type of insert operation, namely the addition of a query result to the *E*-table (provided that all static and dynamic constraints remain intact):

DEFINITION 7.7:
If U is a DB universe and $R \subseteq U \times U$ and $E \in \text{He}(U)$ and q is a set function over U, then:
$\text{Insq}(U, R, E, q) \stackrel{D}{=} \text{Main}(U, R, E, \lambda v \in U : v(E) \cup q(v))$.

Obviously, Definition 7.6 reduces to a special case of Definition 7.7:
$\text{Inst}(U, R, E, t) = \text{Insq}(U, R, E, \lambda v \in U : \{t\})$.

The transaction $\text{Insq}(U, R, E, q)$ thus specifies the attempt to add "in one go" the set $q(v)$ to the *E*-table; it does *not* describe the attempt to add separate elements of the set $q(v)$ one by one. It is, so to speak, an "all-or-nothing" operation.

EXAMPLE 7.3:

The attempt to add in one go the table T1 in Example 1.1 (containing three "candidate employees") to the EMPL-table within the transition relation R_0 (introduced in Example 7.1) on the DB universe EXU can be specified by using the following (constant) function:

$q70 = \lambda v \in \text{EXU: T1}$

The intended transaction is Insq(EXU, R_0, EMPL, q70). In case of a DB state $v \in$ EXU where for example one of the employee numbers from T1 already occurs in v(EMPL), or one of the department numbers from T1 does not occur in v(DEP), no single element of T1 will thus be added.

When trying to add separate elements of T1 one by one, some elements might be added, while others might not be added. For example, maybe department 1 occurs in v(DEP), but department 2 does not. Naming the elements of T1 say t7, t8, and t9 for the moment, the "batch" of attempts to add t7, t8, and t9 in succession, can be specified as:

Inst(EXU, R_0, EMPL, t9) $\circ$ Inst(EXU, R_0, EMPL, t8) $\circ$ Inst(EXU, R_0, EMPL, t7)

□ Example 7.3.

The following operation concerns the removal of a query result from the *E*-table (again provided that all constraints remain intact). Such an operation is called a "delete operation".

DEFINITION 7.8:
If U is a DB universe and $R \subseteq U \times U$ and $E \in \text{He}(U)$ and q is a set function over U, then:
$\text{Del}(U, R, E, q) \stackrel{D}{=} \text{Main}(U, R, E, \lambda v \in U : v(E) - q(v))$.

Making the E-table empty is an important special case: take $q = \lambda v \in U : v(E)$.

EXAMPLE 7.4:

We will give some examples of delete operations within the context of the DB universe EXU and the transition relation EXR in Example 5.1. First we will give the informal descriptions, then the underlying queries, and finally the intended delete operations.

The informal descriptions of the delete operations run like this:

(1) Remove the employee with employee number 3.
(2) Remove all employees of department 3.
(3) Remove all employees of department 3 who do not manage any department.
(4) Remove all departments having no employees.

For sake of convenience, the underlying queries for these delete operations will be called q71, q72, q73, and q74.

(1) $\text{q71} = \lambda v \in \text{EXU} : \{t \in v(\text{EMPL}) \mid t(\text{NO}) = 3\}$.
(2) $\text{q72} = \lambda v \in \text{EXU} : \{t \in v(\text{EMPL}) \mid t(\text{DEPNO}) = 3\}$.
(3) $\text{q73} = \lambda v \in \text{EXU} : \{t \in v(\text{EMPL}) \mid t(\text{DEPNO}) = 3 \text{ en } t(\text{NO}) \notin \{a(\text{MANNO}) \mid a \in v(\text{DEP})\}\}$.
(4) $\text{q74} = \lambda v \in \text{EXU} : \{a \in v(\text{DEP}) \mid a(\text{DNO}) \notin \{t(\text{DEPNO}) \mid t \in v(\text{EMPL})\}\}$.

The formal specifications of the desired delete operations are:

(1) Del(EXU, EXR, EMPL, q71).
(2) Del(EXU, EXR, EMPL, q72).
(3) Del(EXU, EXR, EMPL, q73).
(4) Del(EXU, EXR, DEP, q74).

Taking the definition of EXR into consideration, we observe that delete attempts on the EMPL-table are not influenced by dynamic constraints. We now investigate each of the four delete operations in more detail.

Ad (1): Here at most one tuple is removed. Obviously, nothing is removed if 3 does not occur as an employee number. But if 3 does indeed occur as an employee number in the EMPL-table, it is still possible that, due to a static constraint, nothing is removed, namely if 3 is also a manager number occurring in the DEP-table.

Ad (2): Here zero, one, or more EMPL-tuples are removed simultaneously. If, however, at least one employee of department 3 is also a manager (whether or not of department 3 itself), not a single EMPL-tuple will be removed.

Ad (3): This operation is a refinement of the former case. All relevant EMPL-tuples are removed, without any interference by static or dynamic constraints.

Ad (4): From the dynamic constraint DC1 in the definition of the transition relation EXR it follows that no DNO-values should disappear, and therefore, since {DNO} is a key of DEP in EXU, not a single DEP-tuple! This means then that every deletion attempt concerning the DEP-table is doomed to fail. From this "intrinsic rollback" we conclude that

Del(EXU, EXR, DEP, q74) = id(EXU).

□ Example 7.4.

The last (and most subtle) class of common transactions that we address concerns so-called "update operations". This involves the modification of (parts of) existing tuples. What we need for this purpose is a function q over the DB universe U concerned, where $q(v)$ indicates for each $v \in U$ *which parts* of *which tuples* must be changed in *what way*. More precisely, we require that $q(v)$ is a function over a subset of $v(E)$, namely the set of tuples to be changed, such that $q(v)\,(t)$ for each $t \in \text{dom}(q(v))$ represents the altered tuple *fragment* of t. This leads then to the following general definition:

DEFINITION 7.9:

If U is a DB universe and $R \subseteq U \times U$ and $E \in \text{He}(U)$ and q is a function over U and $\forall v \in U : q(v)$ is a function-valued function such that $\text{dom}(q(v)) \subseteq v(E)$, then:

$$\text{Upd}(U, R, E, q) \stackrel{D}{=} \text{Main}(U, R, E, \lambda v \in U : (v(E) - \text{dom}(q(v))) \cup \{t \,\theta\, q(v)\,(t) \mid t \in \text{dom}(q(v))\}).$$

In other words, each element t of $\text{dom}(q(v))$ is replaced by $t \,\theta\, q(v)\,(t)$, again provided that after the desired changes all constraints must still be met; if not, the state remains unaltered.

EXAMPLE 7.5:

We will give some examples of update operations, using the DB universe UHPT from Chapter 4 and the transition relation RHPT from §5.2. Just as we did in Example 7.4, we will first give the informal descriptions, then the underlying "update queries", and finally the intended update operations.

The informal descriptions of the modification attempts read as follows:

(1) Set for each employee the sick leave to zero again.

(2) Change for the municipality of London the number of dentists into 5, increase the number of region doctors by 2, and double the number of pharmaceutical chemists.

(3) Change the number of patients (on January 1 late) of region doctor 99 into 747, adjust the "increase in the number of patients during the passed year" accordingly (now that a year has passed), and raise the expected increase or decrease by 10 percent (if necessary approximated).

(4) Add for the patient having number 123453 a daughter called Cherelien, born on February 26, 1988.

(5) Decrease for each medicine "the number of units in stock" by the totally prescribed units on May 3, 1989.

The following queries over UHPT concern the update attempts above:

(1) $q75 = \lambda v \in UHPT : \lambda t \in v(EMP) : \{(TSL ; 0)\}$.

(2) $q76 = \lambda v \in UHPT : \lambda t \in v(MUN)$ and $t(CTY) =$ 'London':
$\{(NDT ; 5), (NGP ; t(NGP)+2), (NDP ; 2 * t(NDP))\}$.

(3) $q77 = \lambda v \in UHPT : \lambda t \in v(GP)$ and $t(GPID) = 99$:
$\{(PAT ; 747), (INCR ; 747 - t(PAT)),$
$(EXPI ; t(EXPI) + t(EXPI) \text{ div } 10)\}$.

(4) $q78 = \lambda v \in UHPT : \lambda t \in v(PAT)$ and $t(PNR) = 123453$:
$\{(PROG; t(PROG) \cup \{t78\})\}$,
where $t78 = \{(FNM;$ 'Cherelien'$), (DTB; 19880226), (SEX,$ 'F'$)\}$.

(5) $q79 = \lambda v \in UHPT : \lambda t \in v(MED)$:
$\{(NST ; t(NST) - (\Sigma x \in v(MDP)$ and
$x(MCD) = t(MCD)$ and $x(DAT) = 890503$:
$x(DUR) * x(FREQ) * x(NUT)))\}$.

The update operations asked for are:

(1) Upd(UHPT, RHPT, EMP, q75).

(2) Upd(UHPT, RHPT, MUN, q76).

(3) Upd(UHPT, RHPT, GP, q77).

(4) Upd(UHPT, RHPT, PAT, q78).

(5) Upd(UHPT, RHPT, MED, q79).

We will comment on each of these five alteration attempts. In particular, we will search manually for dynamic and static constraints that could lead to a rollback. (It is, however, the task of the DBMS to verify these constraints "automatically".)

Ad (1): In order to illustrate Definition 7.9 (and some other concepts introduced in this chapter) we would like to "reconstruct" the given solution for this first example explicitly, using the definitions 7.5 and 7.3 and the properties of q75 that dom(q75(v)) = v(EMP) and q75(v) (t) = {(TSL; 0)}.

$$\begin{aligned}
&\text{Upd(UHPT, RHPT, EMP, q75)}\\
&= \text{Main(UHPT, RHPT, EMP,}\\
&\qquad \lambda v \in \text{UHPT}: (v(\text{EMP}) - \text{dom}\,(\text{q75}(v))) \cup\\
&\qquad\qquad \{t\,\theta\,\text{q75}(v)\,(t) \mid t \in \text{dom(q75}(v))\})\\
&= \text{Main(UHPT, RHPT, EMP,}\\
&\qquad \lambda v \in \text{UHPT}: \{t\,\theta\,\{(\text{TSL}\,;0)\} \mid t \in v(\text{EMP})\})\\
&= \text{Ad(UHPT, RHPT,}\\
&\qquad \lambda v \in \text{UHPT}: v\,\theta\,\{(\text{EMP}\,; \{t\,\theta\,\{(\text{TSL}\,;0)\} \mid t \in v(\text{EMP})\})\})\\
&= \text{Id(UHPT)}\,\theta\,(\text{RHPT} \cap \lambda v \in \text{UHPT}: v\,\theta\,\{(\text{EMP}\,; \{t\,\theta\,\{(\text{TSL}\,;0)\}\\
&\qquad\qquad \mid t \in v(\text{EMP})\})\})
\end{aligned}$$

From the definition of UHPT in §4.2 it is rather obvious that $v\,\theta\,\{(\text{EMP}\,; \{t\,\theta\,\{(\text{TSL}\,;0)\} \mid t \in v(\text{EMP})\})\}$ is again an element of UHPT for each $v \in$ UHPT. After all, only the TSL-values of the EMP-table are adapted, and the only constraint on these TSL-values is the requirement that they be members of the set [0 .. 290]. In the new situation, this demand is clearly met. Furthermore, for each $v \in$ UHPT, the pair $(v\,; v\,\theta\,\{(\text{EMP}\,; \{t\,\theta\,\{(\text{TSL}\,;0)\} \mid t \in v(\text{EMP})\})\})$ satisfies the dynamic constraint C12 in §5.2, and (in a trivial way) also all other constraints in the definition of the transition relation RHPT. We can therefore simplify Upd(UHPT, RHPT, EMP, q75) even further:

$$\begin{aligned}
&\text{Upd(UHPT, RHPT, EMP, q75)}\\
&= \lambda v \in \text{UHPT} : v\,\theta\,\{(\text{EMP}\,; \{t\,\theta\,\{(\text{TSL}\,;0)\} \mid t \in v(\text{EMP})\})\}.
\end{aligned}$$

Ad (2): If the municipality of London does not occur in v(MUN), then no tuple must be changed. The state then remains unaltered (without there being any rollback). We will now investigate what would happen when the municipality of London did occur in v(MUN). In §5.2 we encounter no dynamic constraints concerning the MUN-table. Looking at the definition of UHPT in §4.2, we observe that the static (tuple) constraint R44 is the only possible cause of a rollback. When the municipality of London indeed occurs in v(MUN), and when because of the increase of the number of region doctors by two that number is now four or greater - hence, it was two or three before - and in addition the doctor on duty does not have his practice in London, then there will be no change. (Then there will *indeed* be a rollback.)

Ad (3): In case no tuple with registration number 99 occurs in v(GP), no tuples will be altered. We will now investigate what happens when such a tuple does occur. The only dynamic constraint in the definition of the transition relation RHPT concerning the GP-table is C14. The altered tuple t' in the new proposed state indeed satisfies the demand put forward in constraint C14, i.e., t'(INCR) = t'(PAT) − t(PAT), since t'(PAT) = 747. The only static constraints in the definition of the DB universe UHPT that concern the attributes to be altered in the GP-table are the tuple constraints R40 and R41. For the changed tuple t' we have that t'(PAT) − t'(INCR) = 747 − (747 − t(PAT)) = t(PAT). Since the "old" tuple t comes from an element v of UHPT itself, t obeys the demand that t(PAT) $\in \mathbb{N}$, established in the object characterization FGP. Hence t(PAT) ≥ 0. From this we conclude that the tuple constraint R40 cannot lead to a rollback at this transaction. As far as the tuple constraint R41 is concerned, it is required that t'(PAT) + t'(EXPI) ≥ 0 for the changed tuple t', or, in other words, that 747 + t(EXPI) + (t(EXPI) div 10) ≥ 0 for the old tuple t. The latter amounts to the requirement that t(EXPI) > -680. Should therefore the "old expectation" have been a decrease of 680 or more patients, then the proposed change can not be effectuated.

Ad (4): If no tuple with patient number 123453 occurs in v(PAT), then simply no change will take place. But when such a tuple does occur, then the only constraint that could lead to a rollback is the static (attribute) constraint R02. This requirement means in this case that the name Cherelien does not yet occur as an already registered child of patient 123453 (unless having date of birth 19880226 and sex 'F').

Ad (5): Here all MED-tuples qualify for change. The only constraint potentially leading to a rollback in case of this transaction is the static constraint for the attribute NST of the MED-table that the number of units in stock must be greater than or equal to 0. When due to proposed alterations one or more of the stocks would become "negative", then the stock remains unaltered for *all* medicines. (That situation seems to indicate an administrative error which has led, or may soon lead, to inaccurate data, resulting in the decision to carry out no changes at all.)

□ Example 7.5.

EXERCISES

7.4. In this exercise we return to Upd(UHPT, RHPT, EMP, q75), which is the first of the transactions treated in Example 7.5. For now we will call this transaction Φ. Prove that Φ is *idempotent* under function composition, i.e., $\Phi \circ \Phi = \Phi$.

7.5. Assuming that $t \in \Pi(\text{FPAT})$, verify which static and dynamic constraints can lead to a rollback of the transaction Inst(UHPT, RHPT, PAT, *t*). Here, FPAT is the object characterization for the table index PAT as defined in §4.2.

7.6. Give formal specifications of the following transactions on the DB universe EXU within the transition relation EXR in Example 5.1.

(a) Raise all salaries of all employees of the departments 3 and 4 by 5 percent (approximated where needed).

(b) Raise the salary of each manager by 100 pounds.

(c) Raise the salary of each manager by 100 pounds, and raise the salaries of all employees of the departments 3 and 4 by 5 percent. (For the managers attached to department 3 or 4, the extra 100 pounds is *not* further raised by 5 percent).

(d) Raise the salary of each manager by 100 pounds for *each* department that he or she runs.

7.7. This exercise involves Example 2.13. Let $t_A \in \Pi(\text{F4})$ and $t_B \in \Pi(\text{F4})$, where $t_A \neq t_B$.

The municipality represented by t_A will be incorporated by the municipality represented by t_B. This means that t_A inherits the name of t_B, the mayor of t_A becomes a citizen of t_B and the inhabitants of t_A will from now on be citizens of t_B. Places of birth are not changed.

Give a formal definition of the transaction $\text{Annex}(t_A, t_B) \in \text{U1} \twoheadrightarrow \text{U1}$, representing the administrative realization of the outlined municipal reorganization.

7.8. Give a formal definition of the transaction $\text{Delpt}(t_0) \in \text{UHPT} \twoheadrightarrow \text{UHPT}$, where $t_0 \in \Pi(\text{FPT}) \upharpoonright \{\text{PNR, TCD, SNR}\}$, that assigns to each DB state $v \in \text{UHPT}$ the state arising from v by leaving out the patient treatment tuple (if any) having the key value described by t_0, and in addition decreasing the qualifying serial numbers by 1. (There are no dynamic constraints.)

7.9. Give a formal definition of the transaction $\text{Updam}(x_0) \in \text{UHPT} \twoheadrightarrow \text{UHPT}$ within RHPT, where $x_0 \in \text{Snn}(4)$, assigning to each DB state $v \in \text{UHPT}$ the state arising from v when an employee with identity number x_0 takes over the job of his assistant manager, i.e., including his group leadership.
(The assistant manager becomes an ordinary member of his group, and if employee x_0 was already a group leader, then these two groups are considered joined.)

7.10. This exercise concerns Example 3.6.
Give a formal definition of the transaction Make(p) $\in$ UBP $\twoheadrightarrow$ UBP, where $p \in$ [40000 .. 99999], assigning to each DB state $v \in$ UBP the state arising from v when one specimen of the product with product number p has been produced immediately from its direct parts, provided that p is known as a product number and of all direct parts there are sufficient units in stock; should that not be the case, then the state is not altered. (There are no dynamic constraints.)

7.11. Give a formal definition of the transaction Insmdp(x_0) $\in$ UHPT $\twoheadrightarrow$ UHPT, where $x_0 \in \Pi$(FMDP$\nmid$ {SNR}), that assigns to each $v \in$ UHPT the state arising from v by addition of the medicine prescription tuple that is almost completely specified by x_0, where

- the serial number is the first "free" positive number for that patient,
- also the number of units in stock has been adapted, and
- there are no dynamic constraints,

provided that this would result in a state belonging to UHPT; if not, then the state remains the same.

□

CHAPTER 8

Data Dictionaries

The *data dictionary*, also known as the *system catalog*, constitutes a central part of a database management system. It contains *meta-data*, i.e., *data about the data* in the database. The data dictionary may contain data such as

(a) table names, attributes, the allowed values for those attributes, keys, connection requirements and other constraints: in short, a description of the database universe involved,

(b) data on the current database state, for instance, the number of elements per table or the number of different values per attribute of a table,

(c) names and definitions of views, menus, procedures, screens, screen fields, and so on,

(d) (statistical) data on the use of the database so far, possibly specified per department and/or period,

(e) data on the physical structure of the database (unique and non-unique indices, clusters, disk devices, allocated space, occupied pages per table),

(f) authorization data (what may be seen or done by whom?),

(g) creators and owners of tables, views, programs, and so on,

(h) allowed users and user groups, their passwords and privileges,

(i) data on running processes, for example, the data "locked" by the process, the number of disk reads and disk writes, and the requesting user,

(j) data on the distribution of the actual data over the various machines (in case of a distributed database), and

(k) possibly also data on the data dictionary itself.

For more information about the various aspects mentioned above we refer the reader to the literature, for example, [Da 90], [IDT 90/89/88], [NGI 88/87], [We 86], [Ma 84], [ALM 82], [LP 82], [CD 81], [SM 80], [Uh 73], and the references mentioned in them.

In this chapter we will show on the basis of the data definition part of a data dictionary, i.e., on the basis of the meta-data mentioned under (a), not only how a data dictionary can be formally *represented*, but also how its *semantics* can be *formalized.* We conclude this introduction with the remark that this chapter is an adaptation of [Br 88].

8.1 The Data Definition Part of a Data Dictionary

The data definition part of a DD system (data dictionary system) determines the set of DB universes that can be described by means of that DD system: each description that is specifiable in that DD system uniquely determines a DB universe, in a way that is specific to the DD system concerned. Therefore, the data definition part of a DD system can be represented formally by a function that assigns to each description that is allowed in this system the DB universe it is supposed to describe. We will call such a function a *DD function*:

DEFINITION 8.1:
I is a **DD function** $\overset{D}{\Longleftrightarrow}$ I is a function and
$\forall d \in \mathrm{dom}(I) : I(d)$ is a DB universe.

If I is a DD function, then dom(I) is called *the DD universe of I*; if $U \in \mathrm{rng}(I)$, then U is said to be *describable by means of I*. If, in addition, $(d\ ;\ U) \in I$, then d is called a *description of U according to I*; conversely, U is called *the DB universe described by d according to I*, or *the semantics* (or *interpretation*) *of d according to I.*

EXAMPLE 8.1:

We start with a relatively simple example of a DD function. We will call this function I1. Each element of dom(I1) is a DB skeleton in which all table indices and all attributes are strings of at most 16 characters, i.e., dom(I1) = $(\mathrm{Chs}(16) \,\tilde{\twoheadrightarrow}\, \mathbf{P}(\mathrm{Chs}(16)))$. The DD function I1 assigns to each $g \in$ dom(I1) the uniquely determined DB universe over g in which the value of each attribute can be any string of at most 16 characters and in which no other requirements hold. In other words, for every table index $E \in \mathrm{dom}(g)$, an "E-table" can be any subset of $g(E) \twoheadrightarrow \mathrm{Chs}(16)$. In short, the DB universe described by g according to I1 is

$$\Pi\ (\lambda E \in \mathrm{dom}(g) : \mathbf{P}(g(E) \twoheadrightarrow \mathrm{Chs}(16)))$$

The intended DD function I1 can therefore be defined as follows:

$$\mathrm{I1} = \lambda g \in (\mathrm{Chs}(16) \,\tilde{\twoheadrightarrow}\, \mathbf{P}(\mathrm{Chs}(16))) :$$
$$\Pi\ (\lambda E \in \mathrm{dom}(g) : \mathbf{P}(g(E) \twoheadrightarrow \mathrm{Chs}(16))).$$

It turns out that in rng(I1), for every DB skeleton $g \in \mathrm{Chs}(16) \,\tilde{\twoheadrightarrow}\, \mathbf{P}(\mathrm{Chs}(16))$, we have exactly one DB universe over g. Moreover, there is only one way to describe this DB universe by means of I1, since I1 is an *injective* function.

To illustrate this, we will apply I1 to the following small DB skeleton:

$$\begin{array}{ll|l} \text{g3} = \{ & (\text{'EMP'}; \{\text{'ENAME'}, \text{'ADDRESS'}, \text{'CITY'}, \text{'DCODE'}\}), & \text{employees} \\ & (\text{'DEP'}; \{\text{'DNAME'}, \text{'DCODE'}, \text{'MANNAME'}\})\} & \text{departments} \end{array}$$

It is easy to see that g3 is an element of $\text{Chs}(16) \overset{\sim}{\rightarrowtriangle} \mathbf{P}(\text{Chs}(16))$; so g3 $\in$ dom(I1). We will now compute the DB universe described by g3 according to I1. We determine this DB universe I1(g3) by successively applying the definition of I1, the definition of g3, and Lemma 15(a) on page 14:

$$\begin{aligned} & \text{I1(g3)} \\ & = \Pi(\lambda E \in \text{dom(g3)}: \mathbf{P}(\text{g3}(E) \rightarrowtriangle \text{Chs}(16))) \\ & = \Pi(\{(\text{'EMP'}; \mathbf{P}(\text{g3}(\text{'EMP'}) \rightarrowtriangle \text{Chs}(16))), \\ & \qquad (\text{'DEP'}; \mathbf{P}(\text{g3}(\text{'DEP'}) \rightarrowtriangle \text{Chs}(16)))\}) \\ & = \Pi(\{(\text{'EMP'}; \mathbf{P}(\Pi(\{(\text{'ENAME'} \quad ; \text{Chs}(16)), \\ & \qquad\qquad\qquad\qquad (\text{'ADDRESS'} \; ; \text{Chs}(16)), \\ & \qquad\qquad\qquad\qquad (\text{'CITY'} \quad ; \text{Chs}(16)), \\ & \qquad\qquad\qquad\qquad (\text{'DCODE'} \quad ; \text{Chs}(16))\}))), \\ & \qquad (\text{'DEP'}; \mathbf{P}(\Pi(\{(\text{'DNAME'} \quad ; \text{Chs}(16)), \\ & \qquad\qquad\qquad\qquad (\text{'DCODE'} \quad ; \text{Chs}(16)), \\ & \qquad\qquad\qquad\qquad (\text{'MANNAME'}; \text{Chs}(16))\})))\}). \end{aligned}$$

Whereas in the preceding chapters the nature of table indices and attributes seemed hardly relevant, in the examples in this chapter we will explicitly choose strings for table indices and attributes. Consequently, quotes will now be handled with greater care.

□ Example 8.1.

A DD function I is called *at least as expressive as* a DD function I', if I can at least describe all DB universes that can be described by I'.
We call I and I' *DD-equivalent* if they describe exactly the same set of DB universes. Formally:

DEFINITION 8.2:
If I and I' are DD functions, then:

(a) **I is at least as expressive as I'** $\overset{D}{\Leftrightarrow} \text{rng}(I') \subseteq \text{rng}(I)$;

(b) **I is DD-equivalent to I'** $\overset{D}{\Leftrightarrow} \text{rng}(I') = \text{rng}(I)$.

Two DD-equivalent DD functions may not only have different domains (i.e., different sets of descriptions), but they may also have different ways of interpreting their *common* descriptions, should there be any: if I and I' are two DD-equivalent DD functions and $d \in \text{dom(I)} \cap \text{dom}(I')$, $I(d)$ still need not be equal to $I'(d)$. Conversely, two DD functions sharing the same domain need not be DD-equivalent; cf. the examples 8.4 and 8.5.

We note that the range of a DD function I, being a *set* of DB universes, does not include the *class* of *all* DB universes. (For an elaborate treatise on this set-theoretical distinction, the reader is referred to [DDS 76] for example.) As a consequence, for every DD function I there exists a more expressive DD function I', i.e., with which "more" DB universes can be described than with I. We thus draw the interesting conclusion - certainly of interest from a commercial point of view - that there is no such thing as a "universal" DD function with which the class of *all* DB universes could be described.

The following lemma suggests a straightforward way of comparing the expressiveness of two DD functions.

LEMMA 8.1:
If I and I' are DD functions and h is a function such that $I' = I \circ h$,
then I is at least as expressive as I'.

This lemma follows immediately from Definition 8.2(a) and Lemma 9(c) on page 10. The function h "converts" a description according to I' into a description according to I. In this respect, h is called a *DD conversion function*, or, if h is relatively "straightforward", a *DD migration function*.

EXAMPLE 8.2:

We will define a DD function I2 that is DD-equivalent to the DD function I1 in Example 8.1. In fact, I2 is a "sugared" version of I1, in the sense that the DD universe resembles the shape of a *DB universe*. The DD universe of I2, i.e., the set of possible descriptions according to I2, is a DB universe DDU2 with only one "meta-table-index", namely the string 'ATT', and two "meta-attributes", namely the strings 'TNAME' and 'ANAME'. The set of "object-table-indices" of the DB universe described by an element d of dom(I2) is $\{t(\text{'TNAME'}) \mid t \in d(\text{'ATT'})\}$, and the set of attributes of such an "object-table-index" E is $\{x(\text{'ANAME'}) \mid x \in d(\text{'ATT'}) \text{ and } x(\text{'TNAME'}) = E\}$.
The definitions of DDU2 and I2 read as follows:

$$\text{DDU2} = \Pi(\{(\text{'ATT'} ; \mathbf{P}(\{\text{'TNAME'}, \text{'ANAME'}\} \twoheadrightarrow \text{Chs}(16)))\});$$

$$\begin{aligned} \text{I2} = {} & \lambda d \in \text{DDU2}: \\ & \Pi(\lambda E \in \{t(\text{'TNAME'}) \mid t \in d(\text{'ATT'})\}: \\ & \quad \mathbf{P}(\{x(\text{'ANAME'}) \mid x \in d(\text{'ATT'}) \text{ and } x(\text{'TNAME'}) = E\} \twoheadrightarrow \text{Chs}(16))) \end{aligned}$$

The DB universe from Example 8.1 described by g3 according to I1 can also be described according to I2, namely by the function d1 over {'ATT'} for which d1('ATT') is the table over {'TNAME', 'ANAME'} represented in Figure 8.1.

d1('ATT'):

TNAME	ANAME
EMP	ENAME
EMP	ADDRESS
EMP	CITY
EMP	DCODE
DEP	DCODE
DEP	DNAME
DEP	MANNAME

Figure 8.1: A description according to I2

To illustrate the definition of I2, we will now calculate I2(d1). We will do this by successively using the definitions of I2 and d1 (twice), and Lemma 15(a) on page 14:

I2(d1)
= Π(λ*E* ∈ {*t*('TNAME') | *t* ∈ d1('ATT')}:
  P({*x*('ANAME') | *x* ∈ d1('ATT') and *x*('TNAME') = *E*} ⇸ Chs(16)))
= Π(λ*E* ∈ { 'EMP', 'DEP'}:
  P({*x*('ANAME') | *x* ∈ d1('ATT') and *x*('TNAME') = *E*} ⇸ Chs(16)))
= Π({('EMP';**P**({ 'ENAME', 'ADDRESS', 'CITY', 'DCODE'}⇸Chs(16))),
  ('DEP'; **P**({ 'DNAME', 'DCODE', 'MANNAME'} ⇸ Chs(16)))})
= Π({('EMP'; **P**(Π({('ENAME' ; Chs(16)),
  ('ADDRESS' ; Chs(16)),
  ('CITY' ; Chs(16)),
  ('DCODE' ; Chs(16))}))),
  ('DEP'; **P**(Π({('DNAME' ; Chs(16)),
  ('DCODE' ; Chs(16)),
  ('MANNAME'; Chs(16))})))}).

Note that I2(d1) = I1(g3).

It is not a coincidence that the DB universe at the end of Example 8.1, described according to I1, can also be described according to I2, since I2 is DD-equivalent to I1. By Lemma 8.1, this can be proved by defining two conversion functions h12 and h21 such that

I1 = I2 ∘ h12 and I2 = I1 ∘ h21

Here we will only define the conversion function h21. The definition of h12 and the proofs of the two properties above will be left to the reader (in Exercise 8.3).

h21 = λ*d* ∈ DDU2:
  λ*E* ∈ {*t*('TNAME') | *t* ∈ *d*('ATT')}:
    {*x*('ANAME') | *x* ∈ *d*('ATT') and *x*('TNAME') = *E*}

□ Example 8.2.

We note that the DD function I2 from Example 8.2 has the interesting property that the DD universe of I2 is a DB universe itself. The property of a *DD* universe having the same global structure as its *DB* universes can be quite useful in practice. Retrieving and updating the data dictionary on the one hand and the database on the other hand could then be done in the same way! Since *updating* the data dictionary (alias "system-database") in fact amounts to *defining* (or redefining) the actual database (alias "object-database"), it follows that both definition and use of the database could be realized by one and the same mechanism. (By *use* we mean querying and updating the contents.)

DD functions such as I2, whose DD universe is a DB universe itself, will be called *DB-like*:

DEFINITION 8.3:
If I is a DD function, then:
I is **DB-like** $\overset{D}{\Longleftrightarrow}$ dom(I) is a DB universe.

If I is a DB-like DD function, then the DD universe dom(I) is called a *meta-DB-universe*, an element of dom(I) is called a *meta-DB-state*, the table indices of the DB universe dom(I) are called *meta-table-indices*, and the attributes of dom(I) are called *meta-attributes* (as we already did in Example 8.2, by the way).

For any DB-like DD function I we could ask ourselves whether the DB universe dom(I) can itself be described by means of I, in other words, whether there exists some $d_0 \in \text{dom}(I)$ such that $I(d_0) = \text{dom}(I)$, i.e., whether $\text{dom}(I) \in \text{rng}(I)$. In that case, I is called *self-describable*:

DEFINITION 8.4:
If I is a DD function, then:
I is **self-describable** $\overset{D}{\Longleftrightarrow}$ $\text{dom}(I) \in \text{rng}(I)$.

It follows immediately from the definition above that every self-describable DD function is DB-like (and therefore this has not been incorporated as an explicit requirement in the definition).

What self-describability of a DD function I actually amounts to is that the structures *used* in I are no more complex than the structures *described* by means of I. One of the interesting properties of self-describable DD functions is that they can build replicas of their own DD universe. This property can be very useful both when building a DBMS and also when simulating the data dictionary of a given DBMS.

EXAMPLE 8.3:

The DD function I2 in Example 8.2 is self-describable. In order to prove this, we define the following table-valued function:

$$d2 = \{(\text{'ATT'};\{ \{(\text{'TNAME'};\ \text{'ATT'}), (\text{'ANAME'};\ \text{'TNAME'})\},\\ \{(\text{'TNAME'};\ \text{'ATT'}), (\text{'ANAME'};\ \text{'ANAME'})\}\})\}$$

This meta-DB-state d2 can also be represented as follows:

d2('ATT'):

TNAME	ANAME
ATT	TNAME
ATT	ANAME

Figure 8.2: A description according to I2

Using the definitions of I2 and d2, we will now calculate I2(d2):

$$\begin{aligned} I2(d2) &= \Pi(\lambda E \in \{\text{'ATT'}\} : \mathbf{P}(\{\text{'TNAME'}, \text{'ANAME'}\} \twoheadrightarrow Chs(16))) \\ &= \Pi(\quad \{(\text{'ATT'}; \mathbf{P}(\{\text{'TNAME'}, \text{'ANAME'}\} \twoheadrightarrow Chs(16)))\}) \\ &= DDU2 \\ &= dom(I2) \end{aligned}$$

We have thus proved that I2 is indeed self-describable.

The DD function I1 from Example 8.1 is not self-describable, for I1 is not even DB-like:

$$dom(I1) = Chs(16) \overset{\sim}{\twoheadrightarrow} \mathbf{P}(Chs(16)),$$

so not all elements of dom(I1) have the same domain (whereas the elements of a DB universe do have the same domain).

□ Example 8.3.

We will now give a more extensive (and more realistic) example of a DD function.

EXAMPLE 8.4:

We will define a (DB-like) DD function I3 for the description of DB universes having the following features:

(M1) Attributes are either "of type *integer*" (indicated by 'N') or "of type *string*" (indicated by 'C').

(M2) The maximum "field length" can be chosen *per attribute* (though not exceeding 256). We note that in the examples 8.1 and 8.2 the maximum field length in the definition of a DB universe cannot be chosen, but must always be 16. (Nevertheless, the actual field lengths in the tuples of a *DB state* may be less than 16.)

(M3) The field length of an attribute "of type integer", however, must not exceed 9.

(M4) A table (index) can have more than one key, but every key is singular (i.e., consisting of precisely one attribute).

(M5) Connection requirements (of precisely one attribute to precisely one attribute) can be represented; the attributes concerned may occur in the same table.

The definition of DDU3, the DD universe of I3, is preceded by the definitions of two "meta-object-characterizations", FATT3 and FREF3, a "meta-tuple-characterization" TATT3, and a "DD-characterization" DDC3 that assigns to each of the two meta-table-indices 'ATT' and 'REF' the set of allowed "meta-tables" for that meta-table-index:

$$\begin{aligned}
\text{FATT3} = \{ & (\text{'TNAME'} ; \text{Chs}(18)), \\
& (\text{'ANAME'} ; \text{Chs}(16)), \\
& (\text{'TYPE'} ; \{\text{'C'}, \text{'N'}\}), && \text{(M1)} \\
& (\text{'SIZE'} ; [1 .. 256]), && \text{(M2)} \\
& (\text{'KEY'} ; \{\text{'*'}, \text{'–'}\})\};
\end{aligned}$$

$$\begin{aligned}
\text{TATT3} = \{ t \mid\ & t \in \Pi(\text{FATT3}) \text{ and} \\
& \text{if } t(\text{'TYPE'}) = \text{'N'} \text{ then } t(\text{'SIZE'}) \leq 9\}; && \text{(M3)}
\end{aligned}$$

$$\begin{aligned}
\text{FREF3} = \{ & (\text{'TNAME1'} ; \text{Chs}(18)), \\
& (\text{'ANAME1'} ; \text{Chs}(16)), \\
& (\text{'TNAME2'} ; \text{Chs}(18)), \\
& (\text{'ANAME2'} ; \text{Chs}(16))\};
\end{aligned}$$

$$\begin{aligned}
\text{DDC3} = \{ & (\text{'ATT'} ; \{ T \subseteq \text{TATT3} \mid \{\text{'TNAME'}, \text{'ANAME'}\} \text{ is u.i. in } T\}), \\
& (\text{'REF'} ; \mathbf{P}(\Pi(\text{FREF3})))\};
\end{aligned}$$

$$\begin{aligned}
\text{DDU3} = \{ d \mid\ & d \in \Pi(\text{DDC3}) \text{ and} \\
& \{(\text{'TNAME1'} ; \text{'TNAME'}), (\text{'ANAME1'} ; \text{'ANAME'})\} \text{ connects} \\
& \qquad d(\text{'REF'}) \text{ with } d(\text{'ATT'}) \text{ and} \\
& \{(\text{'TNAME2'} ; \text{'TNAME'}), (\text{'ANAME2'} ; \text{'ANAME'})\} \text{ connects} \\
& \qquad d(\text{'REF'}) \text{ with } d(\text{'ATT'})\}.
\end{aligned}$$

We will now define our DD function I3 over DDU3 in the following (top-down) manner:

$$\begin{aligned}
\text{I3} = \lambda d \in \text{DDU3}: & \\
& \{ v \mid v \in \Pi(\text{DBC3}_d) \text{ and} \\
& \ \forall y \in d(\text{'REF'}) : \{(y(\text{'ANAME1'}) ; y(\text{'ANAME2'}))\} \text{ connects} && \text{(M5)} \\
& \qquad\qquad v(y(\text{'TNAME1'})) \text{ with } v(y(\text{'TNAME2'}))\},
\end{aligned}$$

where for each $d \in$ DDU3 the database characterization DBC3_d is defined as follows:

$\text{DBC3}_d =$
$\lambda E \in \{t(\text{'TNAME'}) \mid t \in d(\text{'ATT'})\}$:
$\{T \mid T \subseteq \Pi(\text{FK}_{d,E})$ and
$\forall x \in d(\text{'ATT'})$: if $x(\text{'KEY'}) = \text{'*'}$ and $x(\text{'TNAME'}) = E$ (M4)
then $\{x(\text{'ANAME'})\}$ is u.i. in $T\}$,

where for each $d \in$ DDU3 and each $E \in \{t(\text{'TNAME'}) \mid t \in d(\text{'ATT'})\}$ the object characterization $\text{FK}_{d,E}$ for E is defined as follows:

$\text{FK}_{d,E} =$
$\{(t(\text{'ANAME'}) ; \text{Chs}(t(\text{'SIZE'}))) \mid t \in d(\text{'ATT'})$ and
$t(\text{'TNAME'}) = E$ and $t(\text{'TYPE'}) = \text{'C'}\} \cup$
$\{(t(\text{'ANAME'}) ; \text{Int}(t(\text{'SIZE'}))) \mid t \in d(\text{'ATT'})$ and
$t(\text{'TNAME'}) = E$ and $t(\text{'TYPE'}) = \text{'N'}\}$

Figure 8.3 represents a description d3 according to I3 of a somewhat more refined DB universe than I1(g3) in Example 8.1 (or I2(d1) in Example 8.2, for that matter).

d3('ATT'):

TNAME	ANAME	KEY	TYPE	SIZE
EMP	ENAME	*	C	16
EMP	ADDRESS	–	C	16
EMP	CITY	–	C	16
EMP	DCODE	–	C	16
DEP	DCODE	*	C	16
DEP	DNAME	*	C	16
DEP	MANNAME	–	C	16

d3('REF'):

TNAME1	ANAME1	TNAME2	ANAME2
EMP	DCODE	DEP	DCODE
DEP	MANNAME	EMP	ENAME

Figure 8.3: A description according to I3

To illustrate the definitions of I3, DBC3_d, and $\text{FK}_{d,E}$, we will now elaborate on I3(d3). First, we will elaborate I3 and then d3('REF'):

I3(d3)
$= \{v \mid v \in \Pi(\text{DBC3}_{d3})$ and
$\forall y \in$ d3('REF'): $\{(y(\text{'ANAME1'}); y(\text{'ANAME2'}))\}$ connects
$v(y(\text{'TNAME1'}))$ with $v(y(\text{'TNAME2'}))\}$
$= \{v \mid v \in \Pi(\text{DBC3}_{d3})$ and
$\{(\text{'DCODE'}; \text{'DCODE'})\}$ connects $v(\text{'EMP'})$ with $v(\text{'DEP'})$ and
$\{(\text{'MANNAME'}; \text{'ENAME'})\}$ connects $v(\text{'DEP'})$ with $v(\text{'EMP'})\}$,

where (by the definition of $DBC3_{d3}$ and the properties of d3('ATT'))

$$
\begin{aligned}
&DBC3_{d3}\\
&= \lambda E \in \{t(\text{'TNAME'}) \mid t \in d3(\text{'ATT'})\}:\\
&\qquad \{T \mid T \subseteq \Pi(FK_{d3,E}) \text{ and}\\
&\qquad\qquad \forall x \in d3(\text{'ATT'}): \text{if } x(\text{'KEY'}) = \text{'*'} \text{ and } x(\text{'TNAME'}) = E\\
&\qquad\qquad\qquad \text{then } \{x(\text{'ANAME'})\} \text{ is u.i. in } T\}\\
&= \lambda E \in \{\text{'EMP'}, \text{'DEP'}\}:\\
&\qquad \{T \mid T \subseteq \Pi(FK_{d3,E}) \text{ and}\\
&\qquad\qquad \forall x \in d3(\text{'ATT'}): \text{if } x(\text{'KEY'}) = \text{'*'} \text{ and } x(\text{'TNAME'}) = E\\
&\qquad\qquad\qquad \text{then } \{x(\text{'ANAME'})\} \text{ is u.i. in } T\}\\
&= \{(\text{'EMP'}; \{T \mid T \subseteq \Pi(FK_{d3,\text{'EMP'}}) \text{ and}\\
&\qquad\qquad \{\text{'ENAME'}\} \text{ is u.i. in } T\}),\\
&\quad (\text{'DEP'}; \{T \mid T \subseteq \Pi(FK_{d3,\text{'DEP'}}) \text{ and}\\
&\qquad\qquad \{\text{'DCODE'}\} \text{ is u.i. in } T \text{ and}\\
&\qquad\qquad \{\text{'DNAME'}\} \text{ is u.i. in } T\})\},
\end{aligned}
$$

where (by the definition of $FK_{d3,E}$ and the fact that in d3('ATT') only the type 'C' occurs)

$$
\begin{aligned}
&FK_{d3,E}\\
&= \{(t(\text{'ANAME'}); Chs(t(\text{'SIZE'})) \mid t \in d3(\text{'ATT'}) \text{ and } t(\text{'TNAME'}) = E \text{ and}\\
&\qquad\qquad t(\text{'TYPE'}) = \text{'C'}\} \cup\\
&\quad \{(t(\text{'ANAME'}); Int(t(\text{'SIZE'}))) \mid t \in d3(\text{'ATT'}) \text{ and } t(\text{'TNAME'}) = E \text{ and}\\
&\qquad\qquad t(\text{'TYPE'}) = \text{'N'}\}\\
&= \{(t(\text{'ANAME'}); Chs(16)) \mid t \in d3(\text{'ATT'}) \text{ and } t(\text{'TNAME'}) = E\}
\end{aligned}
$$

hence, by the definition of d3('ATT'),

$$
\begin{aligned}
FK_{d3,\text{'EMP'}} = \{&(\text{'ENAME'} ; Chs(16)),\\
&(\text{'ADDRESS'} ; Chs(16)),\\
&(\text{'CITY'} ; Chs(16)),\\
&(\text{'DCODE'} ; Chs(16))\} \text{ and}\\
FK_{d3,\text{'DEP'}} = \{&(\text{'DCODE'} ; Chs(16)),\\
&(\text{'DNAME'} ; Chs(16)),\\
&(\text{'MANNAME'}; Chs(16))\}.
\end{aligned}
$$

We have completed a full elaboration of the DB universe I3(d3). When we compare this with Example 8.2, we can easily see that I3(d3) $\subset$ I2(d1), since

$$
\begin{aligned}
I2(d1) = \Pi(\{&(\text{'EMP'}; \mathbf{P}(\Pi(FK_{d3,\text{'EMP'}}))),\\
&(\text{'DEP'}; \mathbf{P}(\Pi(FK_{d3,\text{'DEP'}})))\}).
\end{aligned}
$$

The DB universe I3(d3) is clearly a refinement of DB universe I2(d1), since the latter hardly has any constraints.

I3 is an example of a DB-like DD function, because the domain of I3, DDU3, is a DB universe (namely, over {(‘ATT’; dom(FATT3)), (‘REF’; dom(FREF3))}). Nonetheless I3 is not self-describable: by means of I3 we cannot describe "enumeration types" (such as { ‘*’, ‘–’}), nor arbitrary "subrange types" (like [1 .. 256]), nor tuple constraints (like (M3) in the definition of TATT3), nor composite keys (like the key { ‘TNAME’, ‘ANAME’} of ‘ATT’ in DDU3), nor can we describe connection requirements with more than one pair of attributes (like the two requirements of this form occurring in the definition of DDU3).

The DB universe SPSU from Example 2.17 cannot be described according to I3, since by means of I3 no composite keys can be represented.

The DD function I3 is at least as expressive as the DD function I2 in Example 8.2. To prove this, it suffices by Lemma 8.1 to define a function h such that I2 = I3 $\circ$ h. The conversion function h23 below obeys that desired property (see Exercise 8.5):

$$
\begin{aligned}
\text{h23} = \lambda d \in \text{DDU2} : \; & \{(\text{‘ATT’} ; \{t \cup \text{t23} \mid t \in d(\text{‘ATT’})\}), \\
& \;(\text{‘REF’} ; \varnothing)\} ,
\end{aligned}
$$

where $\text{t23} = \{(\text{‘TYPE’} ; \text{‘C’}), (\text{‘SIZE’} ; 16), (\text{‘KEY’} ; \text{‘–’})\}$

Hence, h23 converts each description d according to I2 into the (equivalent) description according to I3 for which the ‘REF’-table is empty and for which the attributes ‘TYPE’, ‘SIZE’, and ‘KEY’ in *each* tuple of the (new) ‘ATT’-table have the (fixed) values ‘C’, 16, and ‘–’, respectively.

□ Example 8.4.

The following example shows that an element of a given DD universe can have more than one "natural" interpretation.

EXAMPLE 8.5:

We will define a second DD function over DDU3, the DD universe over which we have already defined the DD function I3 in Example 8.4. By means of this new DD function we can describe DB universes having almost the same features as the DB universes in Example 8.4; only the feature (M4) has been replaced by the following one:

(M4′) Each table index has at most one key;
this key can be composite, however.

Since we developed our definitions in a rather "modular" way, we only need to introduce one new auxiliary function in order to define our new DD function I4.

The auxiliary function $DBC4_d$, assigning to each table index the set of all allowed tables for that table index, expresses that for each table index E the set of all attributes of E assigned with a star ('*') forms one key, provided that at least one "star-attribute" of E exists.

The definition of our DD function I4 over DDU3 now reads as follows:

$$
\begin{aligned}
&\text{I4} = \\
&\lambda d \in \text{DDU3}: \\
&\quad \{v \mid v \in \Pi(\text{DBC4}_d) \text{ and} \\
&\qquad \forall y \in d(\text{'REF'}): \{(y(\text{'ANAME1'}); y(\text{'ANAME2'}))\} \text{ connects} \qquad \text{(M5)} \\
&\qquad\qquad v(y(\text{'TNAME1'}) \text{ with } v(y(\text{'TNAME2'}))\},
\end{aligned}
$$

where for each $d \in$ DDU3 we define the database characterization $DBC4_d$ as follows:

$$
\begin{aligned}
&\text{DBC4}_d = \\
&\lambda E \in \{t(\text{'TNAME'}) \mid t \in d(\text{'ATT'})\}: \\
&\quad \{T \mid T \subseteq \Pi(\text{FK}_{d,E}) \text{ and} \\
&\qquad \text{if } (\exists x \in d(\text{'ATT'}): x(\text{'KEY'}) = \text{'*'} \text{ and } x(\text{'TNAME'}) = E) \qquad \text{(M4')} \\
&\qquad \text{then } \{x(\text{'ANAME'}) \mid x \in d(\text{'ATT'}) \text{ and } x(\text{'KEY'}) = \text{'*'} \text{ and} \\
&\qquad\qquad x(\text{'TNAME'}) = E\} \text{ is u.i. in } T\}.
\end{aligned}
$$

By way of illustration, Figure 8.4 represents a description d4 (according to I4) of the DB universe SPSU from Example 2.17. Again we point out the difference in interpretation of the stars ('*') in Example 8.4 and those in the current example.

d4('ATT'):

TNAME	ANAME	KEY	TYPE	SIZE
S	S#	*	C	5
S	SNAME	–	C	20
S	STATUS	–	N	4
S	CITY	–	C	15
P	P#	*	C	6
P	PNAME	–	C	20
P	COLOR	–	C	6
P	WEIGHT	–	N	4
P	CITY	–	C	15
SP	S#	*	C	5
SP	P#	*	C	6
SP	QTY	–	N	9

d4('REF'):

TNAME1	ANAME1	TNAME2	ANAME2
SP	S#	S	S#
SP	P#	P	P#

Figure 8.4: A description of SPSU according to I4

Since I4 can describe at most one key per table index, the DB universe I3(d3) from Example 8.4 cannot be described by means of I4.

☐ Example 8.5.

8.2 Summary of the Examples

To conclude this chapter we summarize in Figure 8.5 which DD functions can describe which DB universes, and which DD functions are DB-like or even self-describable.

DD-fu. / DB-un.	I1	I2	I3	I4
I1(g3) (Ex. 8.1)	+	+	+	+
I3(d3) (Ex. 8.4)	-	-	+	-
SPSU (Ex. 8.5)	-	-	-	+
DDU2 (Ex. 8.2)	+	+	+	+
DDU3 (Ex. 8.4)	-	-	-	-
DB-like	-	+	+	+
self-describable	-	+	-	-

Figure 8.5: Summary of the examples

EXERCISES

8.1. If possible, give for each of the following DB universes a description according to I1, I2, I3, or I4; otherwise, if possible, give by means of I3 or I4 an "approximation" of the desired DB universe (preferably in the form of a smallest possible larger DB universe). Should this not be possible either, then indicate the reason(s), and then try to give a "best possible" approximation.

(a) EXU from Example 1.3.

(b) Your EXU2 from Exercise 1.11.

(c) Your EXU3 from Exercise 1.12.

8.2. Prove that every DB universe that can be described by means of the DD function I1 in Example 8.1 also contains "the empty state".

(So prove that $\forall g \in \text{dom}(\text{I1}) : (\lambda E \in \text{dom}(g) : \varnothing) \in \text{I1}(g)$.)

8.3. This exercise refers to Example 8.2.
   (a) Calculate h21(d1).
   (b) Prove that I2 = I1 ∘ h21.
   (c) Define a function h12 such that I1 = I2 ∘ h12 (and prove this property).

8.4. Answer the following questions for each $F \in \{\text{I1}, \text{I2}, \text{I3}, \text{I4}\}$.
   (a) Is each $U \in \text{rng}(F)$ consistent?
   (b) Is each $U \in \text{rng}(F)$ regular? (Hint: $\forall n \in \mathbb{N} : (\text{Chs}(n) \cap \mathbb{Z}) = \varnothing$.)

   In both cases give either a proof or a counterexample.
   (See Exercise 1.5 for the terminology used.)

8.5. Prove that in Example 8.4 the following holds:
   (a) $\forall d \in \text{DDU2} : \text{h23}(d) \in \text{DDU3}$;
   (b) I2 = I3 ∘ h23.

8.6. Show that the DD function I4 in Example 8.5 is not injective: in other words, that there are DB universes that are describable by means of I4 in more than one way. (Hint: consider the key descriptions.)

8.7. (a) Is the DD function I4 in Example 8.5 DB-like?
   (b) Is I4 self-describable?
   Motivate your answers.

8.8. In this exercise we compare the expressive power of the DD functions I3 and I4 in the examples 8.4 and 8.5, respectively.
   (a) Are there any DB universes that are describable according to both I3 and I4?
   (b) Is I3 at least as expressive as I4?
   (c) Is I4 at least as expressive as I3?

   Give in each case either a proof or a suitable counterexample.

8.9. Prove that I3 ∘ h23 = I4 ∘ h23, where h23 is the conversion function defined in Example 8.4.

8.10. Prove that I4 in Example 8.5 is at least as expressive as I2 in Example 8.2.

8.11. (a) Give a description of DDU2 (from Example 8.2) according to I4.

(b) Is that description of DDU2 according to I4 also a description of DDU2 according to I3?

8.12. Motivate all "pluses" and "minuses" in Figure 8.5 by using the properties of those examples mentioned in the material and in the exercises.

□

CHAPTER 9

Directions for Realization in SQL

9.1 Introduction

In this chapter we show how we can implement the mathematical constructions presented in the previous chapters. In particular, we will give directions for implementation in terms of SQL, a standard language for databases. More precisely, we take the version called SQL2, as accepted in 1992 (see the defining document [SQL 92]) as our starting point. We refer the reader who wants to know the details about this version of SQL to the handbook [CO 92]. Although there are still various weaknesses in SQL (see, for instance, *An overview of SQL2* in [DD 92]), the fact that SQL is a widely adopted standard database language makes it an important one. (It is likely that your favourite DBMS also supports at least some dialect of SQL.)

Each of the following sections is dedicated to one of the previous chapters. In particular, §9.2 is devoted to the SQL-counterparts of the constructions for *data definition* as treated in Chapter 3, §9.3 shows how to translate various constructions for *retrieval* presented in Chapter 6, and §9.4 treats the translation of the *maintenance* operations from Chapter 7.

Usually, we give an introductory example as well as a description of the general case. We take the BOM-example developed in Chapter 3 as the running example in this chapter as well.

9.2 Constructing Database Universes

In this section, we explain in which way we can implement database universes in SQL, including their static constraints. We will follow the subdivision used in Chapter 3: in the following subsections we will subsequently treat the implementation of

– attribute constraints,
– tuple constraints,
– table constraints, and
– database constraints.

We start, however, with the so-called *schema definition*.

The Schema

Strictly speaking, our aim is not so much to define a DB universe *U* as such, but rather to declare a variable *D* which has *U* as its type. In other words, we don't want to declare, for example, a (simple) variable of type INTEGER but a (structured) database variable *D* of type *U*. In terms of our example from Chapter 3: we want to declare a database variable, say BOMDB, of type UBP, the DB universe defined in §3.4. In SQL, we can introduce BOMDB as a *schema name* by means of the following *schema definition*:

```
CREATE SCHEMA  BOMDB
```

9.2.1 Attribute Constraints

For the implementation of attribute constraints in SQL, we can use

– domain definitions with domain constraints and
– table definitions with column constraints

as we will show in the following example.

EXAMPLE 9.1:

As an illustration, we give an implementation of the constructions used in Example 3.3. First we implement the set DPN as a so-called "domain":

```
CREATE DOMAIN  DPN  AS INTEGER
CHECK( VALUE >= 10000 AND VALUE < 100000 AND
            VALUE MOD 11 = 0 )
```

Note that we wrote out the definition of the set Snn(5) and that our original variable *k* in the definition of the set DPN in Example 3.3 is replaced by the reserved word VALUE in the SQL-translation.
We implement the infinite set $\mathbb{N}$ "as good as possible" by using the largest available integer set as a basis:

```
CREATE DOMAIN Natset AS INTEGER
CHECK( VALUE >= 0 )
```

Now we are ready to simulate the three object characterizations from Example

3.3 by means of CREATE TABLE statements. In this stage, we also have to introduce the table indexes (which we introduced by way of the DB characterization HBP in Example 3.6).

```
CREATE TABLE PROD
 (PNO   DPN          NOT NULL,
  DES   VARCHAR(30)  NOT NULL,
  TYPE  VARCHAR(6)   NOT NULL,
  CPR   Natset       NOT NULL,
  SPR   Natset       NOT NULL,
  PRFT  Natset       NOT NULL  CHECK( PRFT <> 0 ),
  STK   Natset       NOT NULL,
  COM   VARCHAR(1)   NOT NULL  CHECK( COM IN ( 'Y', 'N' ) ))

CREATE TABLE BAS
 (PNO   DPN          NOT NULL,
  WTU   VARCHAR(2)   NOT NULL  CHECK( WTU IN ( 'GR', 'KG' ) ),
  WT    INTEGER      NOT NULL  CHECK(WT >= 1 AND
                                     WT <= 1000000))

CREATE TABLE BOM
 (PNO   DPN          NOT NULL  CHECK( PNO >= 40000 ),
  PANO  Natset       NOT NULL,
  NUM   INTEGER      NOT NULL  CHECK( NUM >= 1 ))
```

Note that the infinite value set associated with the NUM-attribute in the BOM-table is also "approximated" as good as possible.

□ Example 9.1.

In general, our auxiliary sets (such as $\mathbb{N}$ and DPN in Example 3.3) can be implemented by means of a *domain definition* (i.e., a CREATE DOMAIN statement) provided with a *domain constraint* (a CHECK statement in this case).

Our object characterizations cannot be defined explicitly in SQL, i.e., they cannot be defined as "composite domains" in their own right. However, our object characterizations can be implicitly represented by means of a *table definition* (i.e., a CREATE TABLE statement). A table definition then introduces

- the *table name* (or table index),
- the *column names* (or attributes), and
- their associated value sets, described by
  - a basic *data type* or a user-defined *domain name*,
  - the NOT NULL constraint, and
  - possibly an additional *column constraint* in the form of a CHECK statement.

9.2.2 Tuple Constraints

Tuple constraints can be implemented in SQL by means of a *table constraint definition*: in particular, a CHECK statement at tuple level.

EXAMPLE 9.2:

As an illustration, we implement the tuple constraints specified in Example 3.4. For that purpose, we extend the table definitions in Example 9.1 by adding the following expressions in front of the last character ')' of each table definition:

For the PROD-table:

```
, CHECK( SPR >= 2 * CPR    AND
         PRFT = SPR – CPR  AND
         (STK <= 2 OR STK * CPR <= 1000000) )
```

For the BAS-table:

```
, CHECK( WTU <> 'GR' OR WT < 10000 )
```

For the BOM-table:

```
, CHECK( PANO <> PNO )
```

So, for instance, the table definition for the BOM-table now becomes:

```
CREATE TABLE BOM
 (PNO    DPN        NOT NULL  CHECK( PNO >= 40000 ),
  PANO   Natset     NOT NULL,
  NUM    INTEGER    NOT NULL  CHECK( NUM >= 1 ),

  CHECK( PANO <> PNO )
 )
```

□ Example 9.2.

So, in general, tuple constraints can be implemented in SQL by adding a *table constraint definition* to a *table definition*.

9.2.3 Table Constraints

Table constraints can be implemented in SQL by means of a *table constraint definition* as well. In this case, there are three relevant types of table constraint definitions:

– unique constraint definitions (for specifying keys),
– referential constraint definitions (for specifying internal ssr's), and
– check constraint definitions (for specifying other table constraints).

EXAMPLE 9.3:

As an illustration, we implement the table constraints specified in Example 3.5, except constraint C13. This (recursive) constraint cannot be implemented in a straightforward way in SQL, yet.

We note that the expression "$\Sigma\, t \in T : t(\text{STK}) * t(\text{CPR})$" in constraint C10 will translate to "SELECT SUM(t.STK * t.CPR) FROM PROD t", anticipating §9.3 (in particular Example 9.12), where the SELECT-statement will be treated in detail.

We extend the table definitions in Example 9.2 by adding the following expressions in front of the last character ')' of each table definition:

For the PROD-table:

```
, UNIQUE( PNO )
, CHECK( 100000000 >= (SELECT SUM(t.STK * t.CPR)
                       FROM    PROD t) )
```

For the BAS-table:

```
, UNIQUE( PNO )
```

For the BOM-table:

```
, UNIQUE( PNO, PANO )
```

So, for instance, the table definition for the PROD-table now becomes:

```
CREATE TABLE PROD
 (PNO    DPN          NOT NULL,
  DES    VARCHAR(30)  NOT NULL,
  TYPE   VARCHAR(6)   NOT NULL,
  CPR    Natset       NOT NULL,
  SPR    Natset       NOT NULL,
  PRFT   Natset       NOT NULL  CHECK( PRFT <> 0 ),
  STK    Natset       NOT NULL,
  COM    VARCHAR(1)   NOT NULL  CHECK( COM IN ('Y', 'N') ),

  CHECK( SPR >= 2 * CPR    AND
         PRFT = SPR – CPR  AND
         (STK <= 2 OR STK * CPR <= 1000000) ),
```

```
UNIQUE( PNO ),
CHECK( 100000000 >= (SELECT SUM(t.STK * t.CPR)
                     FROM   PROD t) )
)
```

□ Example 9.3.

As an example of the implementation of an internal ssr by means of a referential constraint definition, we consider constraint R18 for the SP-table in Chapter 4:

R18: {(LOC;IDNR)} connects *T* with *T*

The implementation of constraint R18 in SQL is the following referential constraint definition, to be included in the table definition for the SP-table:

```
FOREIGN KEY (LOC) REFERENCES SP(IDNR)
```

The referential constraint construction in SQL has various options as well as various limitations. Since this book is not intended as a text book on SQL, we will not go into the many details here; we refer the interested reader to, for instance, [CO 92] or [SQL 92].

9.2.4 Database Constraints

Database constraints can be implemented in SQL by means of two relevant types of constraint definitions:

- referential constraint definitions (for specifying simple ssr's), and
- assertion definitions (for specifying other database constraints).

The simple ssr's that can be specified using a referential constraint definition are those of the form treated under (A1) in §3.4.

EXAMPLE 9.4:

As an illustration, we implement the database constraints specified in Example 3.6. We will first analyse each of the four database constraints from Example 3.6 in more detail.

Constraint C14 is of the form treated under (A1) in §3.4. It can therefore be specified using a straightforward referential constraint definition in SQL, associated with the BOM-table:

```
FOREIGN KEY (PANO) REFERENCES PROD(PNO)
```

Constraint C15 is of the form treated under (B2) in §3.4. This constraint consists in fact of two connection requirements (because it is "bilateral"), neither of which is an ordinary referential constraint definition in SQL. On the one hand we require for each $b \in v(\text{BOM})$ that $b(\text{PNO}) \in \{t(\text{PNO}) \mid t \in v(\text{PROD}) \text{ and } t(\text{COM}) = \text{'Y'}\}$, or in other words, that there does not exist a $b \in v(\text{BOM})$ such that $b(\text{PNO}) \notin \{t(\text{PNO}) \mid t \in v(\text{PROD}) \text{ and } t(\text{COM}) = \text{'Y'}\}$. This alternative formulation (with an existential quantifier) can be translated in a direct manner to an *assertion definition*:

```
CREATE ASSERTION C15A
CHECK( NOT EXISTS (SELECT b.*
                   FROM   BOM b
                   WHERE  b.PNO NOT IN (SELECT t.PNO
                                        FROM   PROD t
                                        WHERE  t.COM = 'Y')) )
```

On the other hand we require for each $t \in v(\text{PROD})$ that $t(\text{PNO}) \in \{b(\text{PNO}) \mid b \in v(\text{BOM})\}$ when $t(\text{COM}) = \text{'Y'}$. In other words: there does not exist a $t \in v(\text{PROD})$ such that $t(\text{COM}) = \text{'Y'}$ and $t(\text{PNO}) \notin \{b(\text{PNO}) \mid b \in v(\text{BOM})\}$. This translates to the following assertion definition:

```
CREATE ASSERTION C15B
CHECK( NOT EXISTS (SELECT t.*
                   FROM   PROD t
                   WHERE  t.COM = 'Y'
                     AND  t.PNO NOT IN (SELECT b.PNO
                                        FROM   BOM b)) )
```

A similar argument holds for constraint C16, also resulting in two assertion definitions.

Finally, constraint C17 requires for each PROD-tuple that its CPR-value is at least a certain sum. By writing out the join and the heading transformation, we derive that constraint C17 requires that for no PROD-tuple p

$$\begin{aligned} p(\text{CPR}) < (\Sigma\, (b\,;t) \in\, & v(\text{BOM}) \times v(\text{PROD}) \text{ and} \\ & b(\text{PANO}) = t(\text{PNO}) \text{ and } b(\text{PNO}) = p(\text{PNO}) : \\ & t(\text{CPR}) * b(\text{NUM})\,). \end{aligned}$$

This condition translates to the following assertion definition (anticipating §9.3, in particular Example 9.12, where the SELECT-statement will be treated in detail):

```
CREATE ASSERTION C17
CHECK( NOT EXISTS
        (SELECT p.*
         FROM    PROD p
         WHERE  p.CPR >= (SELECT SUM(t.CPR * b.NUM)
                                    FROM    BOM b, PROD t
                                    WHERE b.PANO = t.PNO
                                       AND  b.PNO   = p.PNO)) )
```

In summary, for the translation of our database constraints into SQL, we introduced five assertion definitions after we extended the table definition of the BOM-table in Example 9.3. There we added the following expression in front of the last character ')':

```
, FOREIGN KEY (PANO) REFERENCES PROD(PNO)
```

□ Example 9.4.

9.2.5 Summary

In §9.2 we have shown how we can translate our specifications of database universes (including their static constraints) into SQL. Our choice of translation results in

one schema definition, including
- a (possibly empty) set of domain definitions,
- a set of table definitions, and
- a set of assertion definitions

of the following forms, respectively. (Here, square brackets ('[ ]') indicate optional components and braces ('{ }') indicate that that part may be repeated zero or more times.)

```
CREATE SCHEMA <schema name>

CREATE DOMAIN <set name> AS <basic data type>
CHECK( <set constraints> )

CREATE TABLE  <table index>
  (  <attribute> <base set> NOT NULL  [CHECK( <attribute constraints> )]
   {,<attribute> <base set> NOT NULL  [CHECK( <attribute constraints> )]}

   [, CHECK( <tuple constraints> )]
```

```
    {,UNIQUE( <attribute set> )}
    {,FOREIGN KEY ( <attribute set> )
        REFERENCES <same  table index> ( <attribute set> )}
    [, CHECK( <table constraints> )]

    {,FOREIGN KEY ( <attribute set> )
        REFERENCES <other table index> ( <attribute set> )}
  )

CREATE ASSERTION  <constraint name>
CHECK( <database constraint> )
```

We recall that a CHECK-statement may contain SELECT-statements. We will treat SELECT-statements in more detail in §9.3.

EXAMPLE 9.5:

As an illustration, we will now present the complete translation of our running example in SQL (that is, without the recursive constraint C13).

```
CREATE SCHEMA  BOMDB

CREATE DOMAIN Natset AS INTEGER
CHECK( VALUE >= 0 )

CREATE DOMAIN  DPN  AS INTEGER
CHECK( VALUE >= 10000 AND VALUE < 100000 AND
          VALUE MOD 11 = 0 )


CREATE TABLE PROD
  (PNO    DPN            NOT NULL,
   DES    VARCHAR(30)    NOT NULL,
   TYPE   VARCHAR(6)     NOT NULL,
   CPR    Natset         NOT NULL,
   SPR    Natset         NOT NULL,
   PRFT   Natset         NOT NULL  CHECK( PRFT <> 0 ),
   STK    Natset         NOT NULL,
   COM    VARCHAR(1)     NOT NULL  CHECK( COM IN ('Y', 'N') ),

   CHECK( SPR >= 2 * CPR    AND
            PRFT = SPR - CPR  AND
            (STK <= 2 OR STK * CPR <= 1000000) ),
```

```
  UNIQUE( PNO ),
  CHECK( 100000000 >= (SELECT SUM(t.STK * t.CPR)
                       FROM   PROD t) )
 )

CREATE TABLE BAS
 (PNO   DPN           NOT NULL,
  WTU   VARCHAR(2)    NOT NULL  CHECK( WTU IN ('GR', 'KG') ),
  WT    INTEGER       NOT NULL  CHECK(WT >= 1 AND
                                      WT <= 1000000),

  CHECK( WTU <> 'GR' OR WT < 10000 ),

  UNIQUE( PNO )
 )

CREATE TABLE BOM
 (PNO   DPN           NOT NULL  CHECK( PNO >= 40000 ),
  PANO  Natset        NOT NULL,
  NUM   INTEGER       NOT NULL  CHECK( NUM >= 1 ),

  CHECK( PANO <> PNO ),

  UNIQUE( PNO, PANO ),

  FOREIGN KEY (PANO) REFERENCES PROD(PNO)
 )

CREATE ASSERTION C15A
CHECK( NOT EXISTS (SELECT b.*
                   FROM   BOM b
                   WHERE  b.PNO NOT IN (SELECT t.PNO
                                        FROM   PROD t
                                        WHERE  t.COM= 'Y')) )

CREATE ASSERTION C15B
CHECK( NOT EXISTS (SELECT t.*
                   FROM   PROD t
                   WHERE  t.COM = 'Y'
                     AND  t.PNO NOT IN (SELECT b.PNO
                                        FROM   BOM b)) )

CREATE ASSERTION C16A
CHECK( NOT EXISTS (SELECT b.*
                   FROM   BAS b
                   WHERE  b.PNO NOT IN (SELECT t.PNO
```

```
                                          FROM   PROD t
                                          WHERE t.COM = 'N')) )

CREATE ASSERTION C16B
CHECK( NOT EXISTS (SELECT t.*
                   FROM   PROD t
                   WHERE  t.COM = 'N'
                     AND  t.PNO NOT IN (SELECT b.PNO
                                        FROM   BAS b)) )

CREATE ASSERTION C17
CHECK( NOT EXISTS
       (SELECT p.*
        FROM   PROD p
        WHERE  p.CPR >= (SELECT SUM(t.CPR * b.NUM)
                         FROM   BOM b, PROD t
                         WHERE  b.PANO = t.PNO
                           AND  b.PNO  = p.PNO)) )
```

□ Example 9.5.

EXERCISES

9.1. Translate the database universe which you constructed step by step in the exercises 3.1, 3.3, 3.9, 3.15, and 3.20 into SQL, using the translation rules from §9.2.

9.2. (a) Check whether our general translation rules in §9.2 also hold in your own favourite database management system.

(b) Adapt, where necessary, our translation rules to your own DBMS as much as possible.

(c) Which kinds of constraints cannot be expressed directly in your own DBMS?

(d) In which alternative way do you have to guard these kinds of constraints in your own DBMS?

9.3. Implement our BOM-example in your own DBMS, using your translation rules from Exercise 9.2.

9.4. Implement your database universe constructed in the exercises 3.1, 3.3, 3.9, 3.15, and 3.20 in your own DBMS, using your translation rules from Exercise 9.2.

□

9.3 Retrieval

In this section, we explain in which way we can translate our queries and views into SQL.

9.3.1 Queries

Often, a query asks for some set described in the form (F1):

(F1) $\{ A \mid B \text{ [and } C\text{] } \}$

where *A* expresses what is *a*sked for,
B expresses the *b*ase set(s) contributing to the answer, and
C expresses some extra *c*ondition for selection (if necessary).

EXAMPLE 9.6:

The query "Give product number and description of each compound product which is still in stock" over our BOM-database from Chapter 3 (and §9.2) can be formally specified as

$$\lambda\, v \in \text{UBP} : \{\, t \upharpoonright \{\text{PNO, DES}\} \mid t \in v(\text{PROD}) \text{ and } t(\text{COM}) = \text{'Y'} \text{ and } t(\text{STK}) > 0 \,\}$$

Here, $A \;=\; t \upharpoonright \{\text{PNO, DES}\}$
$B \;=\; t \in v(\text{PROD})$
$C \;=\; t(\text{COM}) = \text{'Y'} \text{ and } t(\text{STK}) > 0$

□ Example 9.6.

Usually, such specifications of the form $\{ A \mid B \text{ [and } C\text{] } \}$ can be translated to the following *query specification* in SQL:

```
SELECT   DISTINCT <what is asked for>
FROM     <base set(s)>
[WHERE   <condition>]
```

This form represents a wide variety of queries as we will see in the following examples. In Example 9.7 up to Example 9.11 we will subsequently introduce all kinds of new "translation ingredients" within the context of this query form (F1).

EXAMPLE 9.7:

The query from Example 9.6 translates to the following query specification in SQL:

```
SELECT DISTINCT t.PNO, t.DES
FROM   PROD t
WHERE t.COM = 'Y' AND t.STK > 0
```

So, "$t \restriction$ {PNO, DES}" translates to "t.PNO, t.DES",
"$t \in v$(PROD)" translates to "PROD t", and
"t(COM) = 'Y' and t(STK) > 0" translates to
"t.COM = 'Y' AND t.STK > 0".

□ Example 9.7.

In general, the keyword DISTINCT is recommended because a SELECT-statement without the keyword DISTINCT also delivers all duplicate results. In other words, a SELECT-statement delivers a so-called "multi-set". The keyword DISTINCT accounts for the elimination of any redundant duplicate results. So, if we are sure that duplicate results cannot occur then we may drop the keyword DISTINCT. In Example 9.7 we might do this because {PNO} is a key of the table index PROD in the DB universe UBP. In the translation of the first part of constraint C15 in Example 9.4, we dropped the keyword DISTINCT in the translation of the set {t(PNO) | $t \in v$(PROD) and t(COM) = 'Y'} for the same reason, thus resulting in

```
SELECT t.PNO FROM PROD t WHERE t.COM = 'Y'
```

Also if duplicate results do not really matter, the keyword DISTINCT may be dropped. For instance, in the context of the second part of constraint C15 in Example 9.4 (where we only wanted to know whether t(PNO) was a member of the set {b(PNO) | $b \in v$(BOM)}), we dropped the keyword DISTINCT in the translation of this set, yielding

```
SELECT b.PNO FROM BOM b
```

Note that the set expression "{b(PNO) | $b \in v$(BOM)}" also constitutes an example where there is no *C*-part, and hence no WHERE-clause, in the translation.

In the translation to SQL, the variable v and the quantification "$\lambda\, v \in$ UBP" disappeared because the "UBP-context" is usually given. When such a default context is not given, the *schema name* can be mentioned explicitly in the FROM-clause:

```
FROM BOMDB.PROD t
```

where BOMDB is the schema name we introduced on page 189.

In Example 9.7, we already illustrated some elementary, though important translation rules. In the next example, we illustrate some additional translation rules for queries of the form (F1), namely for renaming (in the *A*-part of (F1)), for more than one base set (in the *B*-part of (F1)), and for a so-called "subquery" (in the *C*-part of (F1)).

EXAMPLE 9.8:

Consider the query "Give product number, description, weight, and weight unit (under the names NUMBER, PRODUCT, WEIGHT, and UNIT, respectively) of each base product that is not used as a (direct) part in any product" over our BOM-database from Chapter 3. This query can be formally specified as

$$\begin{array}{l}\lambda\, v \in \text{UBP}:\\ \quad \{\ \{(\text{NUMBER} \quad ; p(\text{PNO})),\\ \qquad (\text{PRODUCT} ; p(\text{DES})),\\ \qquad (\text{WEIGHT} \quad ; b(\text{WT})\ ),\\ \qquad (\text{UNIT} \qquad ; b(\text{WTU}))\}\\ \quad \mid p \in v(\text{PROD}) \text{ and } b \in v(\text{BAS}) \text{ and}\\ \qquad p(\text{PNO}) = b(\text{PNO}) \text{ and}\\ \qquad p(\text{PNO}) \notin \{t(\text{PANO}) \mid t \in v(\text{BOM})\}\ \ \}\end{array}$$

Here we have, in terms of the form (F1):

$$\begin{array}{l}A = \{(\text{NUMBER} \quad ; p(\text{PNO})),\\ \qquad (\text{PRODUCT} ; p(\text{DES})),\\ \qquad (\text{WEIGHT} \quad ; b(\text{WT})\ ),\\ \qquad (\text{UNIT} \qquad ; b(\text{WTU}))\}\\ B = p \in v(\text{PROD}) \text{ and } b \in v(\text{BAS})\\ C = p(\text{PNO}) = b(\text{PNO}) \text{ and}\\ \qquad p(\text{PNO}) \notin \{t(\text{PANO}) \mid t \in v(\text{BOM})\}\end{array}$$

We note that the expression "$\{t(\text{PANO}) \mid t \in v(\text{BOM})\}$" is again of the form (F1); this expression (which has no "*C*-part") can therefore be translated to the query expression

```
SELECT t.PANO
FROM   BOM  t
```

Furthermore, "$\notin$" translates to "NOT IN". Our query now translates to the following query specification in SQL, which contains a *subquery* (i.e., a SELECT-statement within the WHERE-part of another SELECT-statement):

```
SELECT p.PNO   AS NUMBER,
       p.DES   AS PRODUCT,
       b.WT    AS WEIGHT,
       b.WTU   AS UNIT
FROM   PROD p, BAS b
WHERE  p.PNO = b.PNO
   AND p.PNO NOT IN (SELECT t.PANO FROM BOM t)
```

Applied to the DB state v2 from Example 3.2, this query yields the table over {NUMBER, PRODUCT, WEIGHT, UNIT} shown in Figure 9.1.

NUMBER	PRODUCT	WEIGHT	UNIT
62931	Desk chair	9	KG
11099	Pen tray	10	GR

Figure 9.1

□ Example 9.8.

We dropped the keyword DISTINCT, because different PROD/BAS-pairs will always yield different results.
Example 9.8 also lends itself to illustrate the following "minimization rules".

(R1) An occurrence of the form "t." (where t is a tuple variable) in a SELECT-part or a WHERE-part can be dropped if it is clear from the context which tuple was meant.

(R2) If, due to rule R1, a variable t introduced in a FROM-clause does not occur in the SELECT-part or the WHERE-part any more, its occurrence in the FROM-clause can also be dropped.

Applying these rules to the SQL-query in Example 9.8 (rule R1 four times and rule R2 once), we get the following "minimal" result:

```
SELECT p.PNO AS NUMBER,
       DES   AS PRODUCT,
       WT    AS WEIGHT,
       WTU   AS UNIT
FROM   PROD p, BAS b
WHERE  p.PNO = b.PNO
  AND  p.PNO NOT IN (SELECT PANO FROM BOM )
```

For reasons of clarity, we will not apply these rules in the sequel.

The following example shows how to treat an occurrence of the quantifier "∃". It also illustrates the case where we want entire tuples from the base tables as results.

EXAMPLE 9.9:

The query "Give the product data of all products of type C or D that are used as a (direct) part in any product" over our BOM-database from Chapter 3 can be interpreted and formally specified as

$$\lambda\, v \in \text{UBP} : \{\, p \mid p \in v(\text{PROD}) \text{ and } p(\text{TYPE}) \in \{\text{'C'}, \text{'D'}\} \text{ and } \exists\, t \in v(\text{BOM}) : t(\text{PANO}) = p(\text{PNO}) \,\}$$

If S is a set and S' denotes its translation in SQL, then "EXISTS(S')" denotes the condition "$| S | > 0$" in SQL. Knowing this, we rewrite the condition "$\exists t \in v(\text{BOM}) : t(\text{PANO}) = p(\text{PNO})$" as "$|\{ t \mid t \in v(\text{BOM}) \text{ and } t(\text{PANO}) = p(\text{PNO}) \}| > 0$". The translation of the set $\{ t \mid t \in v(\text{BOM}) \text{ and } t(\text{PANO}) = p(\text{PNO}) \}$ into SQL results in

```
SELECT t.*
FROM   BOM t
WHERE t.PANO = p.PNO
```

As a consequence, our original condition "$\exists t \in v(\text{BOM}) : t(\text{PANO}) = p(\text{PNO})$" translates to the following condition in SQL:

```
EXISTS (SELECT t.*
        FROM   BOM t
        WHERE t.PANO = p.PNO)
```

Note that the keyword DISTINCT will never be necessary in such EXISTS-conditions.
Finally, our original query translates to

```
SELECT p.*
FROM   PROD p
WHERE p.TYPE IN ('C', 'D')
   AND EXISTS (SELECT t.*
               FROM   BOM t
               WHERE t.PANO = p.PNO)
```

We note that our query could also be formally specified as follows:

$$\lambda v \in \text{UBP} : \{ p \mid p \in v(\text{PROD}) \text{ and } t \in v(\text{BOM}) \text{ and } p(\text{TYPE}) \in \{ \text{'C'}, \text{'D'} \} \text{ and } t(\text{PANO}) = p(\text{PNO}) \}$$

Here, we vary in fact over all pairs $(p\ ;\ t) \in v(\text{PROD}) \times v(\text{BOM})$. Therefore, the keyword DISTINCT will be necessary because a product might be used as a direct part in several other products, according to the definition of the BOM-table. Our alternative formulation of the original query therefore translates to

```
SELECT DISTINCT p.*
FROM   PROD p, BOM t
WHERE p.TYPE IN ('C', 'D')
   AND t.PANO = p.PNO
```

□ Example 9.9.

In the next example, we treat the special case where we want an entire base table as a result.

EXAMPLE 9.10:

The query "Give the product data of all products" over our BOM-database from Chapter 3 can be formally specified as

$\lambda\, v \in \text{UBP} : v(\text{PROD})$

In the current version of SQL, this query can be formulated as

```
TABLE PROD
```

In older versions of SQL that do not provide the keyword TABLE for this kind of usage, this query can be formulated as

```
SELECT p.* FROM PROD p
```

which is the literal translation of the formal specification

$\lambda\, v \in \text{UBP} : \{\, p \mid p \in v(\text{PROD}) \,\}$

□ Example 9.10.

We continue with the translation of the natural join. The natural join can be directly translated into SQL2, the current version of SQL. It is not possible, however, to introduce one variable varying over the entire natural join tuples in a FROM-clause. Instead, we have to introduce separate variables, one for each of the components of the natural join. We will show this in the following example.

EXAMPLE 9.11:

The query "Give product number, description, weight unit, and stock weight of all base products that are actually in stock" over our database universe UBP can be specified as

$$\lambda\, v \in \text{UBP} : \{\, t \upharpoonright \{\text{PNO, DES, WTU}\} \cup \{(\text{STKWT} \,;\, t(\text{STK}) * t(\text{WT}))\} \mid t \in v(\text{PROD}) \bowtie v(\text{BAS}) \text{ and } t(\text{STK}) > 0 \,\}$$

This specification translates to

```
SELECT p.PNO, p.DES, b.WTU,
       (p.STK * b.WT) AS STKWT
FROM   PROD p  NATURAL JOIN  BAS b
WHERE  p.STK > 0
```

For older versions of SQL that do not have the NATURAL JOIN operator, one has to explicitly write out the join conditions and then use the usual "comma-construction" in the translation to the FROM-clause (a "do-it-yourself-join"). Thus, the formal specification above then changes into

$$\lambda\, v \in \text{UBP}:\\ \{\, p \restriction \{\text{PNO, DES}\} \cup b \restriction \{\text{WTU}\} \cup \{(\text{STKWT}\,;\, p(\text{STK}) * b(\text{WT}))\}\\ \mid (p\,;b) \in v(\text{PROD}) \times v(\text{BAS}) \text{ and } p(\text{PNO}) = b(\text{PNO}) \text{ and } p(\text{STK}) > 0 \,\}$$

and therefore the translation into SQL becomes

```
SELECT p.PNO, p.DES, b.WTU,
       (p.STK * b.WT) AS STKWT
FROM   PROD p,  BAS b
WHERE  p.PNO = b.PNO AND p.STK > 0
```

□ Example 9.11.

Until now we have only considered queries asking for sets described in the form (F1):

(F1) $\{\, A \mid B \text{ [and } C] \,\}$

We will now turn our attention to other query forms as well, e.g. the forms

$\lvert\{\, A \mid B \text{ [and } C] \,\}\rvert$,	the number of elements of that set,
$\min(\{\, A \mid B \text{ [and } C] \,\})$,	the minimum A-value in that set,
$\max(\{\, A \mid B \text{ [and } C] \,\})$,	the maximum A-value in that set,
$\Sigma\, B \text{ [and } C] : A$,	the sum of the As of all Bs (satisfying C), and
$\text{Avg}\, B \text{ [and } C] : A$,	the average of the As of all Bs (satisfying C).

In general, if $\{\, A \mid B \text{ [and } C] \,\}$ translates to
SELECT DISTINCT A' FROM B' [WHERE C']
then $\lvert\{\, A \mid B \text{ [and } C] \,\}\rvert$ translates to
SELECT COUNT(DISTINCT A') FROM B' [WHERE C'],
$\min(\{\, A \mid B \text{ [and } C] \,\})$ translates to
SELECT MIN([DISTINCT] A') FROM B' [WHERE C'],
$\max(\{\, A \mid B \text{ [and } C] \,\})$ translates to
SELECT MAX([DISTINCT] A') FROM B' [WHERE C'],
$\Sigma\, B \text{ [and } C] : A$ translates to SELECT SUM(A') FROM B' [WHERE C'], and
$\text{Avg}\, B \text{ [and } C] : A$ translates to SELECT AVG(A') FROM B' [WHERE C'].

These five operators (COUNT, MIN, MAX, SUM, and AVG) are called *set functions* in SQL. Note that each of the foregoing expressions delivers only one value as result. If there are no Bs (satisfying C) then the minimum, maximum, average, and (in SQL) the sum above are not defined.

The keyword DISTINCT *can* be dropped in combination with MIN and MAX (since duplicates do not influence the answer), and it *must* be dropped in combination with SUM and AVG (for otherwise we would take the sum or average over all *distinct* *A*s only).

We will make each of the forementioned translation rules more concrete in the following example.

EXAMPLE 9.12:

We want to know the number of product types of compound products. Formally:
$\lambda\, v \in$ UBP : |{ t(TYPE) | $t \in v$(PROD) and t(COM) = 'Y'}|.
This translates to
SELECT COUNT(DISTINCT t.TYPE) FROM PROD t WHERE t.COM = 'Y'

We want to know the lowest sales price of any product. Formally:
$\lambda\, v \in$ UBP : min({ t(SPR) | $t \in v$(PROD) }).
This translates to
SELECT MIN(t.SPR) FROM PROD t

We want to know the highest cost price of any compound product of type AUX that is in stock. Formally:
$\lambda\, v \in$ UBP : max({ t(CPR) | $t \in v$(PROD) and t(STK) > 0 and
t(COM) = 'Y' and t(TYPE) = 'AUX' })
This translates to
SELECT MAX(t.CPR) FROM PROD t
WHERE t.STK > 1 AND t.COM = 'Y' AND t.TYPE = 'AUX'

We want to know the total stock value (based on the cost price) of all compound products. Formally:
$\lambda\, v \in$ UBP : $\Sigma\, t \in v$(PROD) and t(COM) = 'Y' : t(STK) * t(CPR).
This translates to
SELECT SUM(t.STK * t.CPR) FROM PROD t WHERE t.COM = 'Y'
In Example 9.3, we already used a similar construction for the formulation of constraint C10.

We want to know the average profit of all products of type C as a percentage of the sales price. Formally:
$\lambda\, v \in$ UBP : Avg $t \in v$(PROD) and t(TYPE) = 'C' : 100 * t(PRFT) / t(SPR).
This translates to
SELECT AVG(100 * t.PRFT / t.SPR) FROM PROD t WHERE t.TYPE = 'C'

These five operators can also be used in subqueries. For instance, the query "Give the product data of each product for which the cost price is at least the sum of the cost prices of its direct components" can be specified as

$\lambda\, v \in \text{UBP} : \{\, p \mid p \in v(\text{PROD}) \text{ and}$
$\quad p(\text{CPR}) \geq (\Sigma\, (b\,;t) \in v(\text{BOM}) \times v(\text{PROD}) \text{ and}$
$\quad\quad b(\text{PANO}) = t(\text{PNO}) \text{ and } b(\text{PNO}) = p(\text{PNO}) :$
$\quad\quad t(\text{CPR}) * b(\text{NUM})\,)\,\}$

This query translates to

```
SELECT p.*
FROM   PROD p
WHERE  p.CPR >= (SELECT SUM(t.CPR * b.NUM)
                 FROM   BOM b, PROD t
                 WHERE  b.PANO = t.PNO
                   AND  b.PNO  = p.PNO)
```

By the way, according to constraint C17, this query should return the product data of *all* products.

□ Example 9.12.

In Example 9.12, we were (among others) interested in the highest cost price of any compound product of type AUX that is in stock. Now suppose that we are in fact interested in the maximum cost price for *each* of the types in stock (and not only for type AUX) and, moreover, for both base products and compound products. In other words, we have to group the products in stock according to their TYPE- and COM-value, and then return the maximum cost price per group.

Before we give a formal specification of the underlying query, we will introduce a general notation which will simplify the formulation of queries concerning such groups.

DEFINITION 9.1:
If T is a set of functions and B is a set, then:

$\text{Part}(T,B) \stackrel{D}{=} \{\, \{t \mid t \in T \text{ and } t \restriction B = w\} \mid w \in T \Vert\!\restriction B \,\}.$

Each element G of Part(T,B) is a nonempty subset of T and $G \Vert\!\restriction B = \{w\}$ for a certain $w \in T \Vert\!\restriction B$. According to Lemma 1.(1) on page 4, we can denote this tuple w by $\bigcup G \Vert\!\restriction B$. We call Part($T$,$B$) *the partition of T according to B.*

EXAMPLE 9.13:
We want to know the highest cost price per type in stock, split up in base products and compound products, in the form of a table over {TYPE, COM, MAXCPR} (i.e., including the TYPE- and COM-values concerned); however, we are only interested in those groups that consist of at least two different products. More precisely:

$\lambda v \in$ UBP :
$\{(\bigcup G \upharpoonright \{$TYPE,COM$\}) \cup \{($MAXCPR; max$(\{t(CPR) \mid t \in G\}))\}$
$\mid G \in$ Part$(\{t \mid t \in v($PROD$)$ and $t($STK$) > 0\}, \{$TYPE, COM$\})$
and $\mid G \mid \geq 2 \}$

In SQL, this query translates to

```
SELECT     t.TYPE, t.COM, MAX(t.CPR) AS MAXCPR
FROM       PROD t
WHERE      t.STK > 0
GROUP BY   TYPE, COM
HAVING     COUNT(*) >= 2
```

□ Example 9.13.

The general form of such a query is

$\{ S_G \mid G \in Part(\{t \mid t \in T$ [and W_t]$\}, B)$ [and H_G] $\}$

where S_G is an expression in terms of G describing the result values, W_t is an extra condition on t (if necessary), and H_G is an extra condition on G (if necessary). In SQL, this query form translates to

```
SELECT     S′
FROM       T′ t
[WHERE     W′]
GROUP BY   B′
[HAVING    H′]
```

where S' is the SQL-translation of S_G, et cetera.

In §2.1.1, we considered various operations on tables, in particular projection (i.e., a generalization of restriction), renaming (i.e., heading transformation), natural join, subset formation, union, intersection, and set difference. In the previous examples, we already treated the translation of projection, renaming, natural join, and subset formation. Generally speaking, projection and renaming translate into the SELECT-part, the natural join translates into the FROM-part, and subset formation translates into the WHERE-part. What remains to be treated from §2.1.1 is the translation of union, intersection, and set difference.

If T and S are sets and T' and S' denote their translations in SQL, then

$T \cup S$ translates to T' UNION S'
$T \cap S$ translates to T' INTERSECT S'
$T - S$ translates to T' EXCEPT S'

We note that the results of the UNION-, INTERSECT-, and EXCEPT-operator, as used above, do not contain duplicate elements in SQL.

EXAMPLE 9.14:

Take T = { t(PNO) | $t \in v$(PROD) and t(TYPE) = 'AUX'}
and S = { t(PNO) | $t \in v$(BOM) and t(PANO) = 44066}.

Then T' = SELECT t.PNO FROM PROD t WHERE t.TYPE = 'AUX'
and S' = SELECT t.PNO FROM BOM t WHERE t.PANO = 44066.

Hence, { t(PNO) | $t \in v$(PROD) and t(TYPE) = 'AUX'} ∪
{ t(PNO) | $t \in v$(BOM) and t(PANO) = 44066}, for instance, translates to

```
SELECT t.PNO FROM PROD t WHERE t.TYPE = 'AUX'
UNION
SELECT t.PNO FROM BOM  t WHERE t.PANO = 44066
```

□ Example 9.14.

9.3.2 Views

We recall from §6.2 that a view ($n;q$) is a "named query", where n is the name and q is the query. In SQL, such a view can be introduced by means of a *view definition*:

CREATE VIEW n AS q'

where q' is the SQL-translation of our specification of the query q. The following example will suffice to illustrate this general translation scheme.

EXAMPLE 9.15:

Consider the view

(STOCKED ; $\lambda\, v \in$ UBP : { $t \upharpoonright$ {PNO, DES} | $t \in v$(PROD) and
t(COM) = 'Y' and t(STK) > 0 }),

inspired by Example 9.6. According to Example 9.7, the SQL-translation of the query is

```
SELECT DISTINCT t.PNO, t.DES
FROM   PROD t
WHERE  t.COM = 'Y' AND t.STK > 0
```

Hence, in SQL, our view can be introduced as follows:

```
CREATE VIEW STOCKED
AS  SELECT DISTINCT t.PNO, t.DES
    FROM    PROD t
    WHERE  t.COM = 'Y' AND t.STK > 0
```

☐ Example 9.15.

Once a view is created, it can be used in SELECT-statements as if it were a base table. For instance, given the view called STOCKED from Example 9.15, the query "Give the product numbers larger than 70000 of all compound products which are still in stock" can be formulated as

```
SELECT x.PNO
FROM    STOCKED x
WHERE  x.PNO > 70000
```

By using views in such a way, we can also decompose complex queries into simpler ones.

EXERCISES

9.5. Determine the results of the queries in the examples 9.7 and 9.9-9.15 when applied to the DB state v2 from Example 3.2. (The result of the query in Example 9.8 when applied to v2 was already determined in that example itself.)

9.6. (a) Check whether our general translation rules in §9.3 also hold in your own favourite database management system.

(b) Adapt, where necessary, our translation rules to your own DBMS as much as possible.

(c) Which kinds of constructions for formulating queries cannot be expressed directly in your own DBMS?

(d) In which alternative way do you have to express these kinds of queries in your own DBMS?

9.7. Implement our examples from §9.3 in your own DBMS, using your translation rules from Exercise 9.6.

☐

9.4 Maintenance

In this section, we give translation rules for the four common classes of transactions introduced in §7.2.

9.4.1 Insertion of a Tuple

The transaction Inst(U,R,E,t), where t will be of the form $\{(a_1;\ w_1), \ldots, (a_n;\ w_n)\}$, specifies the attempt to add the tuple t to the E-table. In the context of a given U (and R), this transaction translates to the following form of *insert statement* in SQL:

INSERT INTO E $(a_1, \ldots ,a_n)$
VALUES $(z_1, \ldots ,z_n)$

where $z_1, \ldots ,z_n$ are the SQL-representations of $w_1, \ldots ,w_n$. If the attribute order $(a_1, \ldots ,a_n)$ is the order in which the attributes were introduced in the *table definition* of E (i.e., the CREATE-statement introducing E), then the expression "$(a_1, \ldots ,a_n)$" in the INSERT-statement can be dropped.

EXAMPLE 9.16:

We want to add the tuple t1 = {(PNO; 87384), (PANO; 40018), (NUM; 2)} to the BOM-table of the database universe UBP. There are no dynamic constraints, so we then use the transition relation UBP × UBP. Let us call this transition relation RBP: RBP = UBP × UBP. We therefore want to apply the transaction Inst(UBP, RBP, BOM, t1). This transaction translates to

```
INSERT INTO BOM (PNO, PANO, NUM)
VALUES (87384, 40018, 2)
```

□ Example 9.16.

9.4.2 Insertion of a Table

The transaction Insq(U,R,E,q) specifies the attempt to add the result of the query q to the E-table in one go. In the context of a given U (and R), this transaction translates to the following form of *insert statement* in SQL:

INSERT INTO E $(a_1, \ldots ,a_n)$
(q')

where q' is the SQL-representation of q and $(a_1, \ldots ,a_n)$ represents the attribute set of the E-table, in the order determined by q'. If the attribute order $(a_1, \ldots ,a_n)$ is also the order in which the attributes were introduced in the *table definition* of E then the expression "$(a_1, \ldots ,a_n)$" in the INSERT-statement can be dropped.

EXAMPLE 9.17:

All compound products in our 50000- and 80000-series should get one piece of the product 40018 as a direct component (assuming that none of them already had 40018 as a direct component). We therefore want to apply the transaction Insq(UBP, RBP, BOM, q1), where q1 is the query

$$\lambda\, v \in \text{UBP}: \{\ \{(\text{PNO}; t(\text{PNO})), (\text{PANO}; 40018), (\text{NUM}; 1)\} \mid t \in v(\text{PROD}) \text{ and } t(\text{PNO}) \text{ div } 10000 \in \{5, 8\} \text{ and } t(\text{COM}) = \text{'Y'}\}$$

The SQL-representation of q1 is

```
SELECT t.PNO, 40018, 1
FROM   PROD t
WHERE  t.PNO DIV 10000 IN (5, 8)
   AND t.COM = 'Y'
```

Hence, the transaction Insq(UBP, RBP, BOM, q1) translates to

```
INSERT INTO BOM (PNO, PANO, NUM)
(SELECT t.PNO, 40018, 1
 FROM   PROD t
 WHERE  t.PNO DIV 10000 IN (5, 8)
    AND t.COM = 'Y')
```

□ Example 9.17.

9.4.3 Deletion

The transaction Del(U,R,E,q) specifies the attempt to delete the result of the query q from the E-table in one go. The query q will typically be of the form $\lambda\, v \in U : \{\ t \mid t \in v(E)$ [and C]$\}$, specifying the E-tuples to be deleted. In the context of a given U (and R), this transaction translates to the following SQL-statement:

```
DELETE FROM E
[WHERE C′]
```

where C' is the SQL-representation of the condition C without the occurrences of "t." (because we are not able in SQL to introduce our variable "t" in the DELETE-statement). In SQL, this statement is called a *delete statement searched.*

We can conclude from the description above that if there is no WHERE-part, all E-tuples are to be deleted.

EXAMPLE 9.18:

It has turned out that less than four thumb screws as direct parts of a product have no effect on its stability. Therefore, we want to delete the thumb screws as direct parts in such cases. In other words, we want to apply the transaction Del(UBP, RBP, BOM, q2), where q2 is the query

$$\lambda\, v \in \text{UBP} : \{\, t \mid t \in v(\text{BOM}) \text{ and } t(\text{NUM}) < 4 \text{ and } t(\text{PANO}) \in \{\, y(\text{PNO}) \mid y \in v(\text{PROD}) \text{ and } y(\text{DES}) = \text{'Thumb screw'} \} \}$$

In this case, the SQL-representation C' is

```
NUM < 4 AND
PANO IN (SELECT y.PNO
         FROM   PROD y
         WHERE  y.DES = 'Thumb screw')
```

Hence, the transaction Del(UBP, RBP, BOM, q2) translates to

```
DELETE FROM BOM
WHERE NUM < 4
   AND PANO IN (SELECT y.PNO
                FROM   PROD y
                WHERE  y.DES = 'Thumb screw')
```

□ Example 9.18.

9.4.4 Update

We consider the transaction Upd(U,R,E,q), where q will typically be of the form $\lambda\, v \in U : \lambda\, t \in v(E)$ [and C] : d. In this case, the transaction Upd(U,R,E,q) represents the attempt to update all E-tuples satisfying the condition C, and d represents the new tuple fragment per E-tuple. Let d be of the form $\{(b_1; w_1), \ldots, (b_k; w_k)\}$. In the context of a given U (and R), this transaction translates to the following SQL-statement:

```
UPDATE E
SET    b1 = z1, ... , bk = zk
[WHERE C']
```

where C' and $z_1, \ldots, z_k$ are the SQL-representations of C and $w_1, \ldots, w_k$ without the occurrences of "t." (because we are not able in SQL to introduce our variable "t" in the UPDATE-statement). In SQL, this statement is called an *update statement searched.*

EXAMPLE 9.19:

We want to increase the cost price and sales price of all compound products in the 50000- and 80000-series with 1000. In other words, we want to apply the transaction Upd(UBP, RBP, PROD, q3), where q3 is

$\lambda\, v \in$ UBP :
  $\lambda\, t \in v$(PROD) and $C : d$

where $C = t$(PNO) div 10000 $\in \{5, 8\}$ and t(COM) = 'Y'
and $d = \{$(CPR; t(CPR) + 1000), (SPR; t(SPR) + 1000)$\}$.
Hence, the transaction Upd(UBP, RBP, PROD, q3) translates to

```
UPDATE PROD
SET    CPR = CPR + 1000,
       SPR = SPR + 1000
WHERE  PNO div 10000 IN (5, 8)
  AND  COM = 'Y'
```

□ Example 9.19.

EXERCISES

9.8. Determine the effect (if any) of the transactions in the examples 9.16-9.19 when applied to the DB state v2 from Example 3.2.

9.9. (a) Check whether our general translation rules in §9.4 also hold in your own favourite database management system.

(b) Adapt, where necessary, our translation rules to your own DBMS as much as possible.

(c) Which kinds of transactions cannot be expressed directly in your own DBMS?

(d) In which alternative way do you have to express these kinds of transactions in your own DBMS?

9.10. Implement our examples from §9.4 in your own DBMS, using your translation rules from Exercise 9.9.

□

References

[AA 93] R. Alhajj and M.E. Arkun:
"An object algebra for object-oriented database systems."
Data Base (1993), pp. 13-22.

[Ab 89] S. Abiteboul et al. (eds.):
"Nested relations and complex objects in databases."
LNCS 361, Springer Verlag, Berlin, 1989.

[ALM 82] F.W. Allen, M.E.S. Loomis, and M.V. Mannino:
"The integrated dictionary/directory system."
ACM Computing Surveys **14**, 2 (1982), pp. 245-286.

[Ar 74] W.W. Armstrong: "Dependency structures of data base relationships."
Proceedings IFIP congress, North-Holland, Amsterdam, 1974,
pp. 580-583.

[Bl 90] A. Blaser (ed.): "Database systems of the 90s."
LNCS 466, Springer Verlag, Berlin, 1990.

[Br 80] E.O. de Brock: "Tables, table variables, and static integrity constraints."
Memorandum, Eindhoven University of Technology, 1980.

[Br 84] E.O. de Brock: "Database models and retrieval languages."
Ph.D. Thesis, Eindhoven University of Technology, 1984.

[Br 88] E.O. de Brock: "Some formal aspects of data dictionaries."
Philips Research, NL-14.638, Eindhoven, 1988.

[Ca 93] R.G.G. Cattel (ed.): "The object database standard."
Morgan Kaufmann, 1993.

[CD 81] R. Curtice and E. Dieckman: "A survey of data dictionaries."
Datamation **27**, 3 (1981), pp. 135-158.

[CO 71] CODASYL Data Base Task Group: "April 71 Report."
ACM, New York, 1971.

[CO 92] S.J. Cannan and G.A.M. Otten: "SQL, the standard handbook." McGraw-Hill, London, 1992.

[Co 70] E.F. Codd: "A relational model of data for large shared data banks." Communications of the ACM **13**, 6 (1970), pp. 377-387.

[Co 72] E.F. Codd: "Further normalization of the data base relational model." In [Ru 72], pp. 33-64.

[Co 72b] E.F. Codd: "Relational completeness of data base sublanguages." In [Ru 72], pp. 65-98.

[Co 74] E.F. Codd: "Recent investigations into relational data base systems." Proceedings IFIP congress, North-Holland, Amsterdam, 1974, pp. 1017-1021.

[CP 87] S. Ceri and G. Pelagatti: "Distributed databases: Principles and systems." McGraw-Hill, New York, 1987.

[Da 86] C.J. Date: "Relational database: Selected writings." Addison-Wesley, Reading (Mass.), 1986.

[Da 90] C.J. Date: "An introduction to database systems (Vol. I)." Addison-Wesley, Reading (Mass.), 1990.

[DD 92] C.J. Date and H. Darwen: "Relational database writings 1989-1991." Addison-Wesley, Reading (Mass.), 1992.

[DDS 76] D. van Dalen, H.C. Doets, and H.C.M. de Swart: "Sets: naive, axiomatic and applied." Pergamon Press, Oxford, 1976.

[DL 80] C. Delobel and W. Litwin (eds.): "Conference on distributed databases." North-Holland, New York, 1980.

[GOV 84] G.E. Geurts-De Haas, H.P.F. van Oorschot, H. van Vondel et al.: "Hospital information model." National Hospital Institute, 84.382, Utrecht, 1984. (In Dutch.)

[HK 87] R. Hull and R. King: "Semantic database modeling: Survey, applications, and research issues." ACM Computing Surveys **19**, 3 (1987), pp. 201-260.

[IDT 88] Independent Database Team - Holland: "Relational database in practice." Proceedings IDT/Codd & Date conference, London, 1988.

[IDT 89] Independent Database Team - Holland: "Evaluation of 16 top RDBMS's using the functional benchmark." Proceedings IDT/Codd & Date conference, Berlin, 1989.

[IDT 90] Independent Database Team - Holland: "A functional evaluation of relational systems using the functional benchmark." Proceedings IDT/EIT conference, Gent, 1990.

[LP 82] B.W. Leong-Hong and B.K. Plagman:
"Data dictionary/directory systems: Administration, implementation, and usage." Wiley, 1982.

[Ma 84] A. Mayne: "Data dictionary systems: A technical review."
NCC Publications, 1984.

[Mai 83] D. Maier: "The theory of relational databases."
Pitman, London, 1983.

[NGI 87] Databaseclub NGI (Dutch Informatics Society):
"The practical usage of relational systems presented."
Proceedings NGI/SIC (C27), Utrecht, 1987. (In Dutch.)

[NGI 88] Databaseclub NGI (Dutch Informatics Society):
"The practical usage of relational systems presented."
Proceedings NGI/SIC (C34), Amsterdam, 1988. (In Dutch.)

[Ol 78] T.W. Olle: "The CODASYL approach to database management."
Wiley and Sons, New York, 1978.

[PM 88] J. Peckam and F. Maryanski: "Semantic data models."
ACM Computing Surveys **20**, 3 (1988), pp. 153-189.

[Re 82] F. Remmen: "Databases: Foundations for the logical structure."
Academic Service, The Hague, 1982. (In Dutch.)

[RKS 88] M.A. Roth, H.F. Korth, and A. Silberschatz:
"Extended algebra and calculus for nested relational databases."
ACM Transactions on Database Systems **13**, 4 (1988), pp. 389-417.

[Ru 72] R. Rustin (ed.): "Data base systems."
Prentice Hall, Englewood Cliffs, 1972.

[Sh 81] D.W. Shipman:
"The functional data model and the data language DAPLEX."
ACM Transactions on Database Systems **6**, 1 (1981), pp. 140-173.

[SM 80] F. Schreiber and G. Martella:
"A data dictionary for distributed databases."
In [DL 80], pp. 17-33.

[SP 89] J.M. Spivey: "The Z notation: A reference manual."
Prentice Hall, Hemel Hempstead, 1989.

[SQL 92] ISO 9075-1992(E): "Database language SQL."
ISO/IEC JTC1/SC21, 1992.

[TK 78] D.C. Tsichritzis and A. Klug (eds.):
"The ANSI/X3/SPARC DBMS framework: Report of the study group on data base management systems."
Information Systems **3**, 1978.

[Uh 73] P.P. Uhrowczik: "Data dictionary/directories."
IBM Systems Journal **12**, 4 (1973), pp. 332-350.

[Ul 82] J.D. Ullman: "Principles of database systems." Computer Science Press, Rockville (Md.), 1982.

[We 86] C.J. Wertz: "The data dictionary: Concepts and uses." North-Holland, Amsterdam, 1986.

[Ya 86] C.C. Yang: "Relational databases." Prentice Hall, Englewood Cliffs, 1986.

List of Definitions

Number		Definiendum	Definiens	Page
1		$\mathbb{N}$	$\{k \in \mathbb{Z} \mid k \geq 0\}$	3
2	(a)	$A \subseteq B$	$\forall x \in A : x \in B$	3
	(b)	$B \supseteq A$	$A \subseteq B$	3
	(c)	$A \subset B$	$A \subseteq B$ and $A \neq B$	3
	(d)	$A \cup B$	$\{x \mid x \in A$ or $x \in B\}$	3
	(e)	$A \cap B$	$\{x \mid x \in A$ and $x \in B\}$	3
	(f)	$A - B$	$\{x \mid x \in A$ and $x \notin B\}$	3
	(g)	$A \times B$	$\{(x ; y) \mid x \in A$ and $y \in B\}$	3
	(h)	$\mathbf{P}(A)$	$\{X \mid X \subseteq A\}$	3
3	(a)	$[m .. n]$	$\{k \in \mathbb{Z} \mid m \leq k$ and $k \leq n\}$	3
	(b)	$[m .. n)$	$\{k \in \mathbb{Z} \mid m \leq k$ and $k < n\}$	3
	(c)	$[m ..)$	$\{k \in \mathbb{Z} \mid m \leq k\}$	3
4	(a)	Snn(n)	$[10^{n-1} .. 10^n - 1]$	3
	(b)	Int(n)	$[-(10^n - 1) .. 10^n - 1]$	3
5		$\bigcup W$	$\{x \mid \exists A \in W : x \in A\}$	4
6	(a)	dom(R)	$\{x \mid (x ; y) \in R\}$	4
	(b)	rng(R)	$\{y \mid (x ; y) \in R\}$	4
	(c)	R^{-1}	$\{(y ; x) \mid (x ; y) \in R\}$	4
7		F is a function	F is a set of ordered pairs and $\forall (x ; y) \in F : \forall (x' ; y') \in F$: if $x = x'$ then $y = y'$	5
8		f and g are joinable	$f \cup g$ is a function	6
9	(a)	f is a function over A	f is a function and dom(f) $= A$	7
	(b)	f is a function from A	f is a function and dom(f) $\subseteq A$	7
	(c)	f is a function into A	f is a function and rng(f) $\subseteq A$	7
	(d)	f is a function onto A	f is a function and rng(f) $= A$	7

No.		Notation	Definition	Page
10		$\text{id}(A)$	$\{(x\,;x) \mid x \in A\}$	7
11	(a)	$A \rightarrowtriangle B$	$\{f \mid f$ is a function and $\text{dom}(f) = A$ and $\text{rng}(f) \subseteq B\}$	8
	(b)	$A \mathrel{\tilde{\rightarrowtriangle}} B$	$\{f \mid f$ is a function and $\text{dom}(f) \subseteq A$ and $\text{rng}(f) \subseteq B\}$	8
12		R is injective	$\forall (x\,;y) \in R : \forall (x'\,;y') \in R$: if $y = y'$ then $x = x'$	8
13		f is a bijection from A to B	f is an injective function and $\text{dom}(f) = A$ and $\text{rng}(f) = B$	9
14		$g \circ f$	$\{(x\,;g(f(x))) \mid x \in \text{dom}(f)$ and $f(x) \in \text{dom}(g)\}$	9
15	(a)	$f \upharpoonright B$	$\{(x\,;y) \in f \mid x \in B\}$	10
	(b)	$f \not\upharpoonright B$	$\{(x\,;y) \in f \mid x \notin B\}$	10
16		$f \equiv g$ on A	$f \upharpoonright A = g \upharpoonright A$	11
17		$f \,\theta\, g$	$(f \not\upharpoonright \text{dom}(g)) \cup g$	11
18		F is a set function	F is a function and $\forall x \in \text{dom}(F) : F(x)$ is a set	13
19	(a)	$\Pi(F)$	$\{f \mid f$ is a function over $\text{dom}(F)$ and $\forall x \in \text{dom}(f) : f(x) \in F(x)\}$	13
	(b)	$\tilde{\Pi}(F)$	$\{f \mid f$ is a function from $\text{dom}(F)$ and $\forall x \in \text{dom}(f) : f(x) \in F(x)\}$	13
20		$\text{He}(V)$	$\bigcup \{\text{dom}(f) \mid f \in V\}$	14
21		r is a sequence of length n	r is a function and $\text{dom}(r) = [0\,..\,n)$	14
22		$R \uparrow n$	$\{(r(0)\,;r(n)) \mid$ r is a sequence of length $n+1$ and $\forall i \in [0\,..\,n) : (r(i)\,;r(i+1)) \in R\}$	15
23	(a)	$\text{Tcl}(R)$	$\bigcup \{R \uparrow n \mid n \in \mathbb{N} - \{0\}\}$	16
	(b)	R is cyclic	$\exists (x\,;y) \in \text{Tcl}(R) : x = y$	16
	(c)	R is acyclic	$\forall (x\,;y) \in \text{Tcl}(R) : x \neq y$	16
1.1		T is a table over A	T is a set and $\forall t \in T : t$ is a function over A	18
1.2		v is a DB state over g	v is a function over $\text{dom}(g)$ and $\forall E \in \text{dom}(g)$: $v(E)$ is a table over $g(E)$	20
1.3		U is a DB universe over g	U is a set of DB states over g	21
2.1		$T \upharpoonright\!\upharpoonright B$	$\{t \upharpoonright B \mid t \in T\}$	26

2.2	$T \bowtie T'$	$\{t \cup t' \mid t \in T$ and $t' \in T'$ and $t \cup t'$ is a function$\}$	27
2.3	$T \infty h$	$\{t \circ h \mid t \in T\}$	30
2.4	$B \rightarrow C$ in T	$\forall t \in T : \forall t' \in T$: if $t \restriction B = t' \restriction B$ then $t \restriction C = t' \restriction C$	35
2.5	B is u.i. in T	$\forall t \in T : \forall t' \in T$: if $t \restriction B = t' \restriction B$ then $t = t'$	39
2.6	B is minimally u.i. in T	B is u.i. in T and $\forall B' \subset B : B'$ is not u.i. in T	39
2.7	h connects T with T'	$T \Vert\!\restriction \mathrm{dom}(h) \subseteq T' \infty h$	42
2.8	h connects T bilaterally with T'	$T \Vert\!\restriction \mathrm{dom}(h) = T' \infty h$	42
2.9	$B \hat{\rightarrow} C$ in W	$\forall T \in W : B \rightarrow C$ in T	46
2.10	B is a key of W	B is a set and $\forall T \in W : B$ is u.i. in T	49
2.11	B is a minimal key of W	B is a key of W and $\forall B' \subset B : B'$ is not a key of W	49
2.12 (a)	Head(W)	He($\bigcup W$)	50
(b)	Mk(W)	$\{B \subseteq \mathrm{Head}(W) \mid B$ is a minimal key of $W\}$	50
2.13 (a)	Prim(W)	$\bigcup$ Mk(W)	50
(b)	Sec(W)	Head(W) – Prim(W)	50
2.14	W is in BCNF	$\forall B \subseteq \mathrm{Head}(W) : \forall a \in \mathrm{Head}(W)$: if $B \hat{\rightarrow} \{a\}$ in W and $a \notin B$ then B is a key of W	51
2.15	W is in 3NF	$\forall B \subseteq \mathrm{Head}(W) : \forall a \in \mathrm{Sec}(W)$: if $B \hat{\rightarrow} \{a\}$ in W and $a \notin B$ then B is a key of W	52
2.16	Un(E, U)	$\{v(E) \mid v \in U\}$	57
2.17	$B \hat{\rightarrow} C$ in E of U	$B \hat{\rightarrow} C$ in Un(E, U)	58
2.18 (a)	B is a key of E in U	B is a key of Un(E, U)	58
(b)	B is a minimal key of E in U	B is a minimal key of Un(E, U)	58
2.19 (a)	Head(E, U)	Head(Un(E, U))	58
(b)	Mk(E, U)	Mk(Un(E, U))	58
(c)	Prim(E, U)	Prim(Un(E, U))	58
(d)	Sec(E, U)	Sec(Un(E, U))	58
2.20 (a)	U is in BCNF	$\forall E \in \mathrm{He}(U) : \mathrm{Un}(E, U)$ is in BCNF	62
(b)	U is in 3NF	$\forall E \in \mathrm{He}(U) : \mathrm{Un}(E, U)$ is in 3NF	62
2.21 (a)	H connects M permanently with D in U	$\forall v \in U : h$ connects $v(M)$ with $v(D)$	63
(b)	H connects M permanently bilaterally with D in U	$\forall v \in U : h$ connects $v(M)$ bilaterally with $v(D)$	63

No.		Term	Definition	Page
2.22		H is a DB function over U w.r.t. $(M\,;D)$	H is a function over U and $\forall v \in U : H(v) \in v(M) \mathrel{-\!\!\rhd} v(D)$	64
2.23		$G \odot H$	$\lambda x \in \mathrm{dom}(G) \cap \mathrm{dom}(H) : G(x) \circ H(x)$	64
5.1	(a)	p is a transition within U	$p \in U \times U$	119
	(b)	R is a transition relation on U	$R \subseteq U \times U$	119
5.2	(a)	$(x\,;y)$ is reversible in R	$(y\,;x) \in \mathrm{Tcl}(R)$	121
	(b)	$(x\,;y)$ is irreversible in R	$(y\,;x) \notin \mathrm{Tcl}(R)$	121
5.3		R is reversible	$\forall p \in R : p$ is reversible in R	121
5.4		$B \overset{\sim}{\rightarrow} C$ at $(T\,;T')$	$\forall t \in T : \forall t' \in T'$: if $t \upharpoonright B = t' \upharpoonright B$ then $t \upharpoonright C = t' \upharpoonright C$	123
5.5		$B \overset{\sim}{\rightarrow} C$ in E at R	$\forall (v\,;v') \in R : B \overset{\sim}{\rightarrow} C$ at $(v(E)\,;v'(E))$	124
6.1		q is a query over U	q is a function over U	135
6.2		p is a view on U	p is an ordered pair and $\pi_2(p)$ is a query over U	151
6.3		V is a view system on U	V is a function and $\forall p \in V : p$ is a view on U	151
7.1		f is a transaction on U	$f \in U \mathrel{-\!\!\rhd} U$	155
7.2		f is a transaction within R	f is a function and $f \subseteq R$	157
7.3		$\mathrm{Ad}(U,R,f)$	$\mathrm{id}(U)\ \theta\ (R \cap f)$	157
7.4		$\mathrm{Adap}(U,f)$	$\mathrm{Ad}(U,\ U \times U, f)$	157
7.5		$\mathrm{Main}(U,R,E,\tau)$	$\mathrm{Ad}(U,R, \lambda v \in U : v\ \theta\ \{(E\,;\tau(v))\})$	164
7.6		$\mathrm{Inst}(U,R,E,t)$	$\mathrm{Main}(U,R,E, \lambda v \in U : v(E) \cup \{t\})$	164
7.7		$\mathrm{Insq}(U,R,E,q)$	$\mathrm{Main}(U,R,E, \lambda v \in U : v(E) \cup q(v))$	165
7.8		$\mathrm{Del}(U,R,E,q)$	$\mathrm{Main}(U,R,E, \lambda v \in U : v(E) - q(v))$	166
7.9		$\mathrm{Upd}(U,R,E,q)$	$\mathrm{Main}(U,R,E, \lambda v \in U : (v(E) - \mathrm{dom}(q(v))) \cup \{t\ \theta\ q(v)(t) \mid t \in \mathrm{dom}(q(v))\})$	167
8.1		I is a DD function	I is a function and $\forall d \in \mathrm{dom}(I) : I(d)$ is a DB universe	174
8.2	(a)	I is at least as expressive as I'	$\mathrm{rng}(I') \subseteq \mathrm{rng}(I)$	175
	(b)	I is DD-equivalent to I'	$\mathrm{rng}(I') = \mathrm{rng}(I)$	175
8.3		I is DB-like	$\mathrm{dom}(I)$ is a DB universe	178
8.4		I is self-describable	$\mathrm{dom}(I) \in \mathrm{rng}(I)$	178
9.1		$\mathrm{Part}(T,B)$	$\{\ \{t \mid t \in T \text{ and } t \upharpoonright B = w\} \mid w \in T \Vert\!\upharpoonright B\ \}$	207

Index of Lemmas, Theorems, Examples, Figures, and Exercises

In view of the large number of references, we give the (initial) pages of all lemmas, theorems, examples, figures, and exercises.

Lemmas

Lemma	Page
1	4
2	5
3	6
4	7
5	7
6	8
7	8
8	8
9	9
10	10
11	10
12	11
13	12
14	12
15	14
16	14
17	15
18	17
2.1	25
2.2	25
2.3	26
2.4	27
2.5	28
2.6	31
2.7	36
2.8	36
2.9	37
2.10	37
2.11	38
2.12	39
2.13	39
2.14	40
2.15	43
2.16	43
2.17	49
2.18	52
2.19	60
2.20	62
2.21	64
2.22	65
5.1	124
5.2	124
8.1	176

Theorems

Theorem	Page
1.1	22
2.1	56
5.1	124
7.1	158

Examples

Example	Page
1	13
2	14
3	16
1.1	18
1.2	20
1.3	21
2.1	26
2.2	27
2.3	29
2.4	30
2.5	35
2.6	39
2.7	41
2.8	45
2.9	46
2.10	49
2.11	50
2.12	52
2.13	54
2.14	58
2.15	63
2.16	63
2.17	70
3.1	76
3.2	78
3.3	82
3.4	84
3.5	86
3.6	88
5.1	119
5.2	121
6.1	135
6.2	136
6.3	138
6.4	140
6.5	143
6.6	146
6.7	151
7.1	155
7.2	160
7.3	165
7.4	166
7.5	167
8.1	174
8.2	176
8.3	178
8.4	179
8.5	183
9.1	189
9.2	191
9.3	192
9.4	193
9.5	196
9.6	199
9.7	199
9.8	201
9.9	202
9.10	204
9.11	204
9.12	206
9.13	207
9.14	209
9.15	209
9.16	211
9.17	212
9.18	213
9.19	214

Figures

Figure	Page
1	16
1.1	18
2.1	27
2.2	28
2.3	29
2.4	30
2.5	35
2.6	41
2.7	46
2.8	47
2.9	48
2.10	69
2.11	71
3.1	79
3.2	79
3.3	82
3.4	94
4.1	99
4.2	117
5.1	129
5.2	129
5.3	129
5.4	130
5.5	131
6.1	150
7.1	161
7.2	162
7.3	163
8.1	177
8.2	179
8.3	181
8.4	184
8.5	185
9.1	202

Exercises

Exercises		Page
1.1	1.2	20
1.3	1.4	21
1.5	1.11	23
1.12	1.13	24
2.1	2.2	31
2.3	2.10	32
2.11	2.16	33
2.17	2.22	34
2.23	2.28	38
2.29	2.34	40
2.35		41
2.36	2.41	44
2.42		45
2.43		47
2.44	2.48	48
2.49	2.56	51
2.57	2.62	53
2.63	2.67	57
2.68	2.71	60
2.72	2.77	61
2.78	2.81	62
2.82	2.86	65
2.87	2.91	66
2.92		67
2.93		72
2.94	2.97	73
2.98	2.102	74
2.103	2.104	75
3.1		80
3.2	3.3	83
3.4	3.9	85
3.10	3.15	87
3.16	3.20	93
3.21	3.23	96
4.1	4.3	114
4.4	4.6	115
4.7	4.12	118
5.1	5.6	125
5.7	5.14	126
5.15	5.19	133
6.1		148
6.2	6.7	149
6.8	6.11	150
6.12	6.14	154
7.1		163
7.2	7.3	164
7.4		170
7.5	7.9	171
7.10	7.11	172
8.1	8.2	185
8.3	8.10	186
8.11	8.12	187
9.1	9.4	198
9.5	9.7	210
9.8	9.10	214

Subject Index

A
acyclic 16
adaptation 157, 157
algebra
  relational - 141
alternate key 123
answer 134
argument 5
Armstrong axioms 36
assertion definition 194
association
  induced - 43
associative 28
atomic 52
attribute 21, 50
  - constraint 77
  - transformation 30
  inspection - 91
  primary - 50
  secondary - 50

B
BCNF 51, 62
bijection 9
bilaterally
  connect - 42
  connect permanently - 63
Boyce-Codd normal form 51, 61
business rule 77

C
calculus
  relational - 141
Cartesian product 3
catalog
  system - 173
characterization
  database - 87
  object - 80
chicken/egg-problem 92
closure
  transitive - 16
column
  - constraint 190
  - name 190
commutative 28
compatible 6
complete domain 14
composition 9
  generalized - 64
connect 42
  - bilaterally 42
  - permanently 63
  - permanently bilaterally 63
connection requirement 89
consistent 23, 23
constantly dependent 124
constraint
  attribute - 77

column - 190
database - 77
domain - 190
dynamic - 120
recursive - 86
referential integrity - 90
static - 77
table - 77
table - definition 191
tuple - 77
coordinate
first - 2
second - 2
cumulative 121, 122
cyclic 16

D

data
- dictionary 173
- model xi
- type 190
database
- characterization 87
- constraint 77
- theory 68
DB function 64
DB-like 178
DB skeleton 21
DB state 20, 21
DB universe 21
DD conversion function 176
DD-equivalent 175
DD function 174
DD migration function 176
DD universe 174
definition
assertion - 194
domain - 190
schema - 189
table - 190
table constraint - 191
view - 151, 209
delete 165
- statement searched 212
dependent
constantly - 124
functionally - 46
incidentally - 46
momentarily - 35
multivalued - 73, 75
permanently - 46, 58
structurally - 46
transition - 123
description 174
dictionary
data - 173
difference 3
differentiation 92
distribute
- to the left 33
- to the right 32
domain 4, 94
complete - 14
- constraint 190
- definition 190
- name 190
dump 147
dynamic constraint 120

E

enumeration 81
error detecting code 99
expressive
at least as - 175
extension 15
external
- schema 146
- SSR 91
- view 153

F

file theory 68
first
- coordinate 2
- normal form 52
fixed point 5
foreign key 90
fourth normal form 75

function 5
DB - 64
DD - 174
DD conversion - 176
DD migration - 176
- from 7
- into 7
- onto 7
- over 7
identity - 7
one-to-one - 8
partial - 7
set - 13, 205
successor - 5
total - 7
functional
- overriding 11
- relationship 141
functionally dependent 46

G
generalization 92
generalized
- composition 64
- product 13
- union 4

H
heading 14, 21, 50
homonymous 78

I
idempotent 170
identity function 7
image 5
incidentally dependent 46
inclusion
set - 3
index
source - 64
table - 21
target - 64
induced association 43
initial subsequence 15
injection 8
injective 8
insert 164, 165
- statement 211
inspection
- attribute 91
- value 91
integer 2
integrity
referential - constraint 90
internal SSR 91
interpretation 174
intersection 3
intrinsic rollback 167
inverse 4
irreflexive 17
irreversible 121

J
join
left outer - 72
natural - 27
joinable 6

K
key 49, 58
alternate - 123
foreign - 90
minimal - 49, 58
primary - 123
knowledge rule 153

L
left
distribute to the - 33
- outer join 72
length 14

M
maintenance 164
match 11
meta-attribute 178
meta-data 173
meta-DB-state 178

meta-DB-universe 178
meta-table-index 178
minimal key 49, 58
minimally u.i. 39
model
  data - xi
  process - xi
modification 11
momentarily dependent 35
multivalued dependent 73, 75

N
name
  column - 190
  domain - 190
  schema - 189
  table - 190
  view - 151
natural
  - join 27
  - number 2
normal form
  Boyce-Codd - 51, 61
  first - 52
  fourth - 75
  second - 75
  third - 51, 61
number
  natural - 2

O
object characterization 80
object-database 178
one-to-one function 8
ordered pair 2
outer
  left - join 72
overriding
  functional - 11

P
pair
  ordered - 2
partial function 7
partition 207
permanently
  connect - 63
  connect - bilaterally 63
  - dependent 46, 58
power set 3
pre-image 5
primary
  - attribute 50
  - key 123
process model xi
product
  Cartesian - 3
  generalized - 13
projection 26

Q
query 135
  - specification 199
  recursive - 146

R
range 4
recursive
  - constraint 86
  - query 146
  - view 154
referential integrity constraint 90
reflexive 119
regular 23
relation 4
  transition - 119
relational
  - algebra 141
  - calculus 141
  - schema 81
remainder 2
requirement
  connection - 89
  subset - 89
restriction 10
retrieval 134
reversible 121
right

distribute to the - 32
rollback 157
intrinsic - 167
rule
business - 77
knowledge - 153

S
schema
external - 146
relational - 81
- definition 189
- name 189
searched
delete statement - 212
update statement - 213
second
- coordinate 2
- normal form 75
secondary attribute 50
self-describable 178
semantics 77, 174
sequence 14
set 1
power - 3
- function 13, 205
- inclusion 3
source index 64
specialization 92
specification
query - 199
SQL view 153
SQL2-standard 164
SSR 89
external - 91
internal - 91
statement
delete - searched 212
insert - 211
update - searched 213
static constraint 77
structurally dependent 46
subquery 201
subschema 147
subsequence
initial - 15
subset
- requirement 89
subskeleton 146
subtype 92
successor function 5
superkey 49
symmetric 126
synonymous 78
system
- catalog 173
view - 151
system-database 178

T
table 18
- constraint 77
- constraint definition 191
- definition 190
- index 21
- name 190
target index 64
theory
database - 68
file - 68
third normal form 51, 61
total function 7
transaction 155, 157
transformation
attribute - 30
transition 119
- dependent 123
- relation 119
transitive closure 16
tuple 18
- constraint 77
type
data - 190

U
u.i. 39
minimally - 39
union 3

generalized - 4
uniquely identifying 38
unit of work 159
universe 57
DB - 21
DD - 174
update 167
- statement searched 213
use 178

V

value 5
inspection - 91
view 151
external - 153
recursive - 154
SQL - 153
- definition 151, 209
- name 151
- system 151

11-test 81
1NF 52
2NF 75
3NF 52, 62
4NF 75